John Ouseley Byrne

Compendium of Irish Sanitary Law

Containing the Sanitary Act, 1866, and the Acts Incorporated Therewith

John Ouseley Byrne

Compendium of Irish Sanitary Law
Containing the Sanitary Act, 1866, and the Acts Incorporated Therewith

ISBN/EAN: 9783337250379

Printed in Europe, USA, Canada, Australia, Japan

Cover: Foto ©Suzi / pixelio.de

More available books at **www.hansebooks.com**

COMPENDIUM

OF

IRISH SANITARY LAW,

CONTAINING

THE SANITARY ACT, 1866, AND THE ACTS INCORPORATED
THEREWITH SO FAR AS THE SAME RELATE
TO IRELAND.

THE ACTS RELATING TO WORKSHOPS, COMMON LODGING
HOUSES, BAKEHOUSES, AND THE ADULTERATION
OF FOOD AND DRINK.

WITH

Explanatory Notes,

A COLLECTION OF LEGAL DECISIONS IN SANITARY CASES,

AND

AN INDEX.

BY

JOHN OUSELEY BYRNE, A.B.

BARRISTER-AT-LAW.

DUBLIN:
WILLIAM McGEE, 18 NASSAU STREET.
1870.

PREFACE.

SANITARY REFORM is a subject of the utmost importance, not only to every Public Body entrusted with the management of a town or district, but also to every Householder, to those engaged in the great variety of trades and manufactures, and, indeed, to every Member of the community. This has been of late years so far recognized by the Legislature that a code of Laws has been enacted, by which most stringent powers are given to the Authorities, and appropriate duties and responsibilities are imposed upon private individuals. The Town Councils in corporate towns, the Town Commissioners in other towns and townships, and the Poor Law Guardians, in their special districts are, entrusted with the execution of these laws, and the Inhabitants of such places are made liable to penalties for their infringement.

A Compendium of this branch of the Law for Ireland, with a full Index for immediate reference, seemed to the author likely to prove useful.

The statutes and portions of statutes which form the basis of this Work are, " The Adulteration of Food and Drink Act, 1860 ;", " The Bakehouse Regulation Act, 1863 ;" the several Acts relating to Common Lodging Houses ; The general " Sanitary Act, 1866," and the several Acts incorporated therewith; and the important but very imperfect statute known as " The Workshop Regulation Act, 1867," which affects the employers of labour in almost every workshop, or place in which any handicraft is carried on by the labour of any child, young person, or woman.

The important legal decisions of the Superior Courts are introduced under the several sections of those statutes to which they refer, and short explanatory notes and references are given where necessary.

The author has endeavoured to afford every information required either by those affected by these statutes, or by those entrusted with carrying them into execution, and, as far as possible, to avoid the technicalities which are almost inseparable from Law books.

J. O. B.

193 GREAT BRUNSWICK STREET, DUBLIN,
24th May, 1870.

CONTENTS.

TABLE OF CASES.

TABLE OF ABBREVIATIONS.

A. & E. . .	Adolphus & Ellis.
B. & Ad. . .	Barnwall & Adolphus.
B. & S. . .	Best & Smith.
C. B. R. . .	Common Bench Reports.
C B. N. S.. .	Common Bench, New Series.
D. & L. . .	Dowling & Lowndes.
Exch. Cham. .	Exchequer Chamber.
El. & Bl. . .	Ellis & Blackburne.
El. & El. . .	Ellis & Ellis.
H. & C. . .	Hurlstone & Coltsman.
J.P. . . .	Justice of the Peace.
Jur. N. S. . .	Jurist New Series.
L. J. N. S. Q. B.	Law Journal, New Series, Queen's Bench.
L. J. Exch. .	Law Journal, Exchequer.
L. J. M. C. N. S.	Law Journal, Magistrates' Cases, New Series
L. J. C. P. . .	Law Journal, Common Pleas.
L. J. Ch. . .	Law Journal, Chancery.
Leg. Rep. . .	Legal Reporter.
L. T., . .	Law Times.
L. T. N. S. Q. B.	Law Times, New Series, Queen's Bench.
L. R. Exch. .	Law Reports, Exchequer.
L. T. N. S. .	Law Times, New Series.
W. R. . .	Weekly Reporter.

PUBLIC HEALTH.

THE SANITARY ACT, 1866.

29 & 30 Victoria, Cap. 90.

An Act to amend the Law relating to the Public Health.

[7th August, 1866.]

WHEREAS it is expedient to amend the Law relating to Public Health : Be it enacted by the Queen's most Excellent Majesty, by and with the Advice and Consent of the Lords Spiritual and Temporal, and Commons, in this present Parliament assembled, and by the authority of the same, as follows :—

Preliminary.

1. This Act may be cited for all purposes as *The Sanitary Act, 1866.** Short title of Act.

* This Act has been amended by 31 & 32 Vic., c. 115, but the Amendment does not extend to either Scotland or Ireland.

PART I.†

Amendment of the Sewage Utilization Act, 1865.

2. " Sewer Authority" in this Act shall have Definition of " Sewer Authority."

† In the application to Ireland of the first part of this Sanitary Act, the changes required by sec. 56 must be observed.

B

SECTION 3. the same meaning as has it in the Sewage Utilization Act, 1865.*

"Lord Lieutenant in Council." The words "Lord Lieutenant in Council" shall mean in this Act the Lord Lieutenant or any Chief Governor or Chief Governors in *Ireland*, acting by and with the Consent of Her Majesty's Privy Council in *Ireland*.

* This definition of Sewer Authority has been amended further as regards Ireland by section 56, which provides that the Sewer Authority in Ireland shall be that contained in the first Schedule to this Act. The "Sewer Authority" in Ireland is also invested with powers to execute the Nuisances Removal Acts, (sec. 57,) to which Part II. of this Sanitary Act relates, and also to execute the powers conferred on the Local Board or Local Boards of Health by the English Acts. (See secs. 11 and 42.)

This part to be construed with 28 & 29 Vic., c. 75. 3. This part of this Act shall be construed as one with the Sewage Utilization Act, 1865, and the expression, "The Sewage Utilization Act, 1865," as used in this or any other Act of Parliament or other Document, shall mean the said Sewage Utilization Act, 1865, as amended by this Act.

This section, by incorporating the Sewage Utilization Act with this Act, considerably enlarges the powers which were conferred on the Authorities ; for instance, the jurisdiction of Boards of Guardians was limited by the Schedule of the Sewage Utilization Act to "any *town* or *village* in any Union not included in the above descriptions ;" but by the Schedule to this Sanitary Act their jurisdiction is enlarged to "such part of each Union as is not under another Sewer or Nuisance Authority." By a comparison of these two Schedules, the exact enlargement of the powers of the Authorities will be seen.

Power to Sewer Authority 4. Any †Sewer Authority may from Time to Time, at any Meeting specially convened for the Purpose, form One or more Committee or Com-

† Inasmuch as the term "Sewer Authority" includes "Nuisance Authority," (sec. 2 note,) this section may be regarded as a supersession of sec. 5 of the Nuisances Removal Act, 1855, which authorizes Nuisance Authorities to appoint Committees, &c.

mittees* consisting wholly of its own Members, or partly of its own Members and partly of such other Persons contributing to the Rate or Fund out of which the Expenses incurred by such Authority are paid, and qualified in such other Manner as the Sewer Authority may determine, and may delegate, with or without Conditions or Restrictions, to any Committee so formed, all or any Powers of such Sewer Authority, and may from Time to Time revoke, add to, or alter any Powers so given to a Committee.

A Committee may elect a Chairman of its Meetings. If no Chairman is elected, or if the Chairman elected is not present at the Time appointed for holding the same, the Members present shall choose One of their Number to be Chairman of such Meeting. A Committee may meet and adjourn as it thinks proper. The Quorum of a Committee shall consist of such Number of Members as may be prescribed by the Sewer Authority that appointed it, or, if no number be prescribed, of Three Members. Every Question at a Meeting shall be determined by a Majority of Votes of the Members present, and voting on that Question; and in case of an equal Division of Votes, the Chairman shall have a Second or Casting Vote.

* The Constitution of the Committees under this section is such as to enable the Authority to associate rate-payers with itself to enforce the provisions of this Act. This provision is especially desirable to Boards of Guardians, in order that they may, in any portions of their Unions in which the Guardians might be few, associate some of the rate-payers with their own members, for the purpose of forming such a Committee as is contemplated by this section. Should any Committee neglect or fail to carry out the requirements of this statute, the Authority who appointed it is the party responsible for the default, and not the Committee itself. The remedy for such default is detailed by Sec. 49.

SECTION 5. The Proceedings of a Committee shall not be invalidated by any Vacancy or Vacancies amongst its Members.

A Sewer Authority may from Time to Time add to or diminish the Number of the Members, or otherwise alter the Constitution of any Committee formed by it, or dissolve any Committee.

A Committee of the Sewer Authority shall be deemed to be the Agents of that Authority, and the Appointment of such Committee shall not relieve the Sewer Authority from any obligation imposed on it by Act of Parliament or otherwise.

Formation of Special Drainage District.

5.* Where the Sewer Authority of a District is a Vestry, Select Vestry, or other Body of Persons acting by virtue of any Act of Parliament, Prescription, Custom, or otherwise as or instead of a Vestry or Select Vestry, it may, by Resolution at any Meeting convened for the Purpose after Twenty-one clear Days' Notice affixed to the Places where Parochial Notices are usually affixed in its District, form any part of such District into a Special Drainage District for the Purposes of the Sewage Utilization Act, and thereupon such Special Drainage District shall, for the Purposes of The Sewage Utilization Act, 1865, and the Powers therein conferred, be deemed to be a Parish in which a Rate is levied for the Maintenance of the Poor, and of which a Vestry is the Sewer Authority, subject, as respects any Meeting of the Inhabitants thereof in Vestry, to the Act of the Fifty-eighth Year of the Reign of King *George* the Third, Chapter Sixty-nine, and the Acts amending the same; and any Officer or

* There being no such bodies in Ireland as here referred to, this section and the two following ones do not appear applicable to Ireland.

Officers who may from Time to Time be appointed by the Sewer Authority of such Special Drainage District for the Purpose, shall have within that District all the Powers of levying a Rate for the Purpose of defraying the Expense of carrying the said Sewage Utilization Act into effect that they would have if such District were such Parish as aforesaid, and such Rate were a Rate for the Relief of the Poor, and they were duly appointed Overseers of such Parish.

6. Where the Sewer Authority of any Place Appeal has formed a Special Drainage District in pursu- against constitution ance of this Act, if any Number of the Inhabi- of Special Drainage tants of such Place, not being less than Twenty, District. feel aggrieved by the Formation of such District, or desire any Modification in its Boundaries, they may, by Petition in Writing under their Hands, bring their Case under the Consideration of One of Her Majesty's Principal Secretaries of State, and the said Secretary of State may after due Investigation annul the Formation of the Special Drainage District, or modify its Boundaries as he thinks just.

7. A Copy of the Resolution of a Sewer Evidence of Authority forming a Special Drainage District formation of Special shall be published by affixing a Notice thereof to Drainage the Church Door of the Parish in which the District. District is situate, or of the adjoining Parish if there be no Church in the said Parish, and by advertising Notice thereof in some Newspaper published or circulating in the County in which such District is situate; and the Production of a Newspaper containing such Advertisement, or a Certificate under the Hand of the Clerk or other

SECTION 8. Officer performing the Duties of Clerk for the Time being of the Sewer Authority which passed the Resolution forming the District, shall be Evidence of the Formation of such District, and after the Expiration of Three Months from the Date of the Resolution forming the District such District shall be presumed to have been duly formed, and no Objection to the Formation thereof shall be entertained in any legal Proceedings whatever.

Power to drain into sewers of Sewer Authority.

8. Any Owner or Occupier of Premises within the District of a Sewer Authority shall be entitled to cause his Drains to empty into the Sewers of that Authority on condition of his giving such Notice as may be required by that Authority of his Intention so to do, and of complying with the Regulations of that Authority in respect of the Mode in which the Communications between such Drains and Sewers are to be made, and subject to the Control of any Person who may be appointed by the Sewer Authority to superintend the making of such Communications; but any Person causing any Drain to empty into any Sewer of a Sewer Authority without complying with the Provisions of this Section shall incur a Penalty not exceeding Twenty Pounds, and it shall be lawful for the Sewer Authority to close any Communication between a Drain and Sewer made in contravention of this Section, and to recover in a summary Manner from the Person so offending any Expenses incurred by them under this Section.

By this section the Owner or Occupier of Premises within the District of a Sewer Authority, being liable for taxation for the construction of the main sewer of the district, and for the keeping of the same in good and serviceable repair, is entitled in SECTION 9. return to cause his drains to empty into those of the Sewer Authority, but upon certain conditions, and if those conditions be not complied with previous to the making of any communication referred to by this section, a penalty is imposed upon the defaulter. In accordance with the provisions of this section, the course prescribed by the Nuisance Authority of Dublin, when the owner or occupier of premises within its district wishes to have his drains to empty into the main sewer, is, first, that the party should ask in writing the Engineer of the Authority to furnish him with an estimate of the expenses necessary to make excavations and to supply drain pipes, &c., from the premises to the main sewer. This estimate is prepared by the engineer according to a fixed schedule of prices, and is furnished with the consent and approval of the Authority. The owner or occupier is then required to deposit the amount of the estimate, which being done, the Authority carries out the work by its own servants under the supervision of the engineer. The works necessary to be done on and within the premises may be done by the owner or occupier *ad lib.*, so as they do not cause a nuisance.

9. Any Owner or Occupier of Premises beyond the Limits of the District of a Sewer Authority may cause any Sewer or Drain from such Premises to communicate with any Sewer of the Sewer Authority upon such Terms and Conditions as may be agreed upon between such Owner or Occupier and such Sewer Authority, or in case of Dispute may, at the option of the Owner or Occupier, be settled by two Justices or by Arbitration, in manner provided by The Public Health Act, 1848, in respect of Matters by that Act authorized or directed to be settled by Arbitration.*

Use of
sewers by
persons
beyond
District.

* See the Public Health Act, 1848, Secs. 133 to 128, (*post.*)

The owner or occupier of premises *beyond* the limits of the district of a Sewer Authority not being liable for its taxation, and not contributing to the cost of the making or repairing of the Sewer of the Authority, is admitted by this section to the same privileges as are possessed by an owner or occupier of premises *within* the district of an Authority, but upon different conditions. The Authority cannot refuse to entertain an appli-

SECTION 10. cation under this section, for the right is conferred upon the owner or occupier of the premises to have such a communication made as that referred to. In case, however, that any dispute should arise on this point, a *mandamus* would be the proper course, and not a reference to Justices or to Arbitrators. A *mandamus* is the proper course to compel the performance of a public duty, whereas the duties of Arbitrators and Justices under the Public Health Act, 1848, are confined to the settlement of disputes as to the conditions to be complied with and the amounts to be paid by the parties respectively.

As to the drainage of houses.

10. If a Dwelling House within the District of a Sewer Authority is without a Drain, or without such Drain as is sufficient for effectual Drainage, the Sewer Authority may by Notice require the Owner of such House, within a reasonable Time therein specified, to make a sufficient Drain emptying into any Sewer which the Sewer Authority is entitled to use, and with which the Owner is entitled to make a Communication, so that such Sewer be not more than One Hundred Feet from the Site of the House of such Owner; but if no such Means of Drainage are within that Distance then emptying into such covered Cesspool or other Place not being under any House, as the Sewer Authority directs; and if the Person on whom such Notice is served fails to comply with the same, the Sewer Authority may itself, at the Expiration of the Time specified in the Notice, do the Work required, and the Expenses incurred by it in so doing may be recovered from such Owner in a summary Manner.

⸚ In addition to this section, it is provided by Sec. 13 of 18 & 19 Vict., 121, (*vide post*,) that Justices, by their order, may require a person to provide sufficient means of drainage, &c., and to drain, empty, cleanse, &c., a water-course, drain, or ashpit, which is a nuisance or injurious to health; and the next section (14) imposes a penalty for contravention of the Justices' order.

11. A Sewer Authority within its District shall have the same Powers in relation to the Supply of Water that a Local Board has within its District, and the Provisions of the Sections herein-after mentioned shall apply accordingly in the same Manner as if in such Provisions "Sewer Authority" were substituted for "Local Board of Health" or "Local Board," and the District in such Provisions mentioned were the District of the Sewer Authority and not the District of the Local Board; that is to say, the Sections numbered from Seventy-five to Eighty, both inclusive, of The Public Health Act, 1848,* Sections Fifty-one, Fifty-two, and Fifty-three of The Local Government Act, 1858,* and Section Twenty of the Local Government Act, 1858,* Amendment Act, 1861.*

Supply of water to District of Sewer Authority.

The Sewer Authority may, if it think it expedient so to do, provide a Supply of Water for the Use† of the Inhabitants of the District by

(1.) Digging Wells;

(2.) Making and maintaining Reservoirs;

(3.) Doing any other necessary Acts;

and they may themselves furnish the same, or contract with any other Persons or Companies to furnish the same: Provided always, that no Land be purchased or taken under this Clause

---

* These sections are appended to Sec. 56.

† "For the use of the inhabitants of the district." It has been held that water used by a defendant for watering his horse and for washing his carriage in his coach-house and stable, situate at the rere of his house, was water for domestic use, within the meaning of a provision in a local Act which empowered a Company to furnish a supply of water for domestic use to the owners and occupiers of houses, at a certain rent. —*Busby* v. *The Chesterfield Water Works and Gas Light Company*, 27 L. J. N. S. M. C. 174.

SECTION 12. except by Agreement or in manner provided by
The Local Government Act, 1858.*

> * See note to Sec. 7 of Sewage Utilization Act.
> It is also provided by Sec. 49 of this Act, that where a
> complaint is made to the Lord Lieutenant that a Sewer
> Authority has made default in providing its district with a
> proper supply of water, the Lord Lieutenant, on the complaint
> being proved, may make an order limiting the time for the
> performance of its duty by the Authority in the matter of such
> complaint ; and if such duty be not performed within the time
> so limited, the Lord Lieutenant may appoint some person to
> perform the same at the cost of the Authority in default.

Expenses
of Sewer
Authority
in supplying
water.

12. Any Expenses incurred by a Sewer Authority in or about the Supply of Water to its District, and in carrying into effect the Provisions herein-before in that Behalf mentioned, shall be deemed to be Expenses incurred by that Authority in carrying into effect The Sewage Utilization Act, 1865, and be payable accordingly.

See Section 6 of the Sewage Utilization Act, 1865, (*post.*)

Wells, &c.,
belonging to
any place
vested in
Sewer
Authority,
&c.
23 & 24 Vict.
c. 77, s 7.

13. All Property in Wells, Fountains, and Pumps, and Powers in relation thereto, vested in the Nuisance Authority by the Seventh Section of the Act passed in the Session of the Twenty-third and Twenty-fourth Years of the Reign of Her present Majesty, Chapter Seventy-seven,† shall vest in the Sewer Authority, where the Sewer Authority supplies Water to its District.

† For this Act see Table of Contents.

29 & 30 *Victoria, Cap.* 90. 11

Part II.*

Amendment of the Nuisances Removal Acts.

Definition of "Nuisances Removal Acts."

14. The Expression "Nuisances Removal Acts"† shall mean the Acts passed in the years following of the Reign of Her present Majesty, that is to say, the one in the Session of the Eighteenth and Nineteenth Years, Chapter One hundred and twenty-one, and the other in the Session of the Twenty-third and Twenty-fourth Years, Chapter Seventy-seven, as amended by this Part of this Act; and this Part of this Act shall be construed as One with the said Acts, and all Expenses incurred by a Nuisance Authority in carrying into effect any of the Provisions of this part of this Act shall be deemed to be Expenses incurred by it in carrying into effect the Nuisances Removal Acts.

* In the application to Ireland of this part of the Sanitary Act, the changes required by Sec. 57 must be observed.
† This expression "Nuisances Removal Acts" has been amended by 32 & 33 Vict., cap. 108, in the application of this Act to Ireland, by including under it "The Nuisances Removal Act for England (Amendment) Act, 1863." The 32 & 33 Vict., cap. 108, is as follows:—

[32 & 33 Vict.] *Sanitary Act (1866) Amendment, (Ireland,) Cap.* 108.

An Act to amend "The Sanitary Act, 1866," so far as the same relates to Ireland.   [11th August, 1869.]

"Nuisances Removal Acts" in Sanitary Act, 1866, to include 26 & 27 Vict., c.

Be it enacted by the Queen's most Excellent Majesty, by and with the advice and consent of the Lords Spiritual and Temporal, and Commons, in this present Parliament assembled, and by the authority of the same as follows:—

1. In the application of "The Sanitary Act, 1866," to Ireland, the term "Nuisances Removal Acts" shall be deemed to include and shall include "The Nuisances Removal Act for England (Amendment) Act, 1863."

117, in application to Ireland.

SECTION 15.

Definition of "Nuisance Authority."

15. "Nuisance Authority" shall mean any Authority empowered to execute the Nuisances Removal Acts.*

＊ The Sewers and Nuisance Authorities in Ireland are described in the first Column of the first Schedule to this Act.

Power of police with respect to nuisances.

16. In any Place within the Jurisdiction of a Nuisance Authority the Chief Officer of Police within that Place, by and under the Directions of One of Her Majesty's Principal Secretaries of State,† on its being proved to his Satisfaction that the Nuisance Authority has made default in doing its Duty, may institute any Proceeding which the Nuisance Authority of such Place might institute with respect to the Removal of Nuisances: Provided always, that no Officer of Police shall be at liberty to enter any House or Part of a House used as the Dwelling of any Person without such Person's Consent, or without the Warrant of a Justice of the Peace, for the Purpose of carrying into effect this Act.

† That is by the Lord Lieutenant or other Chief Governor or Governors of Ireland. See sect. 68.   ·

The course to be adopted in order to have enforced, at the expense of the 'Nuisance Authority, the provisions of this section by any person complaining that the Nuisance Authority has made default in doing its duty, is defined in sect. 49 of this Act.

Sect. 3 of 23 & 24 Vict., c. 77, repealed

17. The Third Section of the said Act of the Session of the Twenty-third and Twenty-fourth Years of the Reign of Her present Majesty, Chapter Seventy-seven, shall be repealed, and all Powers vested in any Highway Board or "Nuisance Removal Committee" under the Nuisance Removal Acts shall determine, and all Property belonging to them for the Purposes of the said Nuisances Removal Acts shall, subject to any

Debts or Liabilities affecting the same, be trans-
ferred to or vested in the Nuisance Authority
under the said Acts: Provided always, that this
Section shall not extend to any Vestry or District Board, under the Act of the Session of
Eighteenth and Nineteenth Years of the Reign 18 & 19 Vict.,
of Her present Majesty, Chapter One hundred c. 120.
and twenty, intituled *An Act for the better Local
Management of the Metropolis,* or to any Committee appointed by such Vestry or District
Board for the Purpose of carrying into effect the
Nuisances Removal Acts or any of them.

18. A requisition in Writing under the Hands Requisition
of any Ten Inhabitants of a Place shall, for the inhabitants
Purposes of the Twenty-seventh Section of "The equivalent
Nuisances Removal Act for *England,** 1855, be of Medical
deemed to be equivalent to the Certificate of the
Medical Officer or Medical Practitioners therein
mentioned, and the said Section shall be enforced
accordingly.

* For this Act see Table of Contents.

19. The Word "Nuisances" under the Nui- Addition to
sance Removal Acts shall include,† nuisance.

(1.) Any House or Part of a House so overcrowded as to be dangerous or prejudicial to the
Health of the Inmates:

(2.) Any Factory, Workshop, or Workplace
not already under the operation of any General
Act for the Regulation of Factories or Bakehouses, not kept in a cleanly State, or not ventilated in such a Manner as to render harmless
as far as practicable any Gases, Vapours, Dust,

† See the definition of Nuisance in Sec. 8 of the Nuisances
Removal Act, 1865. This appears to be an addition to that
definition, and not to supersede it.

SECTION 19. or other Impurities generated in the course of
the Work carried on therein that are a Nuisance
or injurious or dangerous to Health, or so overcrowded while Work is carried on as to be dangerous or Prejudicial to the Health of those
employed therein :

(3.) Any Fire-place or Furnace which does not,
as far as practicable, consume* the Smoke arising
from the Combustible used in such Fire-place or
Furnace, and is used within the District of a
Nuisance Authority for Working Engines by
Steam, or in any Mill, Factory, Dyehouse,
Brewery, Bakehouse, or Gaswork, or in any
Manufactory or Trade Process whatsoever :

    * "Any fireplace or furnace which does not, as far as prac-
ticable, consume," &c. In the Birmingham Improvement Act,
1851, which imposes a penalty for not using smoke-consuming
furnaces, the words *consuming "as far as possible" all the smoke*
was held to mean as far as possible consistently with the carrying on of the manufacture in question ; and it was also held
that where the manufacturer, in using a furnace constructed
to consume its own smoke, has been guilty of no negligence,
but has consumed the smoke as far as he could consistently
with carrying on his manufacture, he ought not to be convicted
in the penalty.—*Cooper* v. *Woolley*, 36 L. J. N. S. M. C. 27.

    The following caution has been extensively served by the
Nuisance Authority in Dublin, on manufacturers with considerable effect :—

CORPORATION OF DUBLIN.

PUBLIC HEALTH COMMITTEE.

           City Hall, Dublin,   1870.

    SIR,—I am directed by the Public Health Committee to
call your immediate attention to the great nuisance caused to
the inhabitants of the neighbourhood of your
by the dense volumes of black smoke which issue from the
chimney belonging thereto, and to request that this serious
inconvenience may be abated without delay.

    The Committee wish to point your attention to the provi-
sions of the 29th & 30th Vic., cap. 90, sec. 19, clause 4, and

4. Any Chimney (not being the Chimney of a private Dwelling House) sending forth Black Smoke in such quantity as to be a Nuisance:

> Provided, first, that in Places where at the Time of the passing of this Act no Enactment is in Force compelling Fireplaces or Furnaces to consume their own Smoke, the foregoing Enactment as to Fireplaces and Furnaces consuming their own Smoke shall not come into operation until the Expiration of One year from the Date of the passing of this Act:

> Secondly, that where a Person is summoned before the Justices in respect of a Nuisance arising from a Fireplace or Furnace which does not consume the Smoke arising from

to inform you that the adoption of an efficient system of stoking would not only tend to abate the annoyance, but would cause a considerable saving in the consumption of fuel ; results with which such a course has already, in some instances, been attended.

I am, Sir, your most obedient servant,

————,

Officer of Health Committee.

These instructions will be found to be most useful for the prevention of the Smoke Nuisance :—

To prevent black smoke issuing from the chimney, when charging the furnace push most of the red coal to the back of the furnace, and spread the remainder evenly to a depth of not less than three inches, and *place the fresh fuel upon the red fire nearest to the door.*

The pieces of fresh fuel must not be larger than the hand when shut ; nor added in such quantity as to choke the furnace.

N.B.—The furnace should never be choked with fuel, as this prevents a sufficient quantity of air from entering, and thereby wastes the fuel, and causes smoke.

If black smoke should issue from the chimney of the furnace, open the furnace door, stir up the black coal, and bring it in contact with the red fire.

the Combustible used in such Fireplace or Furnace, the Justices may hold that no Nuisance is created within the Meaning of this Act, and dismiss the Complaint, if they are satisfied that such Fireplace or Furnace is constructed in such Manner as to consume, as far as practicable,* having regard to the Nature of the Manufacture or Trade, all Smoke arising therefrom, and that such Fireplace or Furnace has been carefully attended to by the Person having the Charge thereof.

* The best available means must be adopted, for it is not enough that the precautions ordinarily adopted in the particular trade or manufacture have been observed.—*Scholefield* v. *Schunck*, 19 J. P. 84.

Duties of Nuisance Authorities as to inspection of nuisances, &c.

20. It shall be the duty of the Nuisance Authority to make from Time to Time, either by itself or its Officers, Inspection of the District, with a view to ascertain what Nuisances exist calling for Abatement under the Powers of the Nuisance Removal Acts, and to enforce the Provisions of the said Acts in order to cause the Abatement thereof, also to enforce the Provisions of any Act that may be in force within its District requiring Fire-places and Furnaces to consume their own Smoke; and any Justice upon Complaint upon Oath may make an Order to admit the Nuisance Authority or their Officers for these Purposes, as well as to ground Proceedings under the Eleventh Section of the Nuisances Removal Act, 1855.*

* "To ground proceedings under the 11th sec. of The Nuisances Removal Act, 1855." For this purpose the sec. of The Nuisances Removal Act here referred to has been amended by The Sanitary Act, 1866, sec. 31, as regards the power of

entry given to the Authorities, especially in relation to nuisances arising from manufactures.   By this last Act, this power of entry may be exercised at any hour when the business in respect of which the nuisance arises is in progress, or is usually carried on : by the former Act, the power of entry was limited to a time between 9 o'clock, A. M. and 6 o'clock, P. M.

This section (20) is compulsory upon the Nuisance Authority to inform themselves of the existence of nuisances, with a view to their abatement by enforcing the provisions of the Nuisances Removal Acts, &c.

21. The Nuisance Authority or Chief Officer of Police shall, previous to taking Proceedings before a Justice under the Twelfth Section of The Nuisances Removal Act, 1855, serve a Notice* on the Person by whose Act, Default,

As to proceedings of Nuisance Authority under sect. 12 of 18 & 19 Vict.. c. 121.

* There is no form of notice, as required by this section, given in the Schedule to the Nuisances Removal Act, 1855. A form is given in the Note to Sec. 12 of that Act.   As regards "The Smoke Nuisance," a notice might be served in this form :—

The Nuisance ⎫   Take Notice, in pursuance of the provisions
 Authority of ⎪   of the Sanitary Act, 1866, and the various
 the _____ ⎪   statutes incorporated therewith, your attention
 _____ ⎬   is requested to the fact that there exists on
 _____ ⎪   your premises situate at   a Nuisance
              ⎪   coming within the meaning and operations of
 To Wit. ____ ⎭   said statutes, an abstract of which is herewith
given, and which is injurious. or dangerous to health, consisting of   and you are hereby required
to take such measures as may be necessary effectually to abate
said Nuisance within   days from this date, otherwise such
proceedings will be instituted under the authority of said statutes as this Nuisance Authority may deem expedient for the
purpose of enforcing such abatement, and for the recovery of
the penalties inflicted by said statutes.
    Dated this   day of   18   .
    To ——, of ——. and to the owner or occupier.
                    Signed ————,
            Officer of said Nuisance Authority.

N. B.—The following are declared to be Nuisances under the provisions of 29 & 30 Vic., chap. 90, section 19·—

1. Any house, or part of a house, so overcrowded as to be dangerous or prejudicial to the health of the inmates.

C

SECTION 21 or Sufferance the Nuisance arises or continues, or, if such Person cannot be found or ascertained, on the Owner or Occupier of the Premises on which the Nuisance arises, to abate the same, and for that Purpose to execute such Works and to do all such things as may be necessary within a Time to be specified in the Notice : Provided,

First, that where the Nuisance arises from the Want or defective Construction of any structural Convenience, or where there is no Occupier of the Premises, Notice under this Section shall be served on the Owner :*

Secondly, that where the Person causing the Nuisance cannot be found, and it is clear that the Nuisance does not arise or continue by the Act, Default, or Sufferance of the Owner or Occupier of the Premises, then the Nuisance Authority may itself abate the same without further Order, and the Cost of so doing shall be part of the Costs of executing the Nuisances Removal Acts, and borne accordingly.

2. Any factory, workshop, or workplace, not kept in a cleanly state, or not ventilated, so as to render harmless gases, vapours, dusts, or other impurities generated in the course of the work carried on therein, or so overcrowded while work is carried on as to be dangerous or prejudicial to health.

3. Any fireplace or furnace which does not, as far as practicable, consume the smoke arising from such fireplace or furnace used for working engines by steam, or in any mill, factory, dyehouse, brewery, bakehouse, or gaswork, or in any manufactory or trade process whatsoever.

4. Any chimney sending forth black smoke in such quantity as to be a Nuisance.

Penalties under the 18th and 19th Victoria, chap. 121, for neglecting to abate Nuisance, £5 per day during the continuance.

* Service of this notice on a person *de facto* receiving the rent is a service on the owner, 33 L. J. M. S. M. C., 11.

Where a nuisance is ascertained by a Nuisance Authority to **SECTION 22.** exist, it is not necessary, before taking proceedings against the owner under this section and Sec. 12 of the Nuisances Removal Act, 1855, to serve him with a notice in the form given in the schedule to the latter Act, (Form C,) which notice is for the examination of the premises by the officers appointed by the Nuisance Authority.—*Amys* v. *Creed*, 38 L. J. N. S. M. C. 22.

22. If the Nuisance Authority shall be of opinion, upon the Certificate of any legally qualified Medical Practioner, that the cleansing and disinfecting of any House or Part thereof, and of any Articles therein likely to retain Infection, would tend to prevent or check infectious or contagious Disease, it shall be the Duty of the Nuisance Authority to give Notice in Writing requiring the Owner or Occupier of such House or Part thereof, to cleanse and disinfect the same as the Case may require; and if the Person to whom Notice is so given fail to comply therewith within the Time specified in the Notice, he shall be liable to a Penalty of not less than One Shilling and not exceeding Ten Shillings for every Day during which he continues to make default; and the Nuisance Authority shall cause such House or Part thereof to be cleansed and disinfected, and may recover the Expenses incurred from the Owner or Occupier in default in a summary Manner; when the Owner or Occupier of any such House or Part thereof as is referred to in this Section is from Poverty or otherwise unable, in the Opinion of the Nuisance Authority, effectually to carry out the Requirements of this Section, such Authority may, without enforcing such Requirements on such Owner or Occupier, with his Consent, at its own Expense, cleanse and disinfect such House or Part thereof and any Articles therein likely to retain Infection.

(margin: Power to cause premises to be cleansed or otherwise disinfected.)

This section is the first of a series of enactments contained

SECTION 23. in this Act, for the purpose of preventing as far as possible the spread of ordinary contagious and infectious diseases. This series consists of Sections 22, 23, 24, 25, 26, 27, 28, 29, 37, 38, 39, and may be divided into two classes—1st. Those which relate to the powers of the Authority with respect to *persons ;* and 2nd. Those which relate to the powers of the Authority with respect to *things :—*

PERSONS.	THINGS.'
Section 25. Power to enforce a penalty on a party who, suffering under an infectious disorder, enters a public conveyance without notifying to the driver or owner that he is so suffering.	[Section 22.' Power] of the authority to cause premises under a penalty to be cleansed or otherwise disinfected.
26. Power to remove to hospital persons sick of infectious disorders, and who are without proper accommodation.	23. Power to provide means of disinfection of clothing, bedding, &c.
29. Power to remove to hospital sick persons brought by ships.	24. Power to provide carriages to convey sick persons to hospital or to their own homes, in order to prevent the use by them of public conveyances.
38. Power to enforce a penalty on persons suffering from infectious disease, or on any person in charge of said sufferer exposing himself in a public place or conveyance.	27. Power to appoint places for the reception of the dead bodies of those who have been sick of infectious disorders, and to appoint a limited time for their burial.
39. Power to enforce a penalty on persons letting houses in which infected persons have been lodging, innkeepers included.	28. Power to appoint places for the reception of dead bodies during the time required for *post-mortem* examinations.
	37. Power to provide hospitals

It is not advisable, in connection with the consideration of those, which are only the ordinary preventive powers given to the Authority, to introduce the Diseases Prevention Act, 1855, or the Nuisances Removal and Diseases Prevention Act, 1860 ; for, the calling into operation of the latter is only provisional, and contingent upon the country being attacked by, or threatened with, any formidable epidemic or contagious disease.

Power to provide means of disinfection.

23. The Nuisance Authority in each District may provide a proper place, with all necessary Apparatus and Attendance, for the Disinfection of Woollen Articles, Clothing, or Bedding which have become infected, and they may cause any Articles brought for Disinfection to be disinfected free of Charge.

As the danger arising from such diseases as fever, smallpox, scarlatina, &c., spreading in a house or neighbourhood, can be in a great measure prevented by disinfecting the clothes and bedding of the sufferers, a hot-air chamber might be constructed by the Authority under this section, and at very little cost, where all such tainted articles could be sent any day in the week for the purpose of disinfection. Such a chamber has been constructed in the city of Dublin, and is under the direction of the Nuisance Authorities and their officers. The entire process is completed in a few hours, and the owners receive the articles back free from infection and without charge.

24. It shall be lawful at all Times for the Nuisance Authority to provide and maintain a Carriage or Carriages suitable for the Conveyance of Persons suffering under any contagious or infectious Disease, and to pay the Expense of conveying any Person therein to a Hospital or Place for the Reception of the Sick or to his own Home.

Nuisance Authorities may provide carriages for conveyance of infected persons.

25. If any Person suffering from any dangerous infectious Disorder shall enter any public Conveyance without previously notifying to the Owner or Driver thereof that he is so suffering, he shall on Conviction thereof before any Justice be liable to a Penalty not exceeding Five Pounds, and shall also be ordered by such Justice to pay to such Owner and Driver all the Losses and Expenses they may suffer in carrying into effect the Provisions of this Act; and no Owner or Driver of any public Conveyance shall be required to convey any Person so suffering until they shall have been first paid a Sum sufficient to cover all such Losses and Expenses.*

Penalty on person suffering from infectious disorder entering public conveyance without notifying to driver that he is so suffering.

Notwithstanding this notice to the driver or owner of the public conveyance, a person suffering from, or any person in charge of any one suffering from an infectious disorder must take proper precaution against the spreading of said disorder under a penalty of £5. (Sec. 38.)

* These losses and expenses, as detailed in Section 38, are

SECTION 26. incurred in having the conveyance thoroughly disinfected after
it has conveyed any such sufferer. The previous section (24)
enables the authority to guard against the spread of infection
in this manner, by providing carriages for the conveyance of
persons to the hospitals or to their own homes.

Removal of persons sick of infectious disorders, and without proper lodging, in any District. 26. Where a Hospital or Place for the Reception of the Sick is provided within the District of a Nuisance Authority, any Justice may, with the Consent of the Superintending Body of such Hospital or Place, by Order on a Certificate signed by a legally qualified Medical Practioner, direct the Removal to such Hospital or Place for the Reception of the Sick, at the Cost of the Nuisance Authority, of any Person suffering from any dangerous contagious or infectious Disorder, being without proper Lodging or Accommodation, or lodged in a Room occupied by* more than One Family, or being on Board any Ship or Vessel.

* The term "in a room occupied by more than one family,"
refers to common lodging-houses. (See note to Sec. 35.)

This section (26) is evidently for the purpose of compelling the
poor, who so frequently are without proper lodging and accommodation in their own dwellings during a dangerous illness, to
go to Hospital. By Sec. 37, the Nuisance Authority is empowered to provide hospital accommodation for all such persons within its district.

Places for the reception of dead bodies may be provided at the public expense. 27. Any Nuisance Authority may provide a proper Place for the Reception of dead Bodies,† and where any such Place has been provided and any dead Body of one who has died of any infectious Disease is retained in a Room in which Persons live or sleep, or any dead Body which is in such a State as to endanger the Health of the

† This place is not to be used for the purpose of holding
post-mortem examinations. (Sec. 28.)

Inmates of the same House or Room is retained in such House or Room, any Justice may, on a Certificate signed by a legally qualified Medical Practitioner, order the Body to be removed to such proper Place of Reception at the Cost of the Nuisance Authority, and direct the same to be buried within a Time to be limited in such Order; and unless the Friends or Relations of the Deceased undertake to bury the Body within the Time so limited, and do bury the same,* it shall be the Duty of the Relieving Officer to bury such Body at the Expense of the Poor Rate, but any Expense so incurred may be recovered by the Relieving Officer in a summary Manner from any Person legally liable to pay the Expense of such Burial.

* This section appears to have been enacted principally with a view to prevent the spread of infection which might be caused by the holding of "wakes." On such occasions a number of persons are usually congregated in the room with the dead body, and, as a consequence, the spread of infection is materially facilitated.

It also provides, though indirectly, for the interment of the remains of destitute persons, which had been left unprovided for by the abolition of the Vestry Cess in Ireland.

28. Any Nuisance Authority may provide a proper Place (otherwise than at a Workhouse or at a Mortuary House as lastly hereinbefore provided for) for the Reception of dead Bodies for and during the Time required to conduct any *Post-mortem* Examination ordered by the Coroner of the District or other constituted Authority, and may make such Regulations as they may deem fit for the Maintenance, Support, and Management of such Place; and where any such Place has been provided, any Coroner or other constituted Authority may order the Removal of

Places for reception of dead bodies during time required for post-mortem examination may be provided.

SECTION 29. the Body for carrying out such *Post-mortem* Examination and the Re-removal of such Body, such Costs of Removal and Re-removal to be paid in the same Manner and out of the same Fund as the Cost and Fees for *Post-mortem* Examinations when ordered by the Coroner.

Power to remove to hospital sick persons brought by ships.

29. Any Nuisance Authority may, with the Sanction of the Privy Council,* signified in manner provided by "The Public Health Act, 1858," lay down Rules for the Removal to any Hospital to which such Authority is entitled to remove Patients, and for keeping in such Hospital so long as may be necessary any Persons brought within their District by any Ship or Boat who are infected with a dangerous and infectious Disorder, and they may by such Rules impose any Penalty not exceeding Five Pounds on any Person committing any Offence against the same.

* In Ireland the Lord Lieutenant in Council. (See Sec. 68.)

There have been no regulations issued by any Authority in Ireland, for the removal to hospital under this section. Masters of vessels (who by Sec. 32 are deemed to be the owners or occupiers thereof) have invariably shown a ready desire to avail themselves of the hospital accommodation which is afforded. The extent of the jurisdiction of the Nuisance Authority as regards ships is detailed in the next section.

Provision as to district of Nuisance Authority extending to places where ships are lying.

30. For the Purposes of this Act any Ship, Vessel, or Boat that is in a place not within the District of a Nuisance Authority shall be deemed to be within the District of such Nuisance Authority as may be prescribed by the Privy Council, and until a Nuisance Authority has been prescribed then of the Nuisance Authority whose District nearest adjoins the Place where such Ship, Vessel, or Boat is lying, the Distance being measured in a straight Line, but nothing

in this Act contained shall enable any Nuisance Authority to interfere with any Ship, Vessel, or Boat that is not in *British* Waters.

SECTION 31.

31. The Power of Entry given to the Authorities by the Eleventh Section of The Nuisances Removal Act, 1855,* may be exercised at any Hour when the Business in respect of which the Nuisance arises is in progress or is usually carried on.

Power of entry to Nuisance Authority or their officer under sec. 11 of 18 & 19 Vict. c. 121.

And any Justice's Order once issued under the said Section shall continue in force until the Nuisance has been abated, or the Work for which the Entry was necessary has been done.

* See Table of Contents.

32. Any Ship or Vessel lying in any River, Harbour, or other Water shall be subject to the Jurisdiction of the Nuisance Authority of the District within which such River, Harbour, or other Water is, and be within the Provisions of the Nuisances Removal Acts, in the same Manner as if it were a House within such Jurisdiction, and the Master or other Officer in charge of such Ship shall be deemed for the Purposes of the Nuisances Removal Acts to be the Occupier of such Ship or Vessel; but this Section shall not apply to any Ship or Vessel belonging to Her Majesty or to any Foreign Government.

Provision as to ships within the jurisdiction of Nuisance Authority.

33. Where the Guardians are the Nuisance Authority for Part of any Parish only, and shall require to expend Money on account of such Part in execution of the Provisions of the said Acts, the Overseers of the Parish shall, upon Receipt of an Order from the said Guardians,

Provision for raising money in divided parishes.

SECTION 34. raise the requisite Amount from the Persons liable to be assessed to the Poor Rate therein by a Rate to be made in like Manner as a Poor Rate, and shall have all the same Powers of making and recovering the same, and of paying the Expense of collecting the Rate when made and shall account to the Auditor of the District for Receipt and Disbursement of the same, in like Manner, and with the same Consequences, as in the Case of the Poor Rate made by them.*

* This Section is not applicable to Ireland.

Nuisance
Authority
may require
payment
of costs or
expenses
from owner
or occupier,
and occupier
paying to
deduct from
rent.
34. That it shall be lawful for the Nuisance Authority, at their Discretion, to require the Payment of any Costs or Expenses which the Owner of any Premises may be liable to pay under the said Nuisances Removal Acts or this Act, either from the Owner or from any Person who then or at any Time thereafter occupies such Premises, and such Owner or Occupier shall be liable to pay the same, and the same shall be recovered in Manner authorized by the Nuisance Removal Acts,* and the Owner shall allow such Occupier to deduct the Sums of Money which he so pays out of the Rent from Time to Time becoming due in respect of the said Premises, as if the same had been actually paid to such Owner as Part of such Rent: Provided always, that no such Occupier shall be required to pay any further Sum than the Amount of Rent for the Time being due from him, or which, after such demand of such Costs or Expenses from such Occupier, and after Notice not to pay his Landlord any Rent without first deducting the Amount of such Costs or

* See Sections 19 and 20 of the Act 18 and 19 Vict., c. 121.

Expenses, becomes payable by such Occupier, SECTION 34. unless he refuse, on Application being made to him for that Purpose by or on behalf of the Nuisance Authority, truly to disclose the Amount of his Rent and the Name and Address of the Person to whom such Rent is payable, but the Burden of Proof that the Sum demanded from any such Occupier is greater than the Rent due by him at the Time of such Notice, or which has since accrued, shall lie upon such Occupier; provided also, that nothing* herein contained shall be taken to affect any Contract made or to be made between any Owner or Occupier of any House, Building, or other Property whereof it is or may be agreed that the Occupier shall pay or discharge all Rates, Dues, and Sums of Money payable in respect of such House, Building, or other Property, or to affect any Contract whatsoever between Landlord or Tenant.

* An agreement for the lease of premises stipulated that the landlord should keep the premises in good and substantial repair, and should pay and discharge all rates, taxes, tithes, and other charges payable in respect of the premises. A piece of ornamental water formed part of the demised premises, in which a deposit of foul mud having accumulated, it became a nuisance. The local Authority, under 18 and 19 Vict., cap. 121, took proceedings against the tenant, and obtained an order of Justices against him, as the person by whose default the nuisance arose, for the removal of the nuisance. The tenant paid £100 to a contractor for the cleansing of the piece of water, and brought an action to recover said sum from the landlord for breach of agreement and for money paid to his use, and it was held that the landlord was not under the agreement to repair, liable to cleanse the piece of water, and that the expense of removing the nuisance was not a charge within the meaning of the agreement.—*Bird* v. *Elwes*, 37 L. J. Exch. 91 ; 3 L. R. Exch. 225.

Part III.*

Miscellaneous.

SECTION 35.

In cities, boroughs, or towns, Secretary of State, on application of Nuisance Authority, may empower them to make regulations as to lodging houses.

35. On Application† to One of Her Majesty's Principal Secretaries of State by the Nuisance Authority‡ of the City of London, or any District or Parish included within the Act for the better Local Government of the Metropolis, or of any Municipal Borough, or of any Place under The Local Government Act, 1858, or any Local Improvement Act, or of any City or Town containing, according to the Census for the Time being in force, a Population of not less than Five Thousand Inhabitants, the Secretary of State may, as he may think fit, by Notice to be published in the *London Gazette,*§ declare the following Enactment to be in force in the District of such Nuisance Authority, and from and after the Publication of such Notice, the Nuisance Authority shall be empowered to make Regulations for the following Matters ; that is to say,

1. For fixing the Number of Persons who may occupy a House or Part of a House which

* In the application of this part of the Sanitary Act to Ireland, the changes prescribed by Sec. 61 must be observed.

† The application mentioned in this section for power to make Regulations as to Lodging Houses may be made by any Nuisance Authority, except a Board of Guardians, (see Sec. 61,) and must be made to the Lord Lieutenant in Council ; and the said Lord Lieutenant in Council shall have the power of declaring the Enactments as to Lodging Houses to be in force in any Nuisance District.—Sec. 68.

‡ For the purpose of this part of this Act, Sewer and Nuisance Authorities in Ireland are incorporated.—Sec. 61.

§ This Notice, as regards Irish Enactments, must be published in the *Dublin Gazette*, in accordance with Sec. 67.

is let in Lodgings, or occupied by Members SECTION 35. of more than one Family:

2. For the Registration of Houses thus let or occupied in Lodgings:

3. For the Inspection of such Houses, and the keeping the same in a cleanly and wholesome State:

4. For enforcing therein the Provision of Privy Accommodation, and other Appliances and Means of Cleanliness, in proportion to the Number of Lodgings and Occupiers, and the Cleansing and Ventilation of the common Passages and Staircases:

5. For the cleansing and lime-whiting at stated Times of such Premises:

The Nuisance Authority may provide for the Enforcement of the above Regulations by Penalties not exceeding Forty Shillings for any One Offence, with an additional Penalty not exceeding Twenty Shillings for every Day during which a default in obeying such Regulations may continue; but such Regulations shall not be of any Validity unless and until they shall have been confirmed by the Secretary of State:*

But this Section shall not apply to Common Lodging Houses† within the Provisions of the Common Lodging Houses Act, 1851, or any Act amending the same.

* That is the Lord Lieutenant in Ireland.

† This section does not apply to Common Lodging Houses. A Common Lodging House is one in which beds are let by the night, to parties who have no fixed residence; and the expression "Common Lodging House" includes, in any case in which only a part of a house is used as a Common Lodging House, the part so used of such house.—14 & 15 Vict., c. 28. One room, therefore, which is occupied by the letting of beds nightly, is a "Common Lodging House" within the meaning of the Act, although the remainder of the house may be occu-

pied by weekly tenants. The distinction drawn by the last
paragraph of this section is for the purpose of confining its
provisions to houses let in lodgings, weekly or for any longer
term, and occupied by members of more than one family.

The following are the Regulations with respect to the latter
which have been approved and enacted by the Lord Lieutenant under this section, upon the application of the Authority
at Dublin :—

*Regulations for Houses and parts of Houses let in Lodgings, and
occupied by members of more than one family, within the Borough of Dublin, under the Sanitary Act, 1866, Sec. 35,
other than Common Lodging Houses, within the provisions of
the Common Lodging House Act, 1851. Made by the Nuisance Authority of the Borough of Dublin, the 4th day of
December, 1866.*

Every house or part of a house let in lodgings, or occupied
by members of more than one family, shall be subject to the
following regulations :—

1. That no greater number of persons shall occupy any room
in any such house than can be accommodated with 300 cubic
feet of space for each, (for example, a room 10 feet high,
15 feet long, and 10 feet wide, contains 1,500 cubic feet of
space, and may therefore accommodate five persons.)

2. That said Authority, or any of its officers, may enter and
inspect any such houses, or any apartments or appurtenances
thereof, without let or hindrance, between the hours of 10 A.M.
and 4 P.M., for the purpose of carrying into effect these regulations and the provisions of said Act, or in special cases at
any other time, upon the signed requisition of the Chairman of
the Committee of said Authority, by vote. of the Committee,
and not otherwise; and may inspect and measure the dimensions of each room, and affix on the door thereof, a description
of the cubic contents of such room, in a form to be provided
by such Authority, and any removal or defacement of such
certificate shall be deemed a breach of these regulations.

3. That the owner of every such house shall have supplied
thereto a properly-constructed ashpit and privy, or water-closet,
or privies or water-closets sufficient to accommodate the inhabitants thereof, and a properly-trapped house-drain communicating with the main sewer, (if any within 100 feet from such
house,) and if no such main sewer, then with a proper cesspool ; and shall cause privies, water-closets, ash-pits, cesspools, and house-drain to be kept cleansed and in proper
repair ; and shall also provide for each such house a sufficient
supply of pure water ; and keep the roof, external walls, and
chimneys of such house in reasonable repair, impervious to

wet ; and shall cause each window of such house to be made SECTION 36.
capable of being opened from the top, or raised from. the
bottom, or otherwise opened to the extent of the half of each
sash, and shall cause the entrance and hall, rooms, staircases,
and lobbies thereof, to be put and kept in good repair. and in
a cleanly and ventilated state; and no room shall be let, or used
as a sleeping apartment unless it shall have at least one window; and all yards, halls, staircases, passages, and rooms, not
papered or oil-painted, he shall cause to be lime-washed at
least every six months. Within the provisions of this regulation the word "owner" shall mean the person or persons who for
the time being shall be in receipt of the rents of the lodgers, or
other occupiers of such premises.

4. That no occupant residing in any such house, nor any
other person, shall throw from any window or other opening
to or upon any roof, shed, yard, passage, or street, any
water, foul liquid, or other offensive matter or thing, or shall
throw or drop same in or upon any common entrance, staircase,
lobby, street, or place, other than that provided for the proper
deposit thereof, and every occupant or other person shall so
use any requisite in or appurtenant to any such house as not to
injure or break same, or render ineffective, or put same out of
order.

5. For every offence against any of these regulations, or any
portion thereof, the party so offending is hereby subjected to a
penalty of not more than 40s. for any one offence, with an
additional penalty not exceeding 20s. for every day during
which a default in obeying such regulation may continue, and
such penalties shall be levied, recovered, and applied as is
provided by said Act.

6. That the said Authority may, with the consent of the
Lord Lieutenant in Council, vary, alter, amend, add to, or
rescind, in part or in the whole, any of the foregoing regulations, as may from time to time be deemed expedient.

Approved of by the Committee.

H. MACLEAN,

Chairman of the said Nuisance Authority
of the Borough of Dublin.

I confirm the above Regulations.

ABERCORN.

36. Where Two Convictions against the Provisions of any Act relating to the over-crowding
of a House, or the occupation of a Cellar as a
separate Dwelling Place, shall have taken place
within the Period of Three Months, whether

Cases in which two convictions have occurred within three months.

the Persons so convicted were or were not the
same, it shall be lawful for any Two Justices
to direct the closing of such Premises for such
Time as they may deem necessary, and, in the
case of Cellars* occupied as aforesaid, to empower
the Nuisance Authority to permanently close the
same, in such Manner as they may deem fit, at
their own Cost.

* For the occupation as to cellars, see extract from Public
Health Act (Table of contents) ; also see Sec. 42 of this Act.

Power to provide hospitals.

37. The Sewer Authority, or in the Metropolis
the Nuisance Authority, may provide for the
Use of the Inhabitants within its District Hospitals or temporary Places for the Reception of
the Sick.

Such Authority may itself build such Hospitals or Places of Reception, or make Contracts
for the Use of any existing Hospital or Part of a
Hospital, or for the temporary Use of any Place
for the Reception of the Sick.

It may enter into any agreement with any
Person or Body of Persons having the Management of any Hospital for the Reception of the
sick Inhabitants of its District, on payment by
the Sewer Authority of such annual or other
Sum as may be agreed upon.

The carrying into effect this Section shall in
the case of a Sewer Authority be deemed to be
one of the Purposes of the said Sewage Utilization Act, 1865, and all the Provisions of the said
Act shall apply accordingly.

Two or more Authorities having respectively
the Power to provide separate Hospitals may
combine in providing a common Hospital, and
all Expenses incurred by such Authorities in

providing such Hospital shall be deemed to be SECTION 38.
expenses incurred by them respectively in carrying into effect the Purposes of this Act.

38. Any Person suffering from any dangerous Penalty on
any person
infectious Disorder who wilfully exposes himself, with infectious disor-
without proper Precaution against spreading the der exposing
said Disorder, in any Street, public Place, or himself, or
on any per-
public Conveyance, and any Person in charge of son in charge
of such suf-
one so suffering who so exposes the Sufferer, and ferer causing
any Owner or Driver of a public Conveyance such exposure.
who does not immediately provide for the Disinfection of his Conveyance after it has, with the
Knowledge of such Owner or Driver, conveyed
any such Sufferer, and any Person who without
previous disinfection gives, lends, sells, trans-
mits, or exposes any Bedding, Clothing, Rags,
or other Things which have been exposed to Infection from such Disorders, shall on Conviction
of such Offence before any Justice, be liable to a
Penalty not exceeding Five Pounds: Provided
that no Proceedings under this Section shall be
taken against Persons transmitting with proper
Precautions any such Bedding, Clothing, Rags,
or other things for the Purpose of having the
same disinfected.

Sec. 23 authorizes the Nuisance Authority in each district to
provide means of disinfection.

39. If any Person knowingly lets any House, Penalty on
persons
Room, or Part of a House in which any Person letting
houses
suffering from any dangerous infectious Disorder in which
has been, to any other Person without having infected persons have
such House, Room, or Part of a House, and all been lodging
Articles therein liable to retain Infection, disinfected to the Satisfaction of a qualified Medical

SECTION 40. Practitioner as testified by a Certificate given by him, such Person shall be liable to a Penalty not exceeding Twenty Pounds. For the Purposes of this Section the Keeper of an Inn shall be deemed to let Part of a House to any Person admitted as a Guest into such Inn.

Guardians &c., of the poor to be the Local Authorities for executing Diseases Prevention Act.

40. Where in any Place Two or more Boards of Guardians or Local Authorities have Jurisdiction, the Privy Council may, by any Order made under the Diseases Prevention Act, 1855, authorize or require such Boards to act together for the Purposes of that Act, and may prescribe the Mode of such joint Action and of defraying the Costs thereof.

This section enables the Lord Lieutenant of Ireland in Council (who is identical with the Privy Council, by Sec. 61,) to authorize or require two or more Boards of Guardians, or other Local Authorities, to act together for the purpose of carrying into effect the 18th & 19th Vic, c. 116* (Diseases Prevention Act, 1855,) as amended by 23rd & 24th Vict., c. 77* (Diseases Prevention Act, 1860.)

The Diseases Prevention Acts of 1855* and 1860* being merely provisional, the power to call them into force is vested in the Lord Lieutenant. The occasions upon which the Lord Lieutenant may exercise that power are detailed in Sec 5 of the 18th & 19th Vict., c. 116 ;* and with reference to the carrying out of the said Diseases Prevention Acts it is provided by Sec. 62 of the Sanitary Act, 1866, that the "Commissioners for Administering the Laws for the Relief of the Poor in Ireland, called the Poor Law Commissioners, shall be the Authority in Ireland for issuing regulations to carry the provisions of said Acts into effect." The purposes of these regulations are clearly explained by Sec. 6 of 18th & 19th Vict., c. 116.

Evidence of family in case of overcrowded houses.

41. In any Proceedings under The Common Lodging Houses Act, 1851,* if the Inmates of any House or Part of a House allege that they are Members of the same Family, the Burden of

---

* For these Acts see Table of Contents.

proving such Allegation shall lie on the Persons SECTION 42
making it.

The opportunity afforded by the passing of this Act was taken by the Legislature to introduce this section by way of amendment to the "Common Lodging Houses Act," for, whenever the officer appointed visited these common lodging houses and found them to be overcrowded, it had been the practice of the keeper of the house, or room, to shield himself from penalties by pleading that the occupants were all members of the same family, and that consequently the house, or room, was exempt from the operation of the Common Lodging House Act and the Bye-laws made thereunder. Now the *onus probandi* is laid upon the defendant. As to Common Lodging Houses see note to Sec. 35, Page 29.

42. The Sixty-seventh Section* of The Public Health Act, 1848, relating to Cellar Dwellings, shall apply to every Place in *England and Ireland* where such Dwellings are not regulated by any other Act of Parliament, and in applying that Section to Places where it is not in force at the Time of the passing of this Act the Expression "this Act" shall be construed to mean the "Sanitary Act, 1866," and not the said "Public Health Act, 1848." In construing the said Sixty-seventh Section as applied by this Act Nuisance Authority shall be substituted for the Local Board. Extension to the whole of England and Ireland of sec. 67 of 11 & 12 Vict., c. 63.

The marginal note to this section is incorrect. The 67th Section of the Public Health Act extends merely to places where cellars are not regulated by any other Act of Parliament; for instance it does not extend to Dublin, inasmuch as the cellar dwellings there are regulated by 12th & 13th Vict., c. 97 (the Dublin Improvement Act, 1847,) Sec 62 of which incorporates therewith 10th & 11th Vict., c. 34, secs. 113, 114, and 115 of which Act relate to such dwellings.

* *Section 67 of the Public Health Act*, 1848, *is as follows:—*

67. And be it enacted, that it shall not be lawful to let or occupy or suffer to be occupied separately as a dwelling any vault, cellar, or underground room built or rebuilt after the Occupation of cellars, &c.

SECTION 42.

Cellars, &c., newly built, not to be let as dwelling rooms.

No cellars, &c., to be let except under certain conditions.

passing of this Act, or which shall not have been so let or occupied before the passing of this Act ; and it shall not be lawful to let or continue to let, or to occupy or suffer to be occupied, separately as a dwelling, any vault, cellar, or under-ground room whatsoever, unless the same be in every part thereof at least seven feet in height, measured from the floor to the ceiling thereof, nor unless the same be at least three feet of its height above the surface of the street or ground adjoining or nearest to the same, nor unless there be outside of and ad-joining the same vault, cellar, or room, and extending along the entire frontage thereof, and upwards from six inches below the level of the floor thereof up to the surface of the said street or ground, an open area of at least two feet and six inches wide in every part, nor unless the same be well and effectually drained by means of a drain the uppermost part of which is one foot at least below the level of the floor of such vault, cellar, or room, nor unless there be appurtenant to such vault, cellar, or room the use of a watercloset or privy and an ashpit, furnished with proper doors and coverings kept and provided according to the provisions of this Act, nor unless the same have a fireplace with a proper chimney or flue, nor unless the same have an external window of at least nine superficial feet in area clear of the sash frame, and made to open in such manner as shall be approved by the Surveyor, except in the case of an inner or back vault, cellar, or room let or oc-cupied along with a front vault, cellar, or room as part of the same letting or occupation, in which case the external window may be of any dimensions not being less than four superficial feet in area clear of the sash frame ; and whosoever lets, occupies, or continues to let, or knowingly suffers it to be occupied for hire or rent, any vault, cellar, or underground room, contrary to this Act, shall be liable for every such offence to a penalty not exceeding twenty shillings for every day during which the same continues to be so let or occupied after notice in writing from the Local Board of Health* in this behalf : Provided always, that in any area adjoining a vault, cellar, or underground room, there may be steps necessary for access to such vault, cellar, or room, if the same be so placed as not to be over, across, or opposite to the said external win-dow, and so as to allow between every part of such steps and the external wall of such vault, cellar, or room, a clear space of six inches at the least, and that over or across any such area there may be steps necessary for access to any building above the vault, cellar, or room to which such area adjoins, if the same be so placed as not to be over, across, or opposite to any

---

* "Nuisance Authority" is substituted for Local Board by Sec. 42 of the Sanitary Act, 1866, Page 35.

such external window: Provided also, that every vault, cellar, SECTION 43.
or underground room in which any person passes the night,
shall be deemed to be occupied as a dwelling within the meaning of this Act: Provided also, that the provisions of this Act **Act not to**
with respect to the letting and occupation of vaults, cellars, **come into**
and underground rooms, shall not, so far as the same relate to **operation until the**
vaults, cellars, and underground rooms which shall have been **expiration of**
let or occupied as dwellings before the passing of this Act, **a certain**
come into force or operation until the expiration of one year **time, in case of cellars, &c.**
from the passing of this Act, nor within any district until the **already**
expiration of six months from the time when this Act shall **occupied as**
have been applied thereto; and all Churchwardens and Over- **dwellings.**
seers of the Poor shall, from time to time after the passing of **Church-**
this Act, cause public notice of the provisions of this Act with **wardens, &c.**
respect to the letting and occupation of vaults, cellars, and **notice of**
underground rooms to be given in such manner as may appear **enactment.**
to them to be best calculated to make the same generally
known.

43. Local Boards* acting in execution of The **Local Board**
Local Government Act, 1858, may adopt the **in certain cases may**
Act to encourage the Establishment of public **adopt Baths and Wash-**
Baths and Wash-houses, and any Act amend- **houses Acts.**
ing the same, for Districts in which those Acts
are not already in force, and when they have
adopted the said Acts they shall have all the
Powers, Duties, and Rights of Commissioners
under the said Acts; and all Expenses incurred
by any Local Board in carrying into execution
the Acts referred to in this Section shall be defrayed out of the General District Rates, and all
Receipts by them under the said Acts shall be
carried to the District Fund Account.

* This power cannot be exercised by Boards of Guardians,
but it may be by all other Sewer or Nuisance Authorities,
Sec. 61.

44. When the District of a Burial Board is **Power of**
conterminous with the District of a Local Board **Burial Boards in**
of Health, the Burial Board may, by Resolution **certain cases**
of the Vestry, and by Agreement of the Burial **to transfer their powers**
Board and Local Board, transfer to the Local **to Local Board.**

SECTION 45. Board all their Estate, Property, Rights, Powers, Duties, and Liabilities, and from and after such Transfer the Local Board shall have all such Estate, Property, Rights, Powers, Duties and Liabilities, as if the Local Board had been appointed a Burial Board by Order in Council under the Fourth Section of the Act of the Session of the Twentieth and Twenty-first Years of the Reign of her present Majesty, Chapter Eighty-one.

Penalty for wilful damage of works.
45. If any Person wilfully damages any Works or Property belonging to any Local Board, Sewer Authority, or Nuisance Authority, he shall be liable to a Penalty not exceeding Five Pounds.

Incorporation of Sanitary Authorities.
46. The following Bodies, that is to say, Local Boards, Sewer Authorities, and Nuisance Authorities, if not already incorporated, shall respectively be Bodies Corporate designated by such Names as they may usually bear or adopt, with Power to sue and be sued in such Names, and to hold Lands for the Purposes of the several Acts conferring Powers on such Bodies respectively in their several Characters of Local Boards, Sewer Authorities, or Nuisance Authorities.

Extent of authority to make provisional orders respecting lands under Sec. 75 of 21 & 22 Vict. cap. 98.
47. The Authority conferred on One of Her Majesty's Principal Secretaries of State by Section Seventy-five of The Local Government Act, 1858, to empower by Provisional Order a Local Board to put in force, with reference to the Land referred to in such Order, the Powers of The Lands Clauses Consolidation Act, 1845, with respect to ithe Purchase and taking of Lands otherwise than by Agreement, shall extend and

apply and shall be deemed to have always extended and applied to every Case in which, by The Public Health Act, 1848, and The Local Government Act, 1858, or either of them, or any Act extending or amending those Acts, or either of them, a Local Board are authorized to purchase, provide, use, or take Lands or Premises for any of the Purposes of the said Acts, or either of them, or of any such Act as aforesaid; and Sections Seventy-three and Eighty-four of The Public Health Act, 1848, shall be construed as if the Words " by Agreement" therein respectively used had been expressly repealed by Section Seventy-five of The Local Government Act, 1858.

The Local Board of Health of Hastings, being desirous of widening a road in that town, presented a petition to the Secretary of State, stating that they proposed under the provisions of the Local Government Act, 1858, and the several Acts incorporated therewith, to widen the road, and praying for that purpose to be allowed to put in force the compulsory powers of the Lands Clauses Consolidation Act to enable them to take land belonging to B. The Secretary of State, in the year 1864, in spite of B.'s opposition, granted a provisional order to take his land contingent, however, upon its being confirmed by Parliament. In 1865, an Act was passed confirming the order, "so far as it was authorized by the Local Government Act, 1858, and the Acts incorporated therewith." Subsequently, this Sanitary Act, 1866, became law, in which, without the knowledge of B., this 47th section was introduced. Upon a motion for an injunction to restrain the defendant from proceeding to take the land, it was held that upon the construction of the 47th section and the Acts referred to, the Board of Health had not power to take B.'s land otherwise than by agreement. The words of V. C. Stuart upon this enactment are somewhat remarkable. He said :— " Section 47 of the Sanitary Act, 1866, is a most extraordinary one. It is a highly difficult section to construe, and from the circumstances under which it was passed seems clearly intended to do what Parliament in the preceding Session refused to do. The section is general in its terms, and deals with all the lands affected by the Acts of 1845 and 1858, and provides that

SECTION 48 — the 73rd and 84th sections of the Public Health Act, 1848, shall be read as if the words 'by agreement' therein respectively used had been expressly repealed by the 75th section of the Local Government Act, 1858. It does not provide for the omission of any other words, and it is quite impossible to read the Act as so altered in any way capable of making it anything else than nonsense. It has, in fact, been perfectly bungled in the attempt to attain the objects proposed, one of which was, perhaps, not of a nature to be avowed."—(*Frewen* v. *Hastings Local Board of Health*, 16, L. T., N. S. 553.)

Appearance of Local Authorities in legal proceedings

48. Any Local Board, Sewer Authority, or Nuisance Authority may appear before any Justice or Justices, or in any legal Proceeding, by its Clerk or by any Officer or Member authorized generally or in respect of any special Proceeding by Resolution of such Board or Authority, and such Person being so authorized shall be at liberty to institute and carry on any Proceeding which the Nuisance Authority is authorized to institute and carry on under the Nuisance Removal Acts or this Act.

In accordance with this section the appointment of an officer of a Nuisance Authority, with power to institute proceedings, ought to be in specific terms, and by resolution signed by the chairman. (See Sec. 5 of the Nuisance Removal Act for England, 1855.)

The resolution might be to this effect :—

RESOLVED,—That pursuant to the powers enabling this Nuisance Authority of   in that behalf, we, the said Nuisance Authority do hereby authorize

And he is hereby authorized to appear on behalf of the said Nuisance Authority generally, before any Justice or Justices, and in any legal proceedings which may be instituted against the said Nuisance Authority, and to institute and carry on any proceedings which the Nuisance Authority is authorized to institute and carry on under the Nuisance Removal Act or the Sanitary Acts, 1866, and Acts incorporated therewith.

This   day of

Chairman of the Nuisance Authority
of the

In case of a complaint to the Justices on behalf of an Authority, the Justices are not bound to adjudicate unless the Clerk SECTION 49. of the Board attends the hearing by himself or by his attorney or counsel.—(*Ex parte* Leamington, 26 J. P. 84.)

49. Where Complaint is made to One of Her Majesty's Principal Secretaries of State* that a Sewer Authority or Local Board of Health has made default in providing its District with sufficient Sewers, or in the Maintenance of existing Sewers, or in providing its District with a Supply of Water in Cases where Danger arises to the Health of the Inhabitants from the Insufficiency or Unwholesomeness of the existing Supply of Water, and a proper Supply can be got at a reasonable Cost, or that a Nuisance Authority has made default in enforcing the Provisions of the Nuisance Removal Acts, or that a Local Board has made default in enforcing the Provisions of The Local Government Act, the said Secretary of State, if satisfied after due Inquiry made by him that the Authority has been guilty of the alleged Default, shall make an Order limiting a Time for the Performance of its Duty in the Matter of such Complaint; and if such Duty is not performed by the Time limited in the Order, the said Secretary of State shall appoint some Person to perform the same, and shall by Order direct that the Expenses of performing the same, together with a reasonable Remuneration to the Person appointed for superintending such Performance, and amounting to a Sum specified in the Order, together with the Costs of the Proceedings, shall be paid by the Authority in default; and any Order made for the Payment of such Costs and Expenses may

Mode of proceeding where Sewer Authority has made default in providing sufficient sewers, &c.

* In Ireland the Lord Lieutenant in Council.

SECTION 50. be removed into the Court of Queen's Bench, and be enforced in the same Manner as if the same were an Order of such Court.

In case a Nuisance Authority has made default in doing its duty with respect to the removal of nuisances in any place within its jurisdiction, the chief officer of police, under the direction of the Lord Lieutenant in Council may institute any proceedings which the Nuisance Authority might institute, &c. (See Sec. 16, page 12.)

Recovery of certain expenses of water supply 50. All Expenses incurred by a Sewers Authority or Local Board in giving a Supply of Water to Premises under the Provisions of the Seventy-sixth Section of The Public Health Act, 1848,* or the Fifty-first Section of The Local Government Act, 1858,† and recoverable from the Owners of the Premises supplied, may be recovered in a summary Manner.

Power to reduce penalties imposed by 6 George IV. cap. 78. 51. All Penalties imposed by the Act of the Sixth Year of King *George* the Fourth, Chapter Seventy-eight, intituled *An Act to repeal the several Laws relating to Quarantine, and to make other Provisions in lieu thereof,* may be reduced by the Justices or Court having Jurisdiction in respect of such Penalties to such Sum as the Justices or Court think just.

Description of vessels within provisions of 6 G. iv, c. 78. 52. Every vessel having on board any Person affected with a dangerous or infectious Disorder shall be deemed to be within the Provisions of the Act of the Sixth Year of King *George* the

Fourth, Chapter Seventy-eight,* although such
Vessel has not commenced her Voyage, or has
come from or is bound for some Place in the
United Kingdom; and the Lords and others of
Her Majesty's Most Honourable Privy Coun-
cil, or any Three or more of them (the Lord
President of the Council or One of Her Majesty's Principal Secretaries of State being One,)
may, by Order or Orders to be by them from
Time to Time made, make such Rules, Orders,
and Regulations as to them shall seem fit, and
every such Order shall be certified under the
Hand of the Clerk in Ordinary of Her Majesty's
Privy Council, and shall be published in the
London Gazette,† and such Publication shall be
conclusive Evidence of such Order to all Intents
and Purposes; and such Orders shall be binding
and be carried into effect as soon as the same
shall have been so published, or at such other
Time as shall be fixed by such Orders, with a
view to the Treatment of Persons affected with
Cholera and epidemic, endemic, and contagious
Disease, and preventing the Spread of Cholera
and such other Diseases as well as on the Seas,
Rivers, and Waters of the United Kingdom,
and on the High Seas within Three Miles of
the Coasts thereof, as on Land; and to declare
and determine by what Nuisance Authority or
Authorities such Orders, Rules, and Regulations
shall be enforced and executed; and any Expenses incurred by such Nuisance Authority or
Authorities shall be deemed to be Expenses incurred by it or them in carrying into effect the
Nuisances Removal Acts.

* The 6 Geo. IV., cap. 78, is an Act to provide for the performance of
Quarantine by foreign vessels.
† In Ireland, the *Dublin Gazette*. See Sec. 67, page 60.

SECTION 53.

Periodical
removal of
manure in
mews, &c.

53. Where Notice* has been given by the Nuisance Authority, or their Officer or Officers, for the periodical Removal of Manure or other refuse Matter from Mews, Stables, or other Premises (whether such Notice shall be by public Announcement in the Locality or otherwise,) and subsequent to such Notice the Person or Persons to whom the Manure or other refuse Matter belongs shall not so remove the same, or shall permit a further Accumulation, and shall not continue such periodical Removal at such Intervals as the Nuisance Authority, or their Officer or Officers shall direct, he or they shall be liable, without further notice, to a Penalty of Twenty Shillings *per* Day for every Day during which

* The Notice may be in this form :—

No.   N O T I C E .

NUISANCE AUTHORITY OF

Notice under 29th & 30th Vic., cap 90 Sec. 53.

To the Owner or Occupier   of Premises at
     You are hereby required by the said Nuisance Authority, pursuant to the provision of the Public Health Act, 29 & 30 Vict., cap. 90, sec. 53, periodically to remove as hereafter re-required all manure or other refuse matter, existing in the premises situated at No.   that is to say
in each   and that said premises be thoroughly cleansed and purified to the satisfaction of the Medical Officer of Health, or other officer of this Nuisance Authority.
     And take notice should you neglect or refuse to comply with the terms of this Notice, you are liable to a penalty of Twenty Shillings for every day during which such refusal or neglect continues.
     And you are further apprized that summary proceedings will be taken without further notice for the enforcing of said penalties incurred as aforesaid.
     Dated this   day of   18
           Signed,

Officer of the said Nuisance Authority.

such Manure or other refuse Matter shall be SECTION 54 permitted to accumulate, such Penalty to be recovered in a summary Manner: Provided always, that this Section shall not apply to any place where the Board of Guardians or Overseers of the Poor are the Nuisance Authority.

The powers conferred upon the Nuisance Authority by this section are very extensive. *One* notice served by it upon parties for the *periodical* removal of manure, &c., is sufficient to call its powers into action. The settlement of the periods at which the manure, &c., should be removed is left to the discretion of the Authority, and any one breach of the terms stated in the notice at any time renders the party, without further notice, liable to a penalty of Twenty Shillings a-day. There is no power that can mitigate this penalty, for it is not discretionary.

Boards of Guardians are expressly deprived of this authority, the section evidently refers only to towns and cities, which districts are invariably under other authorities than Boards of Guardians. If these powers were to be exercised by Boards of Guardians, who are, for the most part, the Nuisance Authority in country districts, it would be a manifest injustice to farmers, &c., to prohibit the keeping of manure in heaps in proper places for agricultural purposes.

This section must be read in conjunction with Sec. 18 of the Nuisance Removal Act, 1855.

54. Penalties under this Act, and Expenses Recovery of penalties. directed to be recovered in a summary Manner, may be recovered before Two Justices in manner directed by an Act passed in the Session holden in the Eleventh and Twelfth Years of the Reign of Her Majesty Queen *Victoria*, Chapter Forty-three intituled *An Act to facilitate the Performance of the Duties of Justices of the Peace out of Sessions within* England *and* Wales *with respect to summary Convictions and Orders*, or any Act amending the same.

By Sec. 60 these penalties and expenses are to be recovered in the manner directed by the Petty Sessions, Ireland, Act. It is imperative that they should be recovered as damages before a Justice, and an action will not lie for their recovery.— *Blackburn* v. *Parkinson*, 28 L.J.M.C.N.S. 7.

SECTION 55.

Powers
of Act
cumulative

55. All Powers given by this Act shall be deemed to be in addition to and not in derogation of any other Powers conferred on any Local Authority by Act of Parliament, Law, or Custom, and such Authority may exercise such other Powers in the same Manner as if this Act had not passed.

PART IV.

Application of Act to Ireland.

56. In applying the First Part of this Act to *Ireland* the following Changes shall be observed :—

(1.) The Provisions of the Sections numbered from Seventy-five to Eighty, both included, of The Public Health Act, 1848,* and Sections Fifty-one, Fifty-two, and Fifty-three of the Local Government Act, 1858,* and Section Twenty of the Local Government Act, 1858, Amendment Act, 1861,* referred to in the First Part of this Act, shall for all Purposes connected with the Execution of this Act be extended to *Ireland* :

(2.) The Sewage Utilization Act, 1865, shall be amended by substituting in *Ireland* the Sewer Authority, as defined by the First Schedule to this Act, for the Sewers Authority as defined by said Act.

* These sections are as follows :—

Extract from Public Health Act, 1848.

75. And be it enacted, That the Local Board of Health† may provide their District with such a Supply of Water as may be proper and sufficient for the Purposes of this Act and for private Use to the Extent required by this Act ; and for those Purposes or any of them the said Local Board† may from Time to Time, with the approval of the General Board of Health, contract with any Person whomsoever, or purchase, take upon Lease, hire, construct, lay down, maintain such Waterworks, and do and execute all such Works, Matters, and Things as shall be necessary and proper ; and any Waterworks Company may contract with the Local Board of Health† to supply Water for the Purposes of this Act in any Manner whatsoever, or may sell and dispose of or Lease their Water-

† In Ireland the Sewer Authority. See Sanitary Act, 1866, sec. 11, page 9.

Extract from Public Health Act, 1848.

works to any Local Board of Health* willing to take the same

In case of waterworks constructed by Local Board, the water may be kept constantly under pressure.
and the said Local Board may provide and keep in any Water-
works constructed or laid down by them under the Powers of
this Act a Supply of pure and wholesome Water, and the
Water so supplied may be constantly laid on at such Pressure
as will carry the same to the top Story of the highest Dwell-
ing-house within the District supplied : Provided always, that
before constructing or laying down any Waterworks† under
the Powers of this Act within any Limits within, for, or in
respect of which any Waterworks Company‡ shall have been
established for supplying Water, the said Local Board shall
give Notice in Writing to every Waterworks Company within
whose Limits the said Local Board may be desirous of laying

Local Board not to construct waterworks, etc., if any waterworks company within their distrct be able and willing to supply water upon terms.
on or supplying Water, stating the Purposes for and (as far as
may be practicable) the extent to which Water is required by
the said Local Board ; and it shall not be lawful for the said
Local Board to construct or lay down any Waterworks within
such Limits, if and so long as any such Company shall be able
and willing to lay on Water proper and sufficient for all reasonable Purposes for which it is required by the said Local Board,
and upon such Terms as shall be certified to be reasonable by
the General Board of Health, after Inquiry and Report by a
Superintending Inspector in this behalf, or (in case such Company shall be dissatisfied with such Certificate) upon such
Terms as shall be settled by Arbitration in the Manner provided by this Act ; and in case any Difference shall arise as to
whether the Water which any such Company is able and willing to supply or lay on is proper and sufficient for the purposes
for which it is required by the said Local Board, or whether the
purposes for which it is required are reasonable, the same shall
be settled by Arbitration in the Manner provided by this Act.

Local Board may require that houses be supplied with water, etc., in certain cases.
76. And be it enacted, That if upon the Report of the Sur-
veyor it appear to the Local Board of Health that any House is
without a proper Supply of Water, and that such a Supply
of Water can be furnished thereto at a Rate not exceeding
Two Pence *per* Week, the said Local Board shall give Notice
in Writing to the Occupier.§ requiring him, within a Time to be

* In Ireland the Sewer Authority. See Sanitary Act, 1866, Sec. 11, page 9.
† *Waterworks* is defined in sec. 2 of Public Health Act to be " streams, springs, wells, pumps, reservoirs, cisterns, tanks, aqueducts, cuts, sluices, mains, pipes, culverts, engines, and all machinery, land, buildings, and things for supplying or used for supplying water ; also the stock-in-trade of any waterworks company.
‡ *Waterworks Company*—"Any corporation, person, or company of persons supplying, or who may hereafter supply, water for their own profit.
§ This notice must be served on the owner. See page 52, and also Sec. 50, page 42.

specified therein, to obtain such Supply, and to do all such Works as may be necessary for that Purpose ; and if such Notice be not complied with the said Local Board may, if they shall think fit, do such Works, and obtain such Supply accordingly, and make and levy Water Rates upon the Premises, not exceeding in the whole the Rate of Two Pence *per* Week, in manner hereinafter provided, as if the Owner or Occupier of the Premises had demanded a Supply of Water, and were willing to pay Water Rates for the same ; and the Expenses* incurred by them in doing such Works as last aforesaid shall be Private Improvement Expenses, and be recoverable as such in the manner hereinafter provided (that is from the owner.—See Page 52.)

* But see Sec. 50 of the Sanitary Act, 1866, page 42.

77. And be it enacted, That the Local Board of Health† may, if they shall think fit, supply Water from any Waterworks purchased or constructed by them under this Act to any Public Baths or Wash-houses, or for trading or manufacturing Purposes, upon such Terms and Conditions as may be agreed upon between the said Local Board and the Persons desirous of being so supplied.

Water for public baths, or trading or manufacturing purposes.

78. And be it enacted, That the Local Board of Health† may cause all existing public Cisterns, Pumps, Wells, Reservoirs, Conduits, Aqueducts, and Works used for the gratuitous Supply of Water to the Inhabitants, to be continued, maintained, and plentifully supplied with Water, or they may substitute, continue, maintain, and plentifully supply with Water other such Works equally convenient ; and the said Local Board† may, if they shall think fit, construct any number of new Cisterns, Pumps, Wells, Conduits, and Works for the gratuitous Supply of any public Baths or Wash-houses established otherwise than for private Profit, or supported out of any Poor or Borough Rates.

Maintenance and construction of public cisterns for gratuitous use.

79. And be it enacted, That whosoever shall wilfully or carelessly break, injure, or open any Lock, Cock, Waste Pipe, or Waterworks belonging to or under the Management or Control of the Local Board of Health,† or constructed, continued, or maintained under this Act, in any Parish or Place in which there shall be no local Board of Health,† or shall unlawfully flush, draw off, divert, or take Water from any Waterworks belonging to or under the Management or Control of the said Local Board,† or so constructed, continued, or maintained in any such Parish or Place, or from any Waters or

Penalty for injuring waterworks, diverting streams, or wasting water.

† In Ireland the Sewer Authority. See Sanitary Act, 1866, sec. 11, page 9

E

Supply of
Water.

Streams by which such Waterworks are supplied, or shall wilfully or negligently waste or cause to be wasted any Water with which he is supplied by the said Local Board,* shall for every such Offence forfeit a Sum not exceeding Five Pounds, and a further Penalty of Twenty Shillings for each Day whilst the Offence is continued after written Notice in that Behalf, which Penalties shall be paid to the said Local Board,* or, in the Case of a Parish or Place in which there shall be no Local Board of Health, to the Churchwardens and Overseers of the Poor, to be by them applied in aid of the Rate for the Relief of the Poor of such Parish or Place: Provided always, that nothing herein contained shall prevent the Owner or Occupier of any Premises through or by which any Streams may flow from using the same as they would have been entitled to do if this Act had not been passed.

Penalties on
persons for
causing
water in
reservoirs to
be fouled:

80. And be it enacted, That whosoever shall bathe in any Stream, Reservoir, Conduit, Aqueduct, or other Waterworks belonging to or under the Management or Control of the Local Board of Health,* or in any Reservoir, Conduit, Aqueduct, or other Waterworks constructed, continued, or maintained under this Act in any Parish or Place in which there shall be no Local Board of Health, or shall wash, cleanse, throw, or cause to enter therein any Animal, Rubbish, Filth, Stuff, or Thing of any kind whatsoever, or shall cause or permit or suffer to run or be brought therein the Water of any Sink, Sewer, Drain, Engine, or Boiler, or other filthy, unwholesome, or improper Water, or shall do anything whatsoever whereby any Water belonging to the said Local Board* or under their Management or Control, or whereby any Water of or contained in any such Reservoir, Conduit, Aqueduct, or other Waterworks so constructed, continued, or maintained in any such Parish or Place as aforesaid shall be fouled, shall for every such Offence forfeit a Sum not exceeding Five Pounds, and a further Sum of Twenty Shillings for each Day whilst the Offence is continued after written Notice in that Behalf; which Penalties shall be paid to the said Local Board, or, in the Case of a Parish or Place in which there shall be no Local Board of Health, to the Churchwardens and Overseers of the Poor, to be by them applied in aid of the Rate for the Relief of the Poor of such Parish or Place; and whosoever, being Pro-

and on pro-
prietors of
gasworks,
&c.

prietor of any Gasworks, or being engaged or employed in the Manufacture or Supply of Gas, causes or suffers to be brought or to flow into any Stream, Reservoir, Conduit, Aqueduct, or Waterworks belonging to or under the Management or Control of the said Local Board, or into any Drain or

---

* In Ireland the Sewer Authority. See Sanitary Act, 1866, Sec 119.

Pipe communicating therewith, any Washing or other Substance produced in the Manufacture or Supply of Gas, or shall wilfully do any Act connected with the Manufacture or Supply of Gas, whereby the Water in any such Stream, Reservoir, Aqueduct, or Waterworks is fouled, shall forfeit to the said Local Board* for every such Offence the sum of Two Hundred Pounds, and, after the Expiration of Twenty-four Hours' Notice in Writing from them in this Behalf, a further sum of Twenty Pounds for every Day during which the Offence is continued, or during the continuance of the Act whereby the Water is fouled ; and every such Penalty shall be recoverable, with full Costs of Suit, by Action of Debt ;† and if any Water supplied by, belonging to, or under the Management or Control of the said Local Board, be fouled in any Manner by the Gas of any such Proprietor or Person as last aforesaid, he shall forfeit to the Local Board for every such Offence a Sum not exceeding Twenty Pounds, and a further Sum not exceeding Ten Pounds for every Day whilst the Offence is continued after the Expiration of Twenty-four Hours' Notice in writing from the said Local Board in this Behalf ; and for the Purpose of ascertaining whether such Water is fouled by the Gas of any such Proprietor or Person, the said Local Board may lay open and examine any Pipes, Conduits, and Works from which the Gas is supposed to escape; provided that before beginning so to do, Twenty-four Hours' Notice in Writing be given to the Person to whom such Pipes, Conduits, or Works belong, or under whose Management or Control they may be, of the Time at which the Examination is intended to be made ; and if upon such Examination it appear that the Water has been fouled by the Gas proceeding from or contained in the Pipes, Conduits, or Works examined, the Expenses of the Examination shall be paid and borne by the Person to whom such Pipes, Conduits, or Works belong, or under whose Management or Control they may be, and be recoverable from him in the summary Manner hereinafter provided; but if it appear that the Water has not been so fouled, then such Expenses, and all Damages occasioned by the Examination, shall be paid by the said Local Board out of the General District Rates levied under this Act, and be recoverable from them in the summary Manner hereinafter provided.

---

* In Ireland the Sewer Authority.   See Sanitary Act, 1866, Sec. 11, Page 9.

† In manner directed by the Petty Sessions, Ireland, Act.   See Sec. of the Sanitary Act, Page 55.

SECTION 56.

EXTRACTS FROM "THE LOCAL GOVERNMENT ACT, 1858."

21 & 22 VICTORIA, CAP. 98.

Water Supply.

Powers of Sec. 76 of 11 & 12 Vict. c. 63, as to water supply, extended to this Act.

51. The Powers given to Local Boards by the Seventy-sixth Section of the Public Health Act, 1848, shall extend to any House within their District to which a Supply of Water can be provided at an* Expense not exceeding the Water Rate authorized by the said Act or any Local Act in force in the District, and Notices under that Section shall be served on Owners of Houses so supplied instead of Occupiers, and Expenses incurred under that Section shall be recoverable from such Owners.

* See Sec. 50 of the Sanitary Act, 1866, Page 42.

Power of carrying water mains.

52. Where the Local Board supply Water to their District they shall have the same Power for carrying Water Mains within the District as they have for carrying Sewers by the Law in force for the Time being.

Power to Directors of Waterworks or Market Company to sell works, &c. to Local Boards.

53. It shall be lawful for any Local Board of Health absolutely to purchase, and for the Directors for the Time being of any Waterworks Company or Market Company, by and with the Authority of Three-fifths of the Shareholders for the Time being in such Company who may be present, either personally or by proxy, at some General Meeting of the Company specially convened for the Purpose, to Sell, Convey, and Transfer unto any Local Board of Health, upon such Terms as shall be mutually agreed upon between the Company and the Local Board,† all the Rights, Powers, and Privileges, and all or any of the Lands and Premises, Works, Matters, and Things, which at the Time of such Purchase shall be the Property of the Company, but subject to all Mortgages, Contracts, or Liabilities to which the same shall be then subject.

† In Ireland the Sewer Authority. See Sanitary Act, Sec. 11, Page 9.

EXTRACT FROM
"THE LOCAL GOVERNMENT ACT (1858) AMENDMENT ACT, 1861."
24 & 25 VICTORIA, CAP. 61.

20. In Districts where no Water Companies are established by Act of Parliament, all Local Boards may make agreements

for the Supply of Water to persons on such Terms as may be SECTION 57.
agreed upon between the Local Board and the persons receiving such Supply, and shall have the same Powers for recovering
Water Rents accruing under such agreements, as they have for
the recovery of Water Rates by the Law in force for the Time
being.

57. The Nuisance Removal Acts as amended *Modifications*
by the Second Part of this Act shall apply to *necessary for*
Ireland; provided, however, that in such Appli- *application of Part 2 to*
cation the following Changes shall be observed: *Ireland.*

(1) Sewer Authority as defined by the Sewage
Utilization Act, 1865, and amended by
this Act, shall in *Ireland* be the Nuisance
Authority for executing the Nuisance Removal Acts :

The Sewer Authority and the Nuisance Authority in Ireland are the
bodies corporate (Sec. 46) mentioned in the first column of the schedule of
this Act, Page 64.

(2) The Expenses of executing the Nuisance
Removal Acts shall be defrayed out of
the Funds hereinafter provided :

These funds are herein-after provided by Sections 58 and 59, and by the
fourth column of the first schedule, Page 64.

(3) The Penalties shall be recovered in the
Manner herein-after provided :

These penalties (Sec. 60) are to be recovered in the manner directed by
the Petty Sessions (Ireland) Act, 1851.

(4) The Expressions "Mayor, Aldermen,
and Burgesses," " Council," " Borough
Rate," " Borough Fund," and " Town
Rate," shall in the First Schedule hereto
have respectively the same Meaning as in
the Acts for the Regulation of Municipal
Corporations in *Ireland :*

" Mayor, Aldermen, and Burgesses" is the new name for the Corporations specified in Schedule A. of 3 & 4 Vict., c. 108. (See Sec. 12 of that Act.)
The Mayor, Aldermen, and Councillors for the time being, or so many
of them as shall at any time be elected, and have accepted the offices,

SECTION 58. shall be and be called the "Council" of such borough. (3 & 4 Vict., c. 108, sec. 57.

The Council, in case the borough fund be insufficient for the municipal purposes to which it is applicable, is empowered to raise the necessary funds by the imposition of a " Borough Rate." (3. & 4 Vict. c. 108, sec. 133.)
" Borough Fund" consists of the rents, profits, and annual proceeds of the real and personal property of the Corporation. (3 & 4 Vict., c. 128, sec. 67.)
" Town Rate" imposed by Commissioners in towns for the purposes of 9 Geo. IV., c. 82, sec. 38.

(5) For the Purposes of the Twenty-second Section of the Nuisance Removal Act, 1855, the Nuisance Authority shall in *Ireland* have the Power of entering Land conferred by The Sewage Utilization Act, 1865, and shall have the same Power of levying Assessments under the said Section that they have of levying any other Rates they are authorized by Law to impose.

This power of entry for the purposes of the 22nd section of the Nuisance Removal Act is set forth under Sec. 5 of the Sewage Utilization Act, 1865.

How expenses to be defrayed in Ireland when Nuisance Authority not a Board of Guardians.

58. In *Ireland*, the Nuisance Authority, not being the Guardians of the Poor, shall pay all Expenses incurred by them in carrying the Nuisance Removal Acts into effect out of the Fund in the First Schedule* in that Behalf mentioned, and where such Fund arises wholly or in part from Rates shall have, in addition to their existing Powers of Rating, all such Powers for making and levying any extra Rate, if necessary, respectively, as in the Case of any Rate authorized to be made under the Provisions of the respective Acts of Parliament under which the Nuisance Authorities are constituted or authorized to levy Rates; and all Provisions of such Acts respectively shall be applicable in respect thereof; provided that when the Rates to be assessed by such Authority are limited by Law to a certain

* See Page 64.

rateable Amount, such Limitation shall not apply or extend to Expenses incurred in carrying this Act into execution; and it shall be lawful for such Authority to assess the Expenses under this Act in addition to such limited Assessment.

This section (58) gives to Nuisance Authorities the power to levy extra rates, if necessary, to carry this Act into operation. Boards of Guardians are expressly excluded from this privilege, but by Sec. 59 *they* are empowered to pay the expenses incurred by them in carrying this Act into effect, out of the Poor Rates of the Union. They are entitled, therefore, to include such expenses in their estimates when striking rates for the relief of the poor, and to levy them accordingly.

59. In *Ireland*, a Nuisance Authority, being Guardians of the Poor, shall pay all Expenses incurred by them in carrying this Act into effect out of the Poor Rates of the Union, and charge the same to the Union, or any Electoral Division or Electoral Divisions thereof, in such Manner as the Poor Law Commissioners shall from Time to Time, by General Orders applicable to Classes of Cases, or by Order in any particular Case, direct.

By the schedule of this Act, Page 64, it would appear that the " Poor Rate of Union" is the fund out of which Boards of Guardians of the Poor may pay all the expenses incurred by them in carrying this Act into effect ; but this section qualifies considerably the expression " The Poor Rate of Union" by providing that those expenses shall be charged to "the Union or any Electoral Division or Electoral Divisions thereof, in such manner as the Poor Law Commissioners shall from time to time by general orders applicable to classes of cases, or by order in any particular case, direct."

60. In *Ireland*, Penalties under this Act and Expenses or Compensation directed to be recovered in a summary Manner, and Nuisances and other Offences liable to be prosecuted summarily, shall be recovered and prosecuted in man-

SECTION 61. ner directed by the Petty Sessions (*Ireland*) Act, 1851,* or any Act amending the same; and all Penalties recovered by any Authority under this Act shall be paid to them respectively, and by them applied in aid of their Expenses under this Act.

Any Order† authorized to be made by Justices under this Act shall be deemed to be an Order made upon a Complaint on which Justices are authorized to make Orders under the last-mentioned Act.

* An action will not lie for their recovery.—*Blackburn* v. *Parkinson*, 28 L.J.M.C.N.S. 7.

† The order is not complete until it is signed by one of the Justices. It is not sufficient for the Justice to sign the book once at the end of several cases. Each order should be signed in the Order Book separately by the Justice making it. An order, or a conviction, made by the Magistrates can be altered on the same day, and in presence of the parties, and before the book has been signed by one of the magistrates.—*Law Adviser's Opinion*, 3rd Jan., 1854.

An order of Justices cannot be acted upon until it is made, and it cannot be considered as made until it has been reduced into writing and signed by the Justices. *Regina* v. *the Justices of Flintshire*, 3, Dowling & Londes, 537.

Williams, J.—I think the word "making" of the order must be understood in its usual sense, and must mean an order properly made under the hands and seals of the Justices.—*Ib.*

Modifications necessary for application of Part 3 to Ireland

61. In applying the Provisions of Part III. of this Act to *Ireland* the following Changes shall be observed:

(1.) Application for Power to make Regulations as to Lodging Houses may be made by any Nuisance Authority except a Board of Guardians, and shall be made to the Lord Lieutenant in Council, and the said Lord Lieutenant in Council shall have the Power of declaring the Enactments as to Lodging Houses in the Third SECTION 62. Part of this Act to be in force in any Nuisance District:*

(2.) The said Lord Lieutenant in Council shall have and exercise the Power, in respect of Boards of Guardians acting together, vested in the Privy Council by the said Third Part of this Act.†

(3.) In *Ireland*, any Nuisance Authority, except a Board of Guardians, may exercise the Powers conferred on Local Boards acting in the Execution of The Local Government Act, 1858, by the said Third Part of this Act.‡

(4.) Sewer and Nuisance Authorities in *Ireland* shall be incorporated for the Purposes of this Act by the Names set forth in the said First Schedule hereto; and such Sewer or Nuisance Authorities may hold Lands by such Names for the Purposes of Burial Ground (*Ireland*) Act, 1856:

(5.) The Penalties under the Third Part of this Act shall be recovered in like Manner as herein-before provided with respect to Penalties under the Second Part of this Act.‖

* See Sec. 35, Page 28.   ‡ See Sec. 43, Page 37.
† See Sec. 40, Page 34.   ‖ See Sec. 60, Page 55.

62. The Diseases Prevention Act, 1855, as amended by the Nuisance Removal and Disease Prevention Amendment Act, 1860, and this Act, shall extend to *Ireland:* Provided, however, that in such Application the following changes shall be observed:

Extension of Disease Prevention Acts and this Act to Ireland.

SECTION 63.

Modifications necessary for application of said Acts to Ireland.

(1.) The Lord Lieutenant in Council shall have the Power with respect to *Ireland* which the Privy Council has under such Provisions for Prevention of Disease in *England* :*

(2.) The Commissioners for administering the Laws for the Relief of the Poor in *Ireland,* hereinafter called the Poor Law Commissioners, shall be the Authority in *Ireland* for issuing Regulations to carry the Provisions of said Act into effect:

(3.) The Regulations of the Poor Law Commissioners shall be authenticated in like manner as Orders of theirs under the Dispensary Act, 1851, Statute 14 & 15 *Vict., c.* 68, Sec. 2:

(4.) In defraying the Expenses of the Prevention of Disease out of the Poor Rate of the Union under this Act the Guardians of the Poor shall charge the same to the Union, or any Dispensary District or Electoral Division or Divisions thereof, in such Manner as the Poor Law Commissioners shall from Time to Time, by General Orders applicable to Classes of Cases, or by Orders in particular Cases, direct.

* See Diseases Prevention Act, 1855, Sec. 5.

Committee and Officers under Dispensaries Act to aid Local Authority in execution of this Act.

63. In *Ireland,* all Committees, Inspectors, Medical Officers, and other Persons appointed or employed under the Powers of Statute Fourteenth and Fifteenth *Victoria,* Chapter Sixty-eight, (the Dispensaries Act, 1851,) shall and they are hereby required within their respective Districts to aid the Local Authority, and such Officers or

Persons as they shall appoint or employ, in the Superintendence and Execution of any Directions and Regulations* which may at any Time be issued by the Poor Law Commissioners for the Time being under the Authority and by virtue of this Act.

* The regulations are those referred to in Parts 2 and 3 of Sec. 62, Page 58.

64. In *Ireland*, the Provisions of The Dispen- The pro-
sary Act, 1851, (Statute 14 & 15 *Vict.*, c. 68,*) visions of
with respect to the Duties and Appointment of c. 68, as
Medical Inspectors, shall be incorporated with appointment
this Act, and the Prevention of Disease and Inspectors
Inquiry into Public Health under this Act shall incorporated
be deemed One of the Purposes for which such with this
Medical Inspectors have been or may be appointed, in like Manner as if its Provisions had
been referred to in the said Act of 1851, instead
of the Provisions of the said Nuisance Removal
and Diseases Prevention Act of 1848.

* EXTRACTS FROM 14 & 15 VICTORIA, CAP. 6S.

3. The said Commissioners may from Time to Time appoint Appoint-
so many fit Persons as the Commissioners of Her Majesty's ment of In-
Treasury shall sanction, being practising Physicians or Sur- spectors.
geons of not less than Seven Years' standing, to be Inspectors
to assist in carrying out the Provisions of this Act, and may
remove all or any of the said Inspectors, and appoint others in
their Place.

Salaries of
Inspectors to
4. There shall be paid to the said Inspectors, such Salaries be paid from
as shall be from Time to Time appointed by the Commis- any funds
sioners of Her Majesty's Treasury, out of any Moneys which Parliament
may from Time to Time be provided by Parliament for that for such pur-
purpose.   pose.
No Medical
Commis-
5. Neither the Medical Commissioner nor any such Inspec- sioner or In-
tor as aforesaid shall, while he continues in such respective spector to
office, practise as a Physician or Surgeon, or in any other practise as
                                                              Physician or
professional capacity.   Surgeon.

Powers and Duties of Medical Inspectors.

[The powers and duties of Medical Inspectors under the Medical Charities Act, which are now made available for the purposes of the Sanitary Act, 1866, are contained in Sections 16, 17, and 18 of the Medical Charities Act.] Those sections are as follow:—

Power of Commissioners and Inspectors to inquire on oath, or require a declaration.

16. The Commissioners or any one of them, and also any such Inspector acting in execution of this Act, by summons under the seal of the Commissioners, or under the separate hand and seal of any Commissioner or Inspector respectively, as the case may be, may require the attendance of all such persons as they or he shall think fit to call before them or any of them respectively, upon any matter connected with the execution of this Act, relating to any Dispensary subject, under this Act, to the authority of the said Commissioners, at such time and place as shall be set forth in the summons, and may make inquiry and returns, and may administer oaths and examine all such persons upon oath, and may require and enforce the production upon oath of books, contracts, agreements, accounts, maps, plans, surveys, valuations, and writings, and copies thereof respectively, in anywise relating to any such matter as aforesaid ; or when the Commissioners or any one of the Commissioners, or any Inspector, shall think fit, instead of requiring such oath as aforesaid, they or he may require any such person to make and subscribe a declaration of

Provisions as to the summoning of witnesses, &c., by Commissioners and Inspectors.

the truth of the matter respecting which he shall have been or shall be so examined : Provided always that no person shall be required, in obedience to any such summons of any of the said Commissioners, to go more than thirty statute miles from the place of his abode, or, in obedience to any such summons of an Inspector, to go more than five miles from the place of his abode : Provided also, that nothing herein contained shall empower the Commissioners, or any Commissioner or Inspector, to require the production of the title, or of any papers or deeds relating to the title of any lands, tenements, or hereditaments, not being property under the authority of or vested in the said Commissioners by this Act : Provided also, that nothing herein contained shall authorize the said Commissioners or any of them, or any such Inspector, to exercise such powers of summons, inquiry, examination, or other such last-mentioned powers as aforesaid, in the case of any Hospital, Infirmary, or Medical Institution, supported by private endowments, bequests, property, or subscriptions.

Penalty for giving false evidence.

17. Every person who upon any such examination as afore-

said, under the authority of this Act, shall wilfully give false Penalty for evidence, or wilfully make or subscribe a false declaration, refusing to shall be deemed guilty of a misdemeanor; and every person attend sum-who shall refuse or wilfully nelgect to attend in obedience to give evi-any such summons as aforesaid of the Commissioners, or any dence. one of the Commissioners, or any Inspector, or to give evidence as aforesaid, or shall wilfully alter, suppress, conceal, destroy, or refuse to produce any books, contracts, agreements, accounts, maps, plans, surveys, valuations, or writings, or copies of the same, which may be required as aforesaid to be produced for the purposes of this Act, to any person authorized by this Act to require the production thereof, shall be liable to forfeit a sum not exceeding five pounds, to be recovered before any Justice or Justices at Petty Sessions, under his or their warrant, by distress and sale of the goods of the party so offending, returning to such party the overplus.

18. Every Inspector acting in execution of this Act shall be Inspectors to entitled to enter at all times into and inspect every Dispensary visit dispen-or Building used for the purposes of this Act, and to attend saries, &c. the meetings of every Board of Guardians or Dispensary Committee on all business arising in the execution of this Act, and Commis-to take part in the proceedings, but not to vote at such meet-sioners and ings; and the said Commissioners, or any Inspector, by their Inspectors to order in writing, shall be empowered (when they deem it Hospitals, expedient) to enter, inspect, and report upon any Infirmary, &c., sup-Hospital, or Medical Institution, supported in the whole or in public funds, part by any public funds, rates, or assessments. rates, &c.

65. In *Ireland,* whenever in compliance with Remunera-any Direction or Regulation of the Poor Law dical Prac-Commissioners which they may be empowered tioners for to make under the Laws for the Time being as under the to the Public Health, any Medical Officer of a and regula-Union or Dispensary District, or any other Me-tions of the dical Practitioner specially employed by the Commis-Guardians for the Purpose, shall perform any Ireland. extra Medical Service in any Union or Part of a Union, it shall and may be lawful for the Guardians of the Union to determine, subject to the Approval of the said Commissioners, and if they shall not approve the Amount determined by the

SECTION 66. Guardians, for the said Commissioners to fix by
Order under their Seal, such Remuneration, pro-
portioned to the Nature and Extent of such Services as aforesaid as to them shall appear just
and reasonable; and the Amount of such Remuneration shall be paid to such Medical Officer
or other Medical Practitioner by the Guardians of
the Union out of the Rates raised for the Relief
of the Poor, and shall be charged either to the
Union at large, or to such Part or Parts of the
Union, according to the Nature of the Case,
as the said Commissioners shall in each Case
direct.

Poor Law
Commis-
sioners to
make in-
quiries as to
public health
in Ireland.

66. The Lord Lieutenant in Council may from
Time to Time direct the Poor Law Commissioners to cause to be made such Inquires as the
Lord Lieutenant in Council see fit in relation to
any Matters concerning the Public Health in
any Place or Places in *Ireland,* and the Poor
Law Commissioners shall report the Result
of such Inquiries to the Lord Lieutenant in
Council.

Publication
in Ireland to
be made in
the *Dublin
Gazette.*

67. Publications shall be made in the *Dublin
Gazette* in any Case in *Ireland,* where Publication in the *London Gazette* is required in *England.*

Powers in
Secretary of
State in Eng-
land to be
exercised in
Ireland by
the Lord
Lieutenant
in Council.

68. All Powers relating to the Execution of
this Act in *England,* and by this Act vested in
One of Her Majesty's Principal Secretaries of
State, shall with regard to the Execution of this
Act in *Ireland,* in all Cases not herein-before expressly provided for, be vested in the Lord Lieutenant or other Chief Governor or Governors of

Ireland; and all Powers relating to the Excution of this Act in *England,* and by this Act vested in the Privy Council in *England,* shall, with regard to the Execution of this Act in *Ireland,* in all Cases not herein-before expressly provided for, be vested in the Lord Lieutenant in Council in *Ireland.*

69. From and after the passing of this Act the Acts set forth in the Second Schedule hereto shall be repealed, so far as they are still in force: Provided always, that all Proceedings commenced or taken under the said Acts and not yet completed may be proceeded with under said Acts, and that all Contracts and Works undertaken by virtue of said Acts shall continue and be effective as if said Acts had not been repealed.

SCHEDULES.

FIRST SCHEDULE.—APPLICATION TO IRELAND.

Description of Sewers and Nuisance Authority in Ireland.*	Description of Sewers and Nuisance District in Ireland.†	Corporate Name, for the purpose of suing or being sued, or holding Property, under the Provisions of this Act.	Rate or Fund out of which Expenses incurred by Sewers or Nuisance Authority under this Act to be defrayed.
The Right Honourable the Lord Mayor, Aldermen, and Burgesses, acting by the Town Council.	The City of Dublin.	The Right Honourable the Lord Mayor, Aldermen, and Burgesses of the City of Dublin.	The Borough Rate or Borough Fund.
The Mayor, Aldermen, and Burgesses, acting by the Town Council.	Towns Corporate, with exception of Dublin.	The Mayor, Aldermen, and Burgesses of the City or Town of ——	The Borough Rate or Borough Fund.
The Town Commissioners.	Towns having Town Commissioners, under the Towns Improvement (Ireland) Act, 1854, (17 & 18 Vict., c. 113,) or under any Local Act.	The Town Commissioners of ——	
The Township Commissioners.	Townships having Commissioners under Local Acts.	The Township Commissioners of ——	
The Commissioners appointed by virtue of an Act made in the 9th Year of the Reign of George the Fourth, intituled "An Act to make Provision for the lighting, cleansing, and watching of Cities and Towns Corporate and Market Towns in Ireland in certain Cases."	Towns under such Commissioners.	The Lighting and Cleansing Commissioners of the Town of ——	Any Rate levied by the Commissioners.
The Municipal Commissioners.	Towns having Municipal Commissioners, under 3 & 4 Vict., c. 108.	The Municipal Commissioners of ——	The Town Fund
The Guardians of the Poor of each Union.	Such part of each Union as is not under another Sewer or Nuisance Authority.	The Guardians of the Poor of the —— Union.	The Poor Rate of Union ‡

* By Section 46, Page 38, these bodies, respectively, are bodies corporate, and are invested with power to sue and be sued in such names as Sewer Authorities, Nuisance Authorities, &c.

† By Sections 30 and 32, Page 24, the district of a Nuisance Authority also extends in certain cases to places where ships are lying.

‡ By the 57th section, Page 53, of this Act the Boards of Guardians pay the expenses out of the Poor Rate of the Union, but shall charge the expenses to the Union or any Electoral Division or Electoral Divisions thereof, *in such manner as the Poor Law Commissioners shall from time to time, by general orders applicable to classes of cases, or by order in any particular case, direct.* See also Section 62, Page 58.

SECOND SCHEDULE.

Statutes Repealed.

Local Boards of Health Act for Ireland, 1818; Statute 58 Geo. III., cap. 47, ss. 10 to 15, inclusive.

Officers of Health Act for Ireland, 1819; Statute 59 Geo. III., c. 41.

Nuisance Removal and Disease Prevention Act, 1848.

Nuisance Removal and Disease Prevention Act, 1849.

THE

SEWAGE UTILIZATION ACT.

———◆———

28 & 29 Victoria, Cap. 75.

An Act for facilitating the more useful Application of Sewage in *Great Britain* and *Ireland.*

[*29th June,* 1865.]

Section 1   Whereas it is expedient to remove Difficulties
under which Local Boards and other Bodies
having the Care of Sewers labour in disposing
of the Sewage of their Districts so as not to be
a Nuisance, and to give Facility to such Authorities to make Arrangements for the Application
of such Sewage to Land for Agricultural Purposes: Be it therefore enacted by the Queen's
Most Excellent Majesty, by and with the Advice and Consent of the Lords Spiritual and
Temporal, and Commons, in this present Parliament assembled, and by the Authority of the
same:

Short title.   1. This Act, for all Purposes, may be cited as
" The Sewage Utilization Act, 1865."*

Application
of Act.   2. This Act shall not extend to any Part of
the Metropolis, as defined by the Act of the

* This title means the Sewage Utilization Act, 1865, as
amended by the Sanitary Act, 1866, (Page 2.)

Session Eighteenth and Nineteenth Years of the present Reign, Chapter One hundred and twenty,* for better Local Management of the Metropolis, and shall not, with the Exception of Clause Fifteen, extend to any Parish as defined in the Schedule to this Act in a Part of which Parish the Public Health Act, 1848, and the Local Government Act, 1858, or One of such Acts, is in force at the Time of the passing of this Act.

Sec. 2. The Public Health Act, 1848, only extended to places where the inhabitants had applied to the authorities to put the same in force in their districts.—(Sec. 8 of Public Health Act, 1848.)

The Local Government Act, 1858, in like manner would not, of necessity, apply to any city, township, or district, the governing bodies of which had not taken steps to adopt it.— (Sec. 12 of Local Government Act, 1858.)

Such district, therefore, in which either of the two said Acts *were* in operation at the time of the passing of the Sewage Utilization Act, 1865, are exempted from the operations of the latter, save as to Clause 15, because they had all their requirements satisfied in relation to the provisions of this Sewage Utilization Act, without need for further legislation.

* The 18th & 19th Vict., c. 120, is a local Act, for the better management of the metropolis.

3. The Expression "Sewer Authority" shall, in the several Places in the Schedule† annexed hereto in that Behalf mentioned, mean the Persons or Bodies of Persons referred to in the First Column of the Schedule annexed hereto ; and the Term "District," in relation to a Sewer Authority, shall, as respects each Authority, mean the Place in that Behalf referred to in the Second Column of the said Schedule.

Definition of Sewer Authority.

† The definition of the expression "Sewer Authority" is amended in the application of the Act to Ireland by the 56th Sec. of the Sanitary Act, 1866, See, therefore, for correct definition the first Schedule to that Act, (Page 64.)

SECTION 4.   "Local Board"* shall mean a Local Board authorized in pursuance of the "Public Health Act, 1848," and the "Local Government Act, 1858," or One of such Acts.

* That is, Sewer Authority.   (See Page 9.)

Powers of Sewer Authorities.   4. Sewer Authorities† shall have Power to construct such Sewers as they may think necessary for keeping their District properly cleansed and drained, and shall, as respects all Sewers constructed by them or under their Control, whether the same were made before or after the· passing of this Act, have all the Powers that Local Boards have, in respect of Sewers vested in or constructed by them, under the Forty-fifth and Forty-sixth Sections of " The Public Health Act, 1848,† the Thirtieth Section of "The Local Government Act, 1858,‡ and the Fourth Section of " The Local Government Act, 1858, Amendment Act, 1861,‡ subject to the Provisions of the Fifth and Sixth Sections of the last-mentioned Act, and to the Saving Clauses in " The Local Government Act, 1858,‡ mentioned, from

† This section is merely permissive as regards the Sewer Authorities, but it is enacted by Sec. 49 of the Public Health Act, 1866, that where complaint is made and proved to the Lord Lieutenant that a Sewer Authority or Board of Health has made default in providing sufficient sewers, the Lord Lieutenant may make an order limiting the time for the performance by the Authority of its duty in the matter of such complaint ; and if that duty is not performed within such limited time, the Lord Lieutenant shall appoint a person to perform the same, at the expense of the Authority in default.   (See Page 39.)

‡ These sections are as follows :—

PUBLIC HEALTH ACT, 1848, SECS. 45 & 46.

Making alteration   Sec. 45. And be it enacted, that the Local Board of Health§ shall, from time to time, repair the sewers vested in them by

§ That is the Sewer Authority. (See Page 68.)

Sixty-eight to Seventy-four, both inclusive; and SECTION 4.
in *Scotland,* in addition to such of the aforesaid
Powers as are applicable to *Scotland,* all the
Powers contained in Section Seven (Public
Sewers) of Part Four of "The General Police
and Improvement (*Scotland*) Act, 1862."

this Act, and shall cause to be made such sewers as may be and discon-
necessary for effectually draining their district for the purposes tinuance of
of this Act; and the said Local Board* may carry any such vested in
sewers through, across, or under any turnpike road, or any Local Board.
street or place laid out as or intended for a street, or under any
cellar or vault which may be under the pavement or causeway
of any street, and after reasonable notice in that behalf, (if
upon the report of the Surveyor it should appear to be necessary,) into, through, or under any lands whatsoever; and the
said Local Board may, from time to time, enlarge, lessen,
alter, arch over, or otherwise improve, all or any of the sewers
vested in them by this Act, and discontinue, close up, or
destroy such of them as they may deem to have become unne-
cessary: Provided always, that the discontinuance, closing up,
or destruction of any sewer be so done as not to create a nuisance; and if by reason thereof any person is deprived of the
lawful use of any sewer, the said Local Board* shall provide
some other sewer as effectual for his use as the one of which
he is so deprived.

Sec. 46. And be it enacted, that the Local Board of Health* As to cleans-
shall cause the sewers vested in them by this Act to be con- ing and emp-
structed, covered, and kept so as not to be a nuisance or inju- tying sewers,
rious to health, and to be properly cleared, cleansed, and &c., by Local
emptied; and for the purpose of clearing, cleansing, and Board.
emptying the same, they may construct and place either above
or under ground such reservoirs, sluices, engines, and other
works as may be necessary, and may cause all or any of such
sewers to communicate with and be emptied into such places
as may be fit and necessary, or to cause the sewage and refuse
therefrom to be collected for sale for any purpose whatsoever,
but so as not to create a nuisance.

THE LOCAL GOVERNMENT ACT, 1858, SEC. 30.

Local Boards* may—
    1. Exercise the powers given by the 46th Sec. of the Public
Health Act, 1848; also without their district, if necessary, for

* That is the Sewer Authority. (See Page 68.)

the purpose of outfall and distribution of sewage, upon making due compensation, to be settled in the manner provided in the 144th Section of the Public Health Act, 1848.

2. Contract with any Company or person for the sale of sewage, or for the distribution of it over any land.

3. Contract for purchase or take on lease any lands, buildings, engines, materials, or apparatus, for the purpose of receiving, storing, disinfecting, or distributing sewage:

Provided always, that these things shall be done so as not to create a nuisance.

THE LOCAL GOVERNMENT ACT, 1858, AMENDMENT ACT, 1861, SECS. 4, 5, & 6.

Sec. 4. Local Boards* may exercise the powers given by the 45th Section of the Public Health Act, 1848 ; also without their district, for the purpose of outfall or distribution of sewage, upon making due compensation, to be settled in the manner provided in the 144th Section of the Public Health Act, 1848: Provided always, that nothing herein contained shall give, or be constructed to give, power to any Local Board* to construct or use any outfall, drain, or sewer, for the purpose of conveying sewage or filthy water into any natural watercourse or stream, until such sewage or filthy or refuse water be freed from all excrementitious or other foul or noxious matter, such as would affect or deteriorate the purity and quality of the water in such stream or watercourse.

Sec. 5. " Provided also, that no sewer or other work shall be constructed or extended under the enactment lastly hereinbefore contained, unless three months at the least before the commencement of such work, notice of the intended work, describing the nature thereof, and stating the intended termini thereof, and the names of the parishes, townships, and places, and the turnpike roads and streets, or places laid out or intended for streets, and other lands, if any, through, across, or under which the work is to be made, and naming a place where a plan of the intended work is open for inspection at all reasonable hours, shall be given by advertisement in one or more of the newspapers usually circulated in the place where the work is to be made ; and a written or printed copy of such notice shall be served, in manner directed by the Public Health Act, 1848, on the owners or reputed owners, lessees or reputed lessees and occupiers of the said lands, and on the overseers of such parishes, townships, or places, and the trustees, surveyors of highways, or others having the care of such roads or streets."

Sec. 6 provides, that if objection be made by any of the

* That is the Sewer Authority. (See Page 68.)

parties interested, and who shall serve notice in writing of such SECTION 4
objection on the Local Board at any time within the said three
months, the work shall not be proceeded with without the
sanction of one of her Majesty's Principal Secretaries of State.

Saving Clauses of the Local Government Act, 1858.

68. The one hundred and forty-fifth section of the Public Section 145
Health Act shall be repealed, and in lieu thereof be it enacted, of 11 & 12
That nothing in this Act shall be construed to authorize any Vict., c. 63
Local Board of Health,* repealed, and
Provisions
(1.) To use, injure, or interfere with any sluices, floodgates, herein
     sewers, groynes, or sea defences, or other works, named in lieu
     already or hereafter made under the authority of any thereof.
     Commissioners of Sewers appointed by the Crown, or
     any sewers or other works already or hereafter made
     and used for the purpose of draining, preserving, or
     improving land under any Local or Private Act of
     Parliament, or for the purpose of irrigating land, or
     in any manner to disturb or interfere with any lands,
     hereditaments, estates, or property vested in Her
     Majesty's principal Secretary of State for the War
     Department for the time being, without consent in
     writing first obtained from such Commissioners or
     Secretary of State, or persons acquiring rights under
     such Local or Private Acts respectively; and nothing
     herein contained shall prejudice or affect the rights,
     privileges, powers, or authorities given or reserved to
     any person under such Local or Private Acts ;
(2.) To interfere with any river, canal, dock, harbour, lock, Saving
     reservoir, or basin, so as to injuriously affect the na- Clause for
     vigation thereon, or the use thereof, or to interfere Proprietors
     with any towing-path so as to interrupt the traffic of Canals,
     thereof, in cases where any corporation, company, &c.
     undertakers, commissioners, conservators, and trus-
     tees, or individuals, are by virtue of any Act of Parlia-
     ment entitled to navigate on or use such river, canal,
     dock, harbour, lock, reservoir, or basin, or in respect
     of the navigation on or use of which river, canal,
     dock, harbour, lock, reservoir, or basin any corpora-
     tion, company, undertakers, commissioners, conser-
     vators, and trustees, or individuals, are entitled by
     virtue of any Act of Parliament to the receipt of any
     tolls or other dues ;
(3.) To interfere with any watercourse in such manner as to
     injuriously affect the supply of water to any river,

---

* That is the Sewer Authority. (See Page 68.)

canal, dock, harbour, reservoir, or basin, in cases where any corporation, company, undertakers, commissioners, conservators, trustees, or individuals (being authorized by virtue of any Act of Parliament to navigate on or use such river, canal, dock, harbour, reservoir, or basin, or to demand any tolls or dues in respect of the navigation on or use of such river, canal, dock, harbour, reservoir or basin,) would, if this Act had not passed, have been entitled by law to prevent or be relieved against such interference;

(4.) To interfere with any bridges crossing any river, canal, dock, harbour, or basin, in cases where any corporation, company, undertakers, commissioners, conservators, trustees, or individuals are authorized by virtue of any Act of Parliament to navigate or use such river, canal, dock, harbour, or basin, or to demand any tolls or dues in respect of the navigation or use of such river, canal, dock, harbour, or basin;

(5.) To execute any works in, through, or under any wharves, quays, docks, harbours, or basins, to the exclusive use of which any corporation, company, undertakers, commissioners, conservators, trustees, or individuals are entitled by virtue of any Act of Parliament, or for the use of which they are entitled by virtue of any Act of Parliament to demand any tolls or dues,

Without the consent in every case of such corporation, company, undertakers, commissioners, conservators, trustees, or individuals as are herein-before in that behalf respectively mentioned, such consent to be expressed in writing, in the case of a corporation under their common seal, and in the case of a company, undertakers, commissioners, conservators, trustees, or individuals, under the hand of their clerk or other duly authorized officer or agent: Provided always, that nothing in this Act contained shall be construed to alter or affect the maintenance of any rights of Local Boards existing at the time of the passing of this Act.

Works not within preceding section, and which interfere with Improvement of Rivers, Canals, &c. to be referred to Arbitration.

69. In cases where any matters or things proposed to be done by any Local Board, and which are not within the prohibition aforesaid, interfere with the improvement of any river, canal, dock, harbour, lock, reservoir, basin, or towing-path which any corporation, company, undertakers, commissioners, conservators, trustees, or individuals are entitled by virtue of any Act of Parliament to navigate on or use, or in respect of the navigation whereon or use whereof to demand any tolls or dues, or interfere with any works belonging to such river, canal, dock, harbour, or basin, or with any land necessary for

the enjoyment or improvement thereof, the Local Board shall give to such corporation, company, undertakers, commissioners, conservators, trustees, or individuals as last aforesaid a notice specifying the particulars of the matters and things so intended to be done; and if the parties on whom such notice is served do not consent to the requisitions thereof, the matter in difference shall be referred to arbitration; and the following questions shall be decided by such arbitration; (that is to say,)

(1.) Whether the matters or things so proposed to be done by the Local Board will cause any injury to such river, canal, dock, harbour, basin, towing-path, works, or land as are herein-before mentioned in this section, or to the enjoyment or improvement of such river, canal, dock, harbour, or basin as aforesaid:

(2.) Whether any injury that may be caused by such matters or things or any of them is or not of a nature to admit of being fully compensated by money.

70. The result of any such arbitration shall be final, and the Local Board shall do as follows; (that is to say,) **Effect of Arbitration.**

If the arbitrators are of opinion that no injury will be caused, the Local Board may forthwith proceed to do the proposed matters and things:

If the arbitrators are of opinion that injury will be caused, but that such injury is of a nature to admit of being fully compensated by money, they shall proceed to assess such compensation; and upon payment of the amount so assessed, but not before, the Local Board may proceed to do the proposed matters and things:

If the Arbitrators are of opinion that injury will be caused, and that it is not of a nature to admit of being fully compensated by money, the Local Board shall not proceed to do any matter or thing in respect of which such opinion may be given.

71. No transfer of powers and privileges under this Act shall deprive any corporation, company, undertakers, commissioners, conservators, trustees, or individuals authorized by virtue of any Act of Parliament to navigate on any river or canal, or to demand for their own benefit in respect of such navigation any tolls or dues, of such powers and privileges as are vested in them by any Act of Parliament in relation to such river or canal. **Provision as to transfer of powers, &c.**

72. Any corporation, company, undertakers, commissioners, conservators, trustees, or individuals authorized by virtue of any Act of Parliament to navigate on or use any river, canal, **Power for Corporation to alter sewers.**

SECTION 5. dock, harbour, or basin, or to demand any tolls or dues in respect of the navigation on such river or canal or the use of such dock, harbour, or basin, may, at their own expense, and on substituting other sewers, drains, culverts, and pipes equally effectual, and certified as such by the Surveyor to the Local Board,* take up, divert, or alter the level of any sewers, drains, culverts, or pipes constructed by any Local Board,* and passing under or interfering with such rivers, canals, docks, harbours, or basins, or the towing-paths of such rivers, canals, docks, harbours, or basins, and do all such matters and things as may be necessary for carrying into effect such taking up, diversion, or alteration.

Preserving water rights of companies or individuals.

73. Nothing in this Act or any Act incorporated therewith shall be construed to authorize any Local Board to injuriously affect any reservoir, river, or stream, or the feeders of any reservoir, river, or stream, or the supply, quality, or fall of water contained in any reservoir, river, stream, or feeders of any reservoir, river, or stream, in cases where any company or individuals would, if this Act had not passed, have been entitled by law to prevent or be relieved against the injuriously affecting such reservoir, river, stream, feeders, supply, quality, or fall of water, unless such Board shall have first obtained the . consent in writing of such company or individuals so entitled as aforesaid.

Arbitration questions under preceding sections.

74. Any difference of opinion that may arise between a Local Board* and any such corporation, company, commissioners, conservators, trustees, or individuals as aforesaid, whether any sewers, drains, culverts, or pipes substituted under the powers of this Act for sewers, drains, culverts, or pipes constructed or laid down by any Local Board, are equally effectual with those for which they are substituted, or whether the supply, quality, or fall of water in any such reservoir, river, or stream as last aforesaid, is injuriously affected by the exercise of powers under this Act, may, at the option of the party complaining, be determined by arbitration in the manner hereinbefore provided ; and in the latter case the Arbitrators shall decide the same questions as to the alleged injury; and the Local Board* shall proceed in the same way as is hereinbefore provided with regard to arbitrations in cases of alleged injury to rivers, canals, docks, harbours, and basins.

Power of entry.

5. The Sewer Authority shall have the Powers of] Entry conferred by the One hundred and forty-third Section of the " Public Health Act

* That is the Sewer Authority. (See Page 68.)

1848,"* for the Purposes of making or keeping in repair any Works made or to be made by them, as well as for the Purposes specified in the said Section.

* The 143rd section of the Public Health Act, 1848, is as follows :—" That in case it shall become necessary to enter, examine, or lay open any lands or premises, for the purpose of making plans, surveying, measuring, taking levels, examining works, ascertaining the course of sewers or drains, or ascertaining or fixing boundaries, and the owner or occupier of such lands or premises shall refuse to permit the same to be entered upon, examined, or laid open for the purposes aforesaid, or any of them, the Local Board† of Health may upon notice to such owner or occupier apply to two Justices (see Section 2 of Nuisances Removal Act, 1855,) for an order authorizing the members of such Local Board and the Superintending Inspector, Surveyor, and Inspector of Nuisances, or any of them, to enter, examine, and lay open the said lands and premises for the purposes aforesaid, or any of them, and if no sufficient cause shall be shown against the same, the Justices may make an order authorizing, and thereupon any Superintending Inspector, the Local Board of Health, or any member thereof, the Surveyor, and Inspector of Nuisances, and any person authorized by any such Superintending Inspector, Local Board, Surveyor, or Inspector of Nuisances may at all reasonable times, between the hours of ten in the forenoon and four in the afternoon, (the time of entry has been extended by Section 31 of the Sanitary Act, 1866, page 25,) enter, examine, and lay open the lands or premises mentioned in such order for such of the said purposes as shall be specified in said order without being subject to any action or molestation for so doing. Provided always that, except in case of emergency, no entry shall be made or works commenced under the powers of this enactment, unless twenty-four hours at the least previously thereto notice of the intended entry and of the object thereof be given to the occupier of the premises intended to be entered."

6 A Sewer Authority shall pay all Expenses incurred by them in carrying this Act into effect out of the Fund or Rate in the Schedule in that Behalf mentioned, and shall have all such Powers of borrowing Money on the Security of such

Payment of expenses.

† That is the Sewer Authority. (See Page 68.)

SECTION 7. Fund or Rate as Local Boards have of borrowing money under "The Local Government Act, 1858,"* and the Acts amending that Act, on the Security of the Funds or Rates in the said Acts in that behalf mentioned, subject to the Conditions and Sanction under which such Powers are exercised by Local Boards under the said Acts.

* Section 78 of the Local Government Act, 1858, enacts that when a Local Board exercising the borrowing powers of the Public Health Act, 1848, or that Act, or any Local Act has contributed to, purchased or executed works of sewerage and water supply, or proposes to contribute, to purchase, or execute such works, and where the cost of such work exceeds one year's assessable value of the premises assessable within the district in respect of which such money may be borrowed, it shall be lawful for such Board to present a petition to one of her Majesty's principal Secretaries of State, (in Ireland to the Lord Lieutenant, Section 68 of Sanitary Act, 1866,) praying for powers to borrow on mortgage of the rates leviable by them an amount not exceeding two years' assessable value of the premises so assessable, such amount to be repaid within such period not exceeding fifty years, as the Board, with the sanction of (in Ireland) the Lord Lieutenant, may determine.

Power to take Lands

7. A Sewer Authority shall, for the Purposes of this Act, have the Powers of taking Lands conferred on Local Boards by the Seventy-fifth Section† of "The Local Government Act, 1858," and any Act amending the same.

† LOCAL GOVERNMENT ACT, 1858, 21 AND 22 VICT., c. 98.

Purchase of Land.

Regulation as to the Purchase of Land.

LXXV. So much of the Eighty-fourth Section of the Public Health Act, 1848, as relates to the Incorporation of the Lands Clauses Consolidation Act, 1845, shall be repealed, and the following Regulations shall be observed with respect to the Purchase of Land by Local Boards for the Purposes of this Act—that is to say :

(1.) The Lands Clauses Consolidation Act, 1845, shall be SECTION 7
incorporated with this Act, except the Provisions relating to Access to the Special Act :

(2.) The Local Board, before putting in force any of the
Powers of the said Lands Clauses Consolidation Act
with respect to the Purchase and taking of Land
otherwise than by Agreement,* shall

Publish once at the least in each of Three consecu- Publication
tive Weeks in the Month of *November* in some of Notices.
Newspaper circulated in the District or some
Part of the District within which such Local
Board has Jurisdiction is situate, an Advertisement describing shortly the Nature of the Undertaking in respect of which the Land is proposed to be taken, naming a Place where a Plan
of the proposed Undertaking may be seen at all
reasonable Hours, and stating the Quantity of
Land that they require ; and shall further in the
Month of *December*

Serve a Notice in manner hereinafter mentioned Service of
on every Owner or reputed Owner, Lessee or re- Notices.
puted Lessee, and Occupier of such Land, defin-
ing in each Case the particular Land intended
to be taken, and requiring an Answer, stating
whether the Person so served assents, dissents,
or is neuter in respect of taking such Land ; such
Notice to be served

By Delivery of the same personally on the Party
required to be served, or, if such Party is absent
abroad, to his Agent ; or

By leaving the same at the usual or last known
Place of Abode of such Party as aforesaid ; or

By forwarding the same by Post in a registered
Letter addressed to the usual or last known Place
of Abode of such Party :

(3.) Upon compliance with the Provisions hereinbefore Power to
contained with respect to Advertisements and Notices, Local Board
the Local Board may, if they shall think fit, present to Petition
a Petition under their Seal to one of Her Majesty's Secretary of
Principal Secretaries of State : The Petition shall State upon
state the Land intended to be taken, and the Pur- Matters
poses for which it is required, and the Names of the herein stated.
Owners, Lessees, and Occupiers of Land who have
assented, dissented, or are neuter in respect of the
taking such Land, or who have returned no Answer
to the Notice : It shall pray that the Local Board

* See Sec. 47 of the Sanitary Act, Page 39.

may, with reference to such Land, be allowed to put in force the Powers of the said Lands Clauses Consolidation Act with respect to the Purchase and taking of Land otherwise than by Agreement, and such Prayer shall be supported by such evidence as the Secretary of State requires :

Secretary of State may direct Inquiry :

(4.) Upon the Receipt of such Petition, and upon due proof of the proper Advertisements having been published and Notices served, the Secretary of State shall take such Petition into consideration, and may either dismiss the same, or direct an Inquiry in the District in which the Land is situate, or otherwise inquire as to the propriety of assenting to the Prayer of such Petition; but until such Inquiry has been made in the District, after such Notice as may be directed by the Secretary of State, no Provisional Order shall be made affecting any Land, without the Consent of the Owners, Lessees, and Occupiers thereof:

and may make Provisional Order:

(5.) After the Completion of the Inquiry as last aforesaid, the Secretary of State may, by Provisional Order, empower the Local Board to put in force with reference to the Land referred to in such Order the Powers of the said Lands Clauses Consolidation Act with respect to the Purchase and taking of Land otherwise than by Agreement, or any of them, and either absolutely or with such Conditions and Modifications as he may think fit, and it shall be the duty of the Local Board to serve a Copy of any Order so made in the Manner and upon the Person in which and upon whom Notices in respect of such Land are hereinbefore required to be served :

No Provisional Order valid until confirmed. by Parliament.

(6.) No Provisional Order so made shall be of any validity unless the same has been confirmed by Act of Parliament, and it shall be lawful for the Secretary of State, as soon as conveniently may be, to obtain such confirmation, and the Act confirming such Order shall be deemed to be a Public General Act of Parliament.

Costs how to be defrayed.

(7.) All Costs, Charges, and Expenses incurred by the said Secretary of State in relation to any such Provisional Order as last aforesaid, shall to such Amount as the Commissioners of Her Majesty's Treasury think proper to direct become a Charge upon the General District Rates levied in the District to which such Order relates, and be repaid to the said Commissioners of Her Majesty's Treasury by annual Instalments not exceeding Five, together with Interest after the yearly Rate of Five Pounds in the Hundred, to be computed from the date of any such last-mentioned Order upon so much of the principal Sum due in respect of the said Costs, Charges, and Expenses as may from Time to Time remain unpaid.

8. Full Compensation shall be made, out of Compensation. any Fund or Rate applicable to the Purposes of this Act, to all Persons sustaining any Damage by reason of the Exercise of any of the Powers of this Act; and in case of Dispute as to Amount, the same shall be settled by Arbitration, as provided in "The Public Health Act, 1848,* or any Act amending the same, or if the Compensation claimed do not exceed the Sum of Twenty Pounds, the same may be ascertained by and recovered before Justices in a summary Manner, in manner provided by the Acts mentioned in this Section.

* See Page 161.

A person abating a nuisance to his property may justify an interference with the property of the wrongdoer, but only so far as is necessary to abate the nuisance ; and it is the duty of a person who enters upon the land of another to abate a nuisance to do it in the way least injurious to the owner of the land entered. When there is an alternative way of abating a nuisance, which involves an interference with the property of an innocent person or a wrongdoer, the interference must be with the property of the wrongdoer. —*Roberts and another* v. *Rose*, 4 Hurlstone and Coltsman, 103.

This section is in substance identical with Sec. 144 of the Public Health Act, England, 1848, and upon this latter section it has been decided that only disputes as to the amount of compensation are to be settled by arbitration or by Justices, not disputes as to the liability to make compensation at all.—*Reg.* v. *Burslem Local Board of Health*, 1 El. & El, 1,077 Exch. Cham.

It has been also held under Sec. 144 of the Public Health Act, 1848, that in order to be entitled to compensation a person must show actionable damage.—*Hall* v *Bristol* (*Mayor*) 36 L. J. C. P. 110.

SECTION 9.

Power of
Sewer Au-
thorities to
combine.

9. Two or more Sewer Authorities, including under that Expression, for the Purposes of this Section, Local Boards, may combine together for the Purpose of executing and maintaining any Works that may be for the Benefit of their respective Districts, and all Monies they may agree to contribute for the Execution and Maintenance of such common Works shall, in the Case of each Authority, be deemed to be Expenses incurred by them in the Execution of Works within their District, and shall be raised accordingly.

A district of one Nuisance Authority, X, might be without a proper fall for drainage or a proper outfall for the exit of sewage. It is therefore hereby enabled to combine with its neighbour Y or Z, or both, for the purpose of completing or maintaining a work which may be for the mutual advantage of all, and the expenses incurred may be divided rateably in proportion to the extent to which each district is benefited.

Sewer Au-
thority may
take pro-
ceedings to
prevent
pollution of
streams.

10. A Sewer Authority, with the Sanction of Her Majesty's Attorney-General in *England*, and of the Attorney-General for *Ireland* in *Ireland*, and of the Lord-Advocate in *Scotland*, may, either in its own Name or in the Name of any other Person, with the Consent of such Person, take such Proceedings by Indictment, Bill in Chancery, Action, or otherwise, as it may deem advisable, for the Purpose of protecting any Watercourse within its Jurisdiction from Pollutions arising from Sewage either within or without its District; and the Costs of and incidental to any such Proceedings, including any Costs that may be awarded to the Defendant, shall be deemed to be Expenses properly incurred by the Sewer Authority in carrying into effect the Purposes of this Act.

The powers of sanction conferred upon the Attorney-General for Ireland under this section are, to a certain degree, an extension of the jurisdiction of a Nuisance Authority. Before the passing of this Act, the Authority had no jurisdiction beyond its own district, and in some cases an injustice was done to the inhabitants of a town by reason of the sewage of another place higher up the river being allowed with impunity to empty itself into the river, and to foul the water, and to cause a nuisance when it reached the town. The proceedings before Justices under Sec. 12 of the Nuisance Removal Act for England, 1855, Page 94, did not afford any remedy to the Authority of the town to have such a nuisance abated, and it has been held that the proceeding before Justices given by this Section 12 of the Act of 1855, for the removal and prevention of nuisances, is confined to cases where the cause and effect of such nuisance exist within the area of the jurisdiction of the local Authority. Therefore, where Ind, Coope, & Co. brewers at Romford, poured their refuse into a river at that place, and the consequential result of that act was the pollution of the water of the river at Dagenham, Essex, and the local Authority at and for Dagenham proceeded before the Justices for the abatement of the nuisance, it was held that as the cause arose out of the jurisdiction of the local Authority prosecuting, the Justices had no power to hear and determine the question.—*The Queen v. Cotton and other Justices of Essex, and Coope and others ;* 28 L. J. N. S. M. C. 22; 1 El. & El. 203. A complete protection, however, against the continuance of such a nuisance is now given by this section to the Authority of any district.

SECTION 11.

11. Nothing contained in this Act, or in the Acts referred to therein, shall authorize any Sewer Authority to make a Sewer so as to drain direct into any Stream or Watercourse.

Sewers not allowed to drain into any stream, &c.

12. The Public Works Loan Commissioners, as defined by "The Public Works Loan Act, 1853," may advance to any Sewer Authority, upon the Security of any Rate applicable to the Purposes of this Act, without any further Security, such sums of money as may be recommended by One of Her Majesty's Principal Secretaries of State, to be applied by such

Power to Public Works Loan Commissioners to lend money to Sewer Authorities.

SECTION 13. Authority in carrying into effect the Purposes of this Act.*

* In Ireland, such sums of money may be recommended by the Commissioners of Public Works. See Sec. 16.

Powers of Act cumulative.

13. All Powers given by this Act shall be deemed to be in addition to and not in derogation of any other Powers conferred on any Sewer Authority by Act of Parliament, Law, or Custom; and the Sewer Authority may exercise such other Powers in the same Manner as if this Act had not passed.

Sewer Authority may enter into contract for supply of sewage.

14. The Sewer Authority of any Place may from Time to Time, for the Purpose of utilizing its Sewage, agree with any Person or Body of Persons, corporate or unincorporate, as to the supply of such Sewage, and Works to be made for the Purpose of that Supply, and the Parties to execute the same and to bear the Costs thereof, and the Sums of Money, if any, to be paid for that Supply; provided that no Contract shall be made for the Supply of Sewage for a Period exceeding Twenty-five Years.

Application of 27 & 28 Vict., c. 114, to works, &c., for supply of sewage.

15. The making of Works of Distribution and Service for the Supply of Sewage to Lands for Agricultural Purposes shall be deemed an "Improvement of Land" authorized by the "Land Improvement Act, 1864," and the Provisions of that Act shall apply accordingly.

Board of Works in Ireland to have power of Secretary of State in sewage matters.

16. The Commissioners of Public Works in *Ireland* shall, in respect to any Sewage Authority or Sewage Matter in *Ireland*, have and exercise all the Powers conferred by this Act, or any Act

incorporated herewith, on One of Her Majesty's Principal Secretaries of State; and all Applications by this Act, or any Act incorporated herewith, authorized or directed to be made to One of Her Majesty's Principal Secretaries of State in respect to Sewage Matters, or the Powers conferred by this Act on Sewage Authorities, shall in *Ireland* be made to the Commissioners of Public Works; and all Orders made on such Applications by said Commissioners shall have the same Force and Effect as Orders made by One of Her Majesty's Principal Secretaries of State on similar Applications in *England* and *Scotland*.

SCHEDULE.

ENGLAND AND WALES.

Description of Local Authority.	Description of Places.	Rate or Fund out of which Expenses to be paid.
The Mayor, Aldermen, and Burgesses acting by the Council.	In Boroughs, with the Exception of the Boroughs of Oxford and Cambridge, not within the Jurisdiction of a Local Board.	The Borough Fund or Borough Rate.
The Commissioners, Trustees, or other Persons intrusted by any Local Act of Parliament with Powers of improving, cleansing, lighting, or paving the Town.	The Boroughs of Oxford and Cambridge, and any Town or Place not included within the above Descriptions, and under the Jurisdiction of Commissioners, Trustees, or other Persons intrusted by any Local Act with powers of improving, cleansing, lighting, or paving any Town.	Any Rate leviable by the Commissioners, Trustees, or other Persons.
The Vestry, Select Vestry, or other Body of Persons acting by virtue of any Act of Parliament, Prescription, Custom, or otherwise, as or instead of a Vestry or Select Vestry.	In Parishes not within the Jurisdiction of any Sewer Authority hereinbefore mentioned, and in which a Rate is levied for the Maintenance of the Poor.	The Poor Rate.

SCOTLAND.

The Town Council.	Places within the Jurisdiction of any Town Council and not subject to the separate Jurisdiction of Police Commissioners or Trustees.	The Revenue of the Burgh, or any Rate applicable to Sewers leviable by the Town Council.
The Police Commissioners or Trustees.	In Places where Police Commissioners or Trustees exercise the Functions of Police Commissioners or Trustees under any General or Local Act.	Any Rate leviable by the Commissioners or Trustees, or any Fund belonging to them.
The Parochial Board.	Any Town or Village not included in the above Descriptions.	The Poor Rate.

IRELAND. *

Description of Local Authority.	Description of Places.	Rate or Fund out of which Expenses to be paid.
The Right Hon. the Lord Mayor, Aldermen, and Burgesses.	The City of Dublin.	The District Sewer Rate.
The Mayor, Aldermen, and Burgesses.	Towns Corporate or Boroughs (with the exception of Dublin.)	Any Rate leviable by the Town Council, or any Fund belonging to them, applicable in the whole or in part to the making or repairing of Sewers within their jurisdiction.
The Town Commissioners or other Governing Body.	Towns having Town Commissioners under 9 G. IV., c. 82, or 17 and 18 Vict., c. 103, or any Acts amending the same, or having Commissioners or other Governing Body under any Local Act.	Any Rate leviable by these bodies, or any Fund belonging to them, applicable in the whole or in part to the making or repairing of Sewers within their jurisdiction.
The Board of Guardians or any Committee thereof appointed by the Board.	Any Town or Village in any Union not included in the above descriptions.	The Poor Rate; but the Expenses to be charged only on the Electoral Division in which the Town or Village is situated.

* This Schedule has been amended by the Sanitary Act, 1866, sec. 56, (p. 47,) and the first Schedule thereto (p. 64.)

NUISANCES REMOVAL AND DISEASES PREVENTION ACTS CONSOLIDATION AND AMENDMENT.

The Nuisances Removal Act for England, 1855.

18 & 19 VICTORIA, CAP. 121.

An Act to consolidate and amend the Nuisances Removal and Diseases Prevention Acts, 1848 and 1849.*

[*14th August,* 1855.]

11 & 12 Vict., c. 123. 12 & 13 Vict., c. 111. WHEREAS the Provisions of "The Nuisances Removal and Diseases Prevention Act, 1848," amended by "The Nuisances Removal and Diseases Prevention Amendment Act, 1849," are defective, and it is expedient to repeal the said Acts as far as relates to *England,* and to substitute other Provisions more effectual in that Behalf: Be it therefore enacted by the Queen's most Excellent Majesty, by and with the Advice and Consent of the Lords Spiritual and Temporal, and Commons, in this present Parliament assembled, and by the Authority of the same, as follows :

* This Act, as amended by the Nuisance Removal and Disease Prevention Amendment Act, 1860, is by the 62nd section of the Sanitary Act, 1866, extended to Ireland, provided, however, that in such application the changes prescribed by that section are observed. (See Page 57.)

1. From and after the passing of this Act the said Acts are by this Section repealed as far as relates to *England* :* Provided always, that all Proceedings commenced or taken under the said Acts, and not yet completed, may be proceeded with under the said Acts ; and all Contracts or Works undertaken by virtue of the said Acts shall continue and be as effectual as if the said Acts had not been repealed.

SECTION 1

Recited Acts repealed as far as relates to England, except as to proceedings commenced.

* These Acts are now repealed as to Ireland by the Sanitary Act, 1866, Sec. 69, Page 63.

2. In this Act the following Words and Expressions have the Meanings by this Section herein-after assigned to them, unless such Meanings be repugnant to or inconsistent with the Context ; (that is to say,) the Word " *Place* "† includes any City, Borough, District under the Public Health Act, Parish, Township, or Hamlet ; or part of any such City, Borough, District, Town, Parish, Township, or Hamlet ; the Word " *Guardians* " includes the Directors, Wardens, Overseers, Governors, or other like Officers having the Management of the Poor for any Parish or Place where the Matter or any Part of the Matter requiring the Cognizance of any such Officer arises ; the Word " *Borough,* " and the Expressions " *Mayor, Aldermen and Burgesses,*" " *Council,*" and " *Borough Fund,*" have respectively the same Meaning as in the

Interpretation of certain terms used in this Act.

† " Place."—A temporary wooden structure, without a roof, and used on a race-course for the purpose of betting, is a place.— *Kelly*, C.B. It does not seem to me to matter whether this structure had a roof or not, or whether it was fastened by some means or other into the earth or not ; it was a structure in which the business of betting could be and was conducted, and in my opinion clearly came within the meaning of the words "Office or Place," as used in the Act.—*Shaw* v. *Morley*, 37 L. J. N. S. M. C. 105.

SECTION 2 Acts for the Regulation of Municipal Corporations, and shall also respectively mean, include,
and apply to any Royal Borough, Royal Town,
or other Town having a Warden, High Bailiff,
Borough Reeve, or other Chief Officer, and Burgesses or Inhabitants, however designated, asso-
ciated with him in the Government or Management thereof, or any Town or Place having a
Governing Body therein in the Nature of a Corporation or otherwise, and to the Chief Officers
and Governing Bodies of such Boroughs, Towns,
and Places, and to the Funds and Property under
the Management of or at the Disposal of such
Chief Officers and Governing Bodies; the Expression *"Improvement Act"* means an Act for
regulating and managing the Police of, and for
draining, cleansing, paving, lighting, watching,
and improving a Place, and an Act for any of
those Purposes; the Word *"Owner"** includes
any Person receiving the Rents of the Property
in respect of which that Word is used from the
Occupier of such Property on his own Account,
or as Trustee or Agent for any other Person, or
as Receiver or Sequestrator appointed by the
Court of Chancery or under any Order thereof,
or who would receive the same if such Property
were let to a Tenant; the Word *"Premises"* extends to all Messuages, Lands, or Tenements,
whether open or inclosed, whether built on or
not, and whether public or private; the Word
"Parish" includes every Township or Place separately maintaining its Poor or separately maintaining its own Highways; the Expression *"Quarter*

* As to the word "Owner" see 27 L. J. N. S. M. C. 211;
33 L. J. N. S. M. C. 11; 36 L. J. N. S. M. C. 105; 30 L.
J. N. S. M. C. 95. See also note to Sec. 19, page 103.

Sessions" means the Court of General or Quarter Sessions of the Peace for a County, Riding, or Division of a County, City, or Borough; the Word "*Person*" and Words applying to any Person or Individual, apply to and include Corporations, whether aggregate or sole; and the Expression "*Two Justices*" shall, in addition to its ordinary Signification, mean One Stipendiary or Police Magistrate acting in any Police Court for the District.

The operative words in this section are "means," "includes," " extends," and " apply to." The effect of the word "means" is to limit the interpretation. The effect of all the other words is to enlarge it.—*Reg.* v. *Kershaw*, 2 El. & Bl., 1007.

Section 3, which defined the Local Authority, related exclusively to England, and has been repealed by the Act of 1860. (23 & 24 Vict., c. 77, s. 1.)

For the constitution of the Local Authority, now called " Nuisance Authority," see the "Sanitary Act, 1866," Sec. 57, page 53.

Section 4 relates exclusively to England.

PART I.

Constitution of Nuisance Authority, Expenses, Description of Nuisances, and Powers of Entry.

And with respect to the Constitution of the Nuisance Authority for the Execution of this Act, the Expenses of its Execution, the Description of Nuisances that may be dealt with under it, and the Powers of Entry for the Purposes of the Act, be it enacted thus:

5. The Nuisance Authority may appoint any Committee of their own Body to receive Notices, take Proceedings, and in all or certain specified

Power to [Nuisance] Authority to appoint Committees.

SECTION 8. respects execute this Act, whereof Two shall be a Quorum; and such Nuisance Authority, or their Committee, may, in each particular Case, by Order in Writing under the Hand of the Chairman of such Body or Committee, empower any Officer or Person to make Complaints and take Proceedings on their Behalf.

The first portion of this section is altered to such an extent by Sec. 4 of the Sanitary Act, 1866 (Page 3,) as to be almost practically superseded. The latter portion is also superseded by Sec. 48 of the Sanitary Act, 1866, Page 40.

Sections 6 and 7 are repealed by the Act of 1860, 23 & 24 Vict., c. 77, Sec. 1.

What are deemed Nuisances under this Act.

8. The Word "Nuisance" under this Act shall include—

> Any Premises in such a State as to be a Nuisance or injurious to Health :
>
> Any Pool, Ditch, Gutter, Watercourse, Privy, Urinal, Cesspool, Drain, or Ashpit, so foul as to be a Nuisance or injurious to Health :
>
> Any Animal so kept as to be a Nuisance or injurious to Health :
>
> Any Accumulation or Deposit which is a Nuisance or injurious to Health :

Provided always, that no such Accumulation or Deposit as shall be necessary for the effectual carrying on of any Business or Manufacture shall be punishable as a Nuisance under this Section, when it is proved to the Satisfaction of the Justices that the Accumulation or Deposit has not been kept longer than is necessary for the Purposes of such Business or Manufacture, and that

the best available means have been taken for
protecting the Public from Injury to Health
thereby.*

* The word " Nuisance" has been further defined in Sec. 19
of the Sanitary Act, 1866, Page 13.

[Sec. 9 is repealed by the Act of 1860.]

10. †Notice of Nuisance may be given to the Notice of
Nuisance Authority by any Person aggrieved Nuisance to
thereby, or by any of the following Persons: the [Nuisance]
Sanitary Inspector or any paid Officer under the &c., to
said Nuisance Authority; Two or more Inhabi- ground
tant Householders of the Parish or Place to
which the Notice relates; the Relieving Officer
of the Union or Parish; any Constable or any
Officer of the Constabulary or Police Force of
the District or Place; and in case the Premises
be a Common Lodging House,‡ any Person appointed for the Inspection of Common Lodging
Houses; and the Nuisance Authority may take
cognizance of any such Nuisance after Entry
made as herein-after provided, or in conformity
with any Improvement Act under which the Inspector has been appointed.

† The Form of Notice to be served upon the Nuisance Authority acquainting it of the existence of a Nuisance is given
in the Schedule to this Act (Form B, Page 124.)
‡ As to Common Lodging Houses see Note to Sec. 35 of
the Sanitary Act, 1866, Page 29.

11. The Nuisance Authority shall have power Power of
of Entry for the following Purposes of this Act, Entry to
and under the following Conditions:—§ Authority or
their Officer.

§ The hours specified in the conditions mentioned in this
section, during which the Nuisance Authority, or their Officer,
may exercise their powers of entry for the purposes of this Act,

(1.) To ground Proceedings.

For this Purpose, when they or any of their Officers have reasonable Grounds for believing that a Nuisance exists on any private Premises, Demand may be made by them or their Officer, on any Person having Custody of the Premises, of Admission to inspect the same at any Hour between Nine in the Morning and Six in the Evening,* and if Admission be not granted any Justice having Jurisdiction in the Place may, on Oath made before him of Belief in the Existence of the Nuisance, and after reasonable Notice of the intended Application to such Justice being given in Writing to the Party on whose Premises the Nuisance is believed to exist, by Order† under his Hand require the Person having the Custody of the Premises to admit the Nuisance Authority or their Officer; and if no Person having Custody of the Premises can be discovered, any such Justice may and shall, on Oath made before him of Belief in the Existence of such Nuisance, and of the Fact that no Person having Custody of the Premises can be discovered, by Order under his Hand authorize the

---

* have been extended in relation to Nuisances arising from a trade or business to any hour when the business in respect of which the Nuisance arises is in progress, or is usually carried on. The Sanitary Act, 1866, Sec. 31, Page 25.

† The Form of this order is given in the Schedule to this Act, at Page 124 ; and when once issued under this section it shall continue in force until the Nuisance has been abated or the work for which the entry of the Nuisance Authority was necessary has been done (the Sanitary Act, 1866, Sec. 31.) Care must be taken that the order of the Justices is not acted upon until it has been reduced into writing and signed by the Justice.   See Note on Sec. 60 of the Sanitary Act, 1866, Page 55.

Nuisance Authority or their Officers to enter the Premises between the Hours aforesaid.

(2.) To examine Premises where Nuisances exist, to ascertain the Course of Drains, and to execute or inspect Works ordered by Justices to be done under this Act.

For these Purposes, whenever, under the Provisions of this Act, a Nuisance has been ascertained to exist, or when an Order of Abatement or Prohibition under this Act has been made, or when it becomes necessary to ascertain the Course of a Drain, the Nuisance Authority may enter on the Premises, by themselves or their Officers between the Hours aforesaid, until the Nuisance shall have been abated, or the Course of the Drain shall have been ascertained, or the Works ordered to be done shall have been completed, as the Case may be.

(3.) To remove or abate a Nuisance in case of Non-compliance with or Infringement of the Order of Justices, or to inspect or examine any Carcase, Meat, Poultry, Game, Flesh, Fish, Fruit, Vegetables, Corn, Bread, or Flour, under the Powers and for the Purposes of this Act.

For this Purpose the Nuisance Authority or their Officer may from Time to Time enter the Premises where the Nuisance exists, or the Carcase, Meat, Poultry, Game, Flesh, Fish, Fruit, Vegetables, Corn, Bread, or Flour is found, at all reasonable Hours, or at all Hours during

SECTION 12. which Business is carried on on such Premises, without Notice.

PART II.

With regard to the Removal of Nuisances, be it enacted thus :—

Proceedings by [Nuisance] Authority before Justices in the case of Nuisances likely to recur, &c.

12. In any Case where a Nuisance is so ascertained by the [Nuisance] Authority to exist, or where the Nuisance in their Opinion did exist at the Time when the Notice was given, and, although the same may have been since removed or discontinued, it is in their Opinion likely to recur or to be repeated on the same Premises or any Part thereof, they shall cause Complaint thereof* to be made before a Justice of the Peace; and such Justice shall thereupon issue a

---

* The Nuisance Authority must, (Sec. 21 of the Sanitary Act, 1866,) before taking proceedings under this section before ∴ Justice, serve a notice on the person by whose act, default, or sufferance the nuisance arises, or, if such person cannot be ascertained, on the owner or occupier of the premises upon which the nuisance arises, to abate the same, and for that purpose to execute such works, &c., as may be necessary within a time to be specified in the notice; but in a case where the nuisance arises through the want or defective construction of any structural convenience, or where there is no occupier of the premises, the notice must be served on the owner. In a case where the person causing the nuisance cannot be found, and it is clear that the nuisance does not arise or continue, &c., by the act of the owner or occupier of the premises, the Nuisance Authority *may* itself abate the same without further order, and the cost of doing so shall be paid as directed by Secs. 58 and 59 of the Sanitary Act, 1866. The form of the notice to be served in such cases as prepared by the Nuisance Authority for the Borough of Dublin is as follows, (except in the case of a smoke or other nuisance, as defined by Sec. 19 of the Sanitary Act, 1866, the form for which see Page 17.)

Summons,* requiring the Person by whose Act, Default, Permission, or Sufferance the Nuisance arises or continues, or if such Person cannot be found or ascertained, the Owner or Occupier of the Premises on which the Nuisance arises, to appear before any Two Justices, in Petty Sessions

BOROUGH OF DUBLIN.

To ————————   NOTICE.

of No. ——— ———
                            Under 29 & 30 *Vict.,Cap.* 90.
and to the Owner or Occupier.

The Lord Mayor, Aldermen, and Burgesses, being the Nuisance Authority of this Borough, having ascertained that a nuisance exists in or upon the house or premises at
that is to say

so as to be a nuisance or injurious to health, and that such nuisance exists by reason of your acts, default, or sufferance.
Now, take notice, that you are hereby required to remove or abate the same, and for that purpose to do all such things as may be necessary within   days, otherwise proceedings will be taken against you by the said Nuisance Authority without further notice, under the provisions of the Sanitary Act, 1866, 29 & 30 Vict., cap. 90, and the several Acts incorporated therewith for the abatement and removal of such nuisance, and to enforce the provisions of said Acts against you, and for the recovery of the penalties thereby imposed, in the event of your refusal or neglect to comply with the terms of this notice.
Dated this   day of   18
                    Signed ————,
          Officer of the said Nuisance Authority.

This notice is addressed " And to the owner or occupier ;" the propriety of this will be seen by looking at the 35th section of this Act (Page 117), which provides that it shall be sufficient in any proceeding to designate a party as the owner or occupier without further description.

* The proper forms of " Summons" and "Order of Justices" are given in the schedule (Forms D. and E.) to this Act. (Pages 126 and 128.)

SECTION 12.

If proved to Justices that Nuisance exists, &c., they shall issue order for abatement, &c.

assembled, at the usual Place of Meeting, who shall proceed to inquire into the said Complaint; and if it be proved to their Satisfaction that the Nuisance exists, or did exist at the Time when the Notice was given, or, if removed or discontinued since the Notice was given, that it is likely to recur or to be repeated, the Justices shall make an order in Writing under their Hands and Seals on such Person, Owner, or Occupier, for the Abatement or Discontinuance and Prohibition of the Nuisance as herein-after mentioned, and shall also make an Order for the Payment of all Calls incurred up to the Time of hearing or making the Order for Abatement or Discontinuance or Prohibition of the Nuisance.

This section (12.) points out the proceedings of the Nuisance Authority before Justices to procure an order *in writing under their hands and seals* on such *person,* owner, or occupier by whose act, default, permission, or sufferance a nuisance arises, continues, or is likely to recur, for the abatement, prohibition, or discontinuance of the same. The meanings of the words "person," "owner," and "justices" are clearly defined in Sec. 2 (Page 88), but there has been some litigation as to the extent of the meaning or scope of the words "by whose act, default, permission, or sufferance." The occupiers of a brewery had for upwards of twenty years discharged the refuse from it into a barrel-drain, which, after passing along a road, entered land belonging to another proprietor. The proprietor of this land did not get rid of the refuse as his predecessors had done, and it became after it reached his land a nuisance. Held, that the occupier of the brewery was the person by whose act, default, permission, or sufferance the nuisance was caused, and that an order of the Justices under next section, (13) directing him to abate the nuisance by cutting off all communication between the drains of his premises and the barrel-drain, was valid. —*Brown* v. *Bussell,* 37 L. J. N. S. M. C. 65.

The Dean and Chapter of St. Paul's are lords of the manor of Barnes, Surrey, in which manor there is a common called Barnes' Common, on which there was a pond which had become a nuisance. The common was managed and regulated by conservators appointed by the copyhold jury and tenants with the assent of the lords at the Court Baron; proceedings having been taken under this section against the Dean and Chapter in respect of the nuisance in question. Held that as the common was managed and regulated by conservators they were not liable.—*Richmond Union* v. *St. Paul's Chapter*, 18 L. T. N. S. 522, Q. B.

The harbour of Margate was vested in the Margate Pier and Harbour Company, and by the action of the sea a quantity of seaweed was drifted into the harbour, and, being left there, became a nuisance. Held that the company was bound to remove it, and that, not having effectually done so, an order was rightly made upon them under this section.—*Proprietors of Margate Pier* v. *The Town Council of Margate*, 20 L. T. N. S. 564, Q. B.

An owner of a market allowed sheep to be penned there, and he found the hurdles for the pens, and derived a profit in addition to the toll on the sheep. The sheep droppings created a nuisance on the part where they were penned. Held that the owner of the market was liable to an order for the removal of the nuisance as being the person within the meaning of Sec. 12, "by whose act, default, permission, or sufferance" the nuisance arose. — *Draper* v. *Sperring*, 10 C. B. N. S. 113.

B. owned property on which were several houses let to weekly tenants. From these houses a quantity of sewage flowed into cesspools also on his property. Sewage from other houses also flowed into these cesspools, and in rainy weather they overflowed. The sewage thus escaping passed through pipes laid under the public highway into an open ditch or dike in a field not belonging to B., where it caused the nuisance complained of. Held that the Justices properly declined to make an order on B. for the abatement of the nuisance under this section.—*Hendon (Guardians)* v. *Bowles*, 16, W. R. 510. 17, L. T. N. S. 597, Q. B.

An order may be made under Sec. 12 upon a person who causes a nuisance, though it arises at a distance from his premises. —*Brown* v. *Bussell* and *Francomb* v. *Freeman*, 9, B. & S. 1.

Where several persons drain into one place, an order under Sec. 12 may be made upon one whose drainage by itself causes a nuisance.—*Ib.*

But if, though the aggregate drainage is a nuisance, the drainage in each is not by itself enough to cause a nuisance; *quære* whether an order should be made under Sec. 12, or a sewer be laid down under Sec. 22.—Per Blackburn, J., it is for the Local Authority to determine which.—*Ib.*

H

SECTION 13.   An order under Sec. 12 may be made upon a person who claims an easement to drain through the land of A .nto a watercourse on land of B.—*Ib.*

F, the owner of six houses let to yearly tenants, made a drain from them, by leave of the owner of adjoining land through his land into a watercourse on W.'s land, where the drainage became a nuisance. Held that an order under Sec. 12 was rightly made on F.—*Ib.*

Justices' order for abatement.   13. By their Order* the Justices may require the Person on whom it is made to provide sufficient Privy Accommodation, Means of Drainage or Ventilation, or to make safe and habitable, or to pave, cleanse, whitewash, disinfect, or purify the Premises which are a Nuisance or injurious to Health, or such Part thereof as the Justices may direct in their Order, or to drain, empty, cleanse, fill up, amend, or remove the injurious Pool, Ditch, Gutter, Watercourse, Privy, Urinal, Cesspool, Drain, or Ashpit which is a Nuisance and injurious to Health, or to provide a Substitute for that complained of, or to carry away the Accumulation or Deposit which is a Nuisance or injurious to Health, or to provide for the cleanly and wholesome keeping of the Animal kept so as to be a Nuisance or injurious to Health, or if it be proved to the Justices to be impossible so to provide, then to remove the Animal, or any or all of these Things (according to the Nature of the Nuisance,) or to do such other Works or Acts† as are necessary to

* The form of the order of Justices is given in the Schedule, Form E, to this Act, Page 128. See note on Sec. 60 of the Sanitary Act, 1866.

† Under this section an order of Justices was made upon a corporation which is included in the word "person," (Sec. 2,) "within three months to abate and discontinue the nuisance, and do such works and acts as are necessary to abate the same." The terms of the order were construed strictly in the superior court, and it was held to be an order to abate

abate the Nuisance complained of, in such Manner and within such Time as in such Order shall
be specified; and if the Justices are of opinion
that such or the like Nuisance is likely to recur,
the Justices may further prohibit the Recurrence
of it, and direct the Works necessary to prevent
such Recurrence, as the case may in the Judgment of such Justices require; and if the Nuisance proved to exist be such as to render a
House or Building, in the Judgment of the Justices, unfit for Human Habitation, they may
prohibit the using thereof for that Purpose until
it is rendered fit for that Purpose in the Judgment of the Justices, and on their being satisfied
that it has been rendered fit for such Purpose
they may determine their previous Order by
another declaring such House habitable, from
the Date of which other Order such House may
be let or inhabited.

merely, and not an order for structural works, such as are referred to by Sec. 16, and that consequently there was no
appeal against it.—Ex parte *The Mayor, Aldermen, and Burgesses of Liverpool*, 27. L. J. N. S. M. C. 89. In a case,
therefore, where *structural* works are necessary, the order
should specify the works by using the word structural in order
to enable the defendant to appeal under Sec. 16.

The nature and extent of the works required to be done by
the order of the Justices under this section ought to be in accordance with those described in the notice of the Nuisance
Authority referred to in Sec. 21 of the Sanitary Act, 1866,
Page 17.

14 Any Person not obeying the said Order for
Abatement shall, if he fail to satisfy the Justices
that he has used all due Diligence to carry out
such Order, be liable for every such Offence to a
Penalty of not more than Ten Shillings *per* Day
during his Default; and any Person knowingly

SECTION 14. and wilfully acting contrary to the said Order of Prohibition shall be liable for every such Offence to a Penalty not exceeding Twenty Shillings *per* Day during such contrary Action; and the [Nuisance] Authority may, under the Powers of Entry given by this Act, enter the Premises to which the Order relates, and remove or abate the Nuisance condemned or prohibited, and do whatever may be necessary in execution of such Order, and charge the Cost to the Person on whom the Order is made, as hereinafter provided.

[Nuisance] Authority may enter and remove or abate Nuisance.

This order of Justices (see Page 128) is addressed "to the owner or occupier of the premises, or to the Nuisance Authority, or to their servants or agents, and to all whom it may concern ;" but the fact of its being addressed to the Nuisance Authority of the district does not relieve the owner or occupier from any portion of his responsibility under that order either for the abatement of the nuisance or for the penalty imposed under this section during his default. An order to abate a nuisance by removing offensive privies was directed to the owner or to the Nuisance Removal Committee, the owner being directed to remove the same within seven days, and if such order was not complied with the Committee was authorized and required to enter and remove it. The seven days elapsed, and neither the owner nor the Committee removed the Nuisance. Held that the Justices had power to fine the owner under this section for disobedience of the order, notwithstanding that it was addressed to the Nuisance Committee as well as to the owner.—*Tomlins* v. *Great Stanmore Nuisance Committee,* 12 L. T. N. S. 118 Q.B.; but penalties which are imposed under this section for disobeying an order to abate a nuisance cannot be enforced without previously summoning the owner under Sec. 20.—*The Queen* v. *Jenkins,* 32 L. J. N. S. M. C. I.

This section as far as the Nuisance Authority is concerned is merely permissive. The penalty is imposed solely on the person by whose act, default, permission, or sufferance the nuisance exists, and who has been made a defendant before the Justices. The Local Authority is authorized to enter upon the premises to which the order relates and abate the nuisance, and a *mandamus* will not be granted to compel the Local Authority to enforce the order of the Justices on the default of the persons upon whom it is made. —In re *The Local Board of Health of the Parish of Ham,* 26 L. J. N. S. M. C. 64.

See also ex-parte *Bassett,* 7 El. & Bl. 280.

15. Any* such Order of Prohibition may be appealed against as provided in this Act.

* This liberty to appeal appears to be confined to that class of nuisances which require the execution of structural works to prevent their recurrence. An example of that class is given in the latter portion of Sec. 13. There is also an appeal within seven days given under this Act, Sec. 16, against an order of Justices for the *abatement* of a nuisance by the execution of structural works.

16. When it shall appear to the Justices that the Execution of structural Works is required for the Abatement of a Nuisance, they may direct such Works to be carried out under the Direction or with the Consent or Approval of any Public Board, Trustees, or Commissioners having Jurisdiction in the Place in respect of such Works,† and if within Seven Days from the Date of the Order the Person on whom it is made shall have given Notice to the Nuisance Authority of his Intention to appeal against it as provided in this Act, and shall have entered into Recognizances to try such Appeal as provided by this Act, and shall appeal accordingly, no Liability to Penalty shall arise, nor shall any Work be done nor Proceedings taken under such Order until after the Determination of such Appeal, unless such Appeal cease to be prosecuted.

Appeal
against order
of abatement
when struc-
tural works
are required.

† The first schedule of the Sanitary Act, 1866, defines the public bodies having jurisdiction in the place in respect of such works.

To entitle a party to an appeal from the orders of Justices it is necessary that the order should expressly state that structural works are to be executed for the abatement of a nuisance. An order was made by Justice on a Corporation within three months "to abate and discontinue the nuisance, and to do such works and acts as are necessary to abate the same," and such order was construed strictly and held to be an order to abate merely, and not an order for structural works, within this section, and that consequently there was no appeal from it.— Ex-parte *The Mayor, Aldermen, and Burgesses of Liverpool*, 27 L. J N. S. M. C. 89.

The Local Authority is not bound for the purpose of executing structural works for the abatement of a *public* nuisance to obtain an order of Justices under this section, this section applying only to the abatement by structural works of nuisances upon private premises.—*Reg.* v. *Middleton Nuisance Removal Committee*, 1 El. & El. 98.

If person causing Nuisance cannot be found, [Nuisance] Authority to execute order at once.

17. Whenever it appears to the Satisfaction of the Justices that the Person by whose Act or Default the Nuisance arises, or the Owner or Occupier of the Premises is not known or cannot be found, then such Order may be addressed to and executed by such [Nuisance] Authority, and the Cost defrayed out of the Rates or Funds applicable to the execution of this Act.

This section appears to be merely permissive, giving, as it does, the Nuisance Authority power to execute an order of Justices for abatement of a nuisance, and containing no express command to that effect.—See Page 100. The funds out of which the several authorities may defray the costs of the execution of the order are given in the fourth column of the Schedule, Page 64.

Manure, &c., to be sold.

18. Any Matter or Thing removed by the [Nuisance] Authority in pursuance of this Enactment may be sold by Public Auction, after not less than Five Days' Notice by Posting Bills distributed in the Locality, unless in Cases where the Delay would be prejudicial to Health, when the Justices may direct the immediate Removal, Destruction, or Sale of the Matter or Thing; and the Money arising from the Sale retained by the [Nuisance] Authority, and applied in payment of all Expenses incurred under this Act

with reference to such Nuisance, and the surplus, if any, shall be paid on Demand, by the [Nuisance] Authority to the Owner of such Matter or Thing.

Section 53 of the Sanitary Act, 1866, Page 44, obviates, to a certain extent, the necessity for putting this section into force, so far as manure or other refuse matter from mews, stables, or other premises are concerned, for it provides for the *periodical* removal of manure, &c., by the owner thereof, upon notice merely given to that effect by the Nuisance Authority, under a penalty of twenty shillings per day (not less) for every day such is allowed to accumulate.

19. All reasonable Costs and Expenses from Time to Time incurred in making a Complaint, or giving Notice, or in obtaining an Order of Justices under this Act, or in carrying the same into effect under this Act, shall be deemed to be Money paid for the Use and at the Request of the Person on whom the Order is made, or if the Order be made on the [Nuisance] Authority, or if no Order be made, but the Nuisance be proved to have existed when the Complaint was made or the Notice given, then of the Person by whose Act or Default the Nuisance was caused; and in case of Nuisances caused* by the Act or Default

Costs and expenses of works to be paid by person on whom order is made, or owner or occupier

* This section only makes the expenses for carrying out an order of Justices for the removal of a nuisance a charge upon the premises in the case of Nuisances caused by the default of the *owner* of the premises.—Bird *v.* Gleves, 18 L. T. N. S., 727. Upon the meaning of the word owner in this section, the following case may be instructive. In June, 1861, an order of Justices was made under Section 13 of this Act on " the owner" of certain premises to remove a nuisance, and in default, the Authority commenced the necessary works on the 16th July, 1861 and completed them in the following September. The real owner of the premises was abroad, and on the 21st of May in same year, he had executed a power of attorney to his solicitor, the defendant, to receive the rents for him. This power of

SECTION 19. of the Owner of Premises, the said Premises shall be and continue chargeable with such Costs and Expenses, and also with the Amount of any Penalties incurred under this Act, until the same be fully discharged, provided that such Costs and Expenses shall not exceed in the whole One Year's Rackrent of the Premises; and such Costs and Expenses, and Penalties, together with the Charges of suing for the same, may be recovered in any County or Superior Court, or if the [Nuisance] Authority think fit, before any Two Justices of the Peace; and the said Justices shall have Power to divide such Costs, Expenses, and Penalties between the Persons by whose Act or Default the Nuisance arises, in such Manner as they shall consider reasonable; and if it appear to them that a Complaint made under this Act is frivolous or unfounded, they may order the Payment by the [Nuisance] Authority or Person making the Complaint of the Costs incurred by the Person against whom the Complaint is made, or any part thereof.

attorney reached the defendant on the 22nd July following, and he duly received the yearly rents for the owner at the Michaelmas in the same year. By the 2nd section of this Act, "owner" includes the person receiving the rents for himself or as agent. The action was brought by the Nuisance Authority to recover from the defendent the sum of £21 12s., amount of expenses incurred in carrying out the order of Justices. Upon the trial the defendant contended that he was not liable as "the owner" of the premises, inasmuch as he had not received the power of attorney till after the orders of Justices to abate the nuisance was made and executed. Judgment was given against the defendant for the full amount claimed, and on appeal, it was held that the defendant was not "the owner" within the meaning of Section 2 of this Statute at the time the order was made, and that therefore he was not liable under this 19th section to an action for money paid for his use.— The Guardians of the Blything Union *v.* Warton, 32 L. J. N. S. M. C., 133.

20. Where any Costs, Expenses, or Penalties
are due under or in consequence of any Order of Proceedings
Justices* made in pursuance of this Act as afore- tices to re-
said, any Justice of the Peace, upon the appli- cover ex-
cation of the [Nuisance] Authority, shall issue
a summons, requiring the Person from whom
they are due to 'appear before Two Justices at a
Time and Place to be named therein; and upon
Proof to the Satisfaction of the Justices present that any such Costs, Expenses, or Penalties
are so due, such Justices,.unless they think fit†
to excuse the Party summoned upon the Ground
of Poverty or other special Circumstances, shall
by Order in Writing under their Hands and Seals,
order him to pay the Amount to the [Nuisance]
Authority at once, or by such Instalments as the
Justices think fit, together with the Charges attending such Application, and the Proceedings
thereon; and if the Amount of such Order, or
any Instalment thereof, be not paid within Four-

* See Form I, in the Schedule to this Act, page 134.
† " Unless they think fit," The discretion to be exercised by
Justices under powers conferred by an Act similar to this does
not warrant them in entering into the consideration of the
justness or unjustness of the operation of the Act. Thus, in
an extra-parochial place, which was made by due course of
law part of the union, the Justices having refused to levy by
distress certain money ordered by the Guardians of the Union
to be paid by one Carne, the Overseer of the Poor of the
Parish, from the poor rates of said parish towards the relief of the poor thereof, and as the contribution of the said
parish to the common fund of the said union, it was held
that the Justices could not refuse to issue their warrant to
distress the goods of the overseer, merely because they thought
it unjust that such extra-parochial place should be com-
pelled to contribute to the common fund of the union.—33
L. J. N. S. M. C., 101. Penalties imposed under this Act for
disobeying an order to abate a nuisance cannot be enforced
without previously summoning the offender under this section.
—The Queen *v.* Catherine Jenkins, 32 L. J. N. S. M. C. I.

teen days after the Sum is due, the same may,
by Warrant of the said or other Justices, be
levied by Distress and Sale.

> Under this section, the Justices prescribed as the proper
> tribunal have *exclusive jurisdiction* to try an action for money
> paid in pursuance of Section 19 by the authorities for the use of
> the defendant, even in a case where the title to the land may
> be in question, (the Guardians of Headfort Union *v.* Kingston
> and another)—25 L. J. N. S. M. C. 41 ; see also *The Queen* v.
> *Harden*, 2 El. & El. 881.   And it is a general rule where an
> Act of Parliament creates an obligation, and enforces the per-
> formance in a specified manner, that performance cannot be
> enforced in any other manner.—Lord Tenterden in Doe. d.,
> the Bishop of Rochester *v.* Bridges, 1 B. & Ad., 847.

Surveyors of highways to cleanse, ditches, &c., paying owners, &c., for damages.

21. All Surveyors and District Surveyors may
make, scour, cleanse, and keep open all Ditches,
Gutters, Drains, or Watercourses in and through
any Lands or Grounds adjoining or lying near to
any Highway, upon paying the owner or Occupier of such Lands or Grounds, provided they
are not Waste or Common, for the Damages,
which he shall thereby sustain, to be settled and
paid in such Manner as the Damages for getting
Materials in enclosed Lands or Grounds are
directed to be settled and paid by the Law in
force for the Time being with regard to Highways.

> This section is an extension of the powers of County Sur-
> veyors in relation to surface drainage works under their super-
> vision.

Power to [Nuisance] Authority to cover and improve open ditches, &c

22. Whenever any Ditch, Gutter, Drain, or
Watercourse used or partly used for the Conveyance of any Water, Filth, Sewage, or other
Matter from any House, Buildings, or Premises
is a Nuisance within the Meaning of this Act,
and cannot, in the Opinion of the [Nuisance]
Authority, be rendered innocuous without the

laying down of a Sewer or of some other Structure along the same or Part thereof or instead thereof, such [Nuisance] Authority shall and they are hereby required to lay down such Sewer or other Structure, and to keep the same in good and serviceable Repair ;* and they are hereby declared to have the same Powers as to entering Lands for the Purposes thereof, and to be entitled to recover the same Penalties in case of Interference, as are contained in the Sixty-seventh and Sixty-eighth Sections of the Act passed in the Fifth and Sixth Years of the Reign of King *William* the Fourth, intituled *An Act for consolidating and amending the Laws relating to Highways in* England; and such [Nuisance] Authority are hereby authorized and empowered to assess† every House, Building, or Premises then or at any Time thereafter using for the Purposes aforesaid the said Ditch, Gutter, Drain, Watercourse, Sewer, or other Structure, to such Payment, either immediate or annual, or distributed over a Term of Years, as they shall think just and reasonable, and, after Fourteen Days' No-

---

* The expression "Repair" does not mean the reconstruction of a sewer which has been originally defectively made, but the keeping of the original sewer in proper repair.—*Reg* v. *Epsom Union,* 8 L. T. N. S. 383.

† This power to assess is confined to the district of the Nuisance Authority, and the jurisdiction of a Nuisance Authority terminates with the boundary of the district. The drainage of two houses in Parish P was carried by a covered drain into an open ditch in Parish H. This ditch being a nuisance was made into a covered sewer by the Local Authority of H, who assessed under this section, amongst others, the two houses in Parish P as using the said drain or structure so made. Held that the assessment was illegal, and that the Local Authority of Parish H had no jurisdiction.—*Reg.* v. *Warner,* 27 L. J. M. C. 144. See also *Hornsley Board of Health,* 8 El. & Bl. 915.

SECTION 22. tice* at the least left on the Premises so assessed, to levy and collect the Sum and Sums so assessed in the same Manner, and with the same Remedies in case of Default in Payment thereof, as Highway Rates are by the Law in force for the Time being leviable and collectable, and with the same Right and Power of Appeal against the Amount of such Assessments reserved to the Person or Persons so assessed as by the Law for the Time being in force shall be given against any Rate made for the Repair of the Highways; and the Provisions contained in this Section shall be deemed to be Part of the Law relating to Highways in *England:* Provided always, that where such Ditch, Gutter, Drain, or Watercourse shall, as to Parts thereof, be within the

---

* The assessing the premises, and the giving notice of the assessment, are two successive acts going to make up the liability of the person so assessed, and the words "after fourteen days" refer to the latter.—*Reg* v. *Middleton*, 5 Jur. N.S. 623; and both days must be excluded in reckoning the fourteen days.—*Reg.* v. *Shropshire J.J.*; 8 A. and E. 173. A watercourse at Bury having become a nuisance, which it was impossible to remove without constructing a sewer, the defendants, who were the Improvement Commissioners, under the Bury Local Act, carried a new sewer for some distance alongside the watercourse and for the remainder of the length across the land of the plaintiff, where no sewer had passed before. It was not shown that the nuisance could not have been abated without going through the plaintiff's land. By the Local Act they were required to give notice of their intention, but they omitted to do so, and justified under this section. Held by Kelly, C. B., and Channell, B., that, although the Bury Commissioners were the Local Authority, under Sec. 3 of the Nuisances Removal Act, that Act did not repeal the provisions of the Local Act, and that the defendants had not authority to carry a new sewer through the close of plaintiff.—Per Martin, B., that the operation of Sec. 22 was not restrained by their Local Act.

By this section Authorities have not only the power to construct new sewers, but also, if they think fit, to compel people to drain into them.—*Wood V. C.; Attorney-General* v. *Richmond,* 12 Jur. N. S. 544.

See the case of the Bury Commissioners, Page 122.

Jurisdiction of different [Nuisance] Authorities, this Enactment shall apply to each [Nuisance] Authority only as to so much of the Works hereby required, and the Expenses thereof, as is included within the respective Jurisdiction of that Authority: Provided also, that such Assessment shall in no Case exceed a Shilling in the Pound on the Assessment to the Highway Rate, if any.*

* See Sec. 57 of the Sanitary Act, 1866 (page 54,) by which it is provided that for the purposes of this section the Nuisance Authority shall in Ireland have the power of entering Land, conferred by the Sewage Utilization Act, 1865, and shall have the same power of levying assessments under this section that they have of levying any other rates they are authorized by Law to impose.

For the purposes of this section the Nuisance Authority in Ireland are armed with the powers of entry, conferred by the Sewage Utilization Act, 1865, Sec 5. (See note, Page 75.) But that power of entry refers only to cases of private nuisances, and the order of Justices is only required when it becomes necessary to enter on private premises to abate the nuisance. — *R. V. Middleton Committee*, 5 Jur. N. S. 622, 28 L. J. M. C., N. S. 41.

Penalty for causing water to be corrupted by gas washings

23. Any Person or Company engaged in the Manufacture of Gas who shall at any Time cause or suffer† to be brought or to flow into any Stream, Reservoir, or Aqueduct, Pond, or Place for Water, or into any Drain communicating therewith, any Washing or other Substance produced in making or supplying Gas, or shall wilfully do any Act connected with the making or supplying of Gas whereby the Water in any such Stream, Reservoir, Aqueduct, Pond, or Place for Water shall be fouled, shall forfeit for every such Offence the Sum of Two Hundred Pounds.

† This word "suffer" includes an act done involuntarily by by the manufacturers of gas. — *Hipkins* v. *The Birmingham Gas Company*, 30, L. J. Exch. 60.

SECTION 24.

Penalty to be sued for in Superior Courts within six months.

24. Such Penalty may be recovered, with full Costs of Suit, in any of the Superior Courts, by the Person into whose Water such Washing or other Substance shall be conveyed or shall flow, or whose Water shall be fouled by any such Act as aforesaid, or if there be no such Person, or in default of Proceedings by such Person, after Notice to him from the [Nuisance] Authority of their Intention to proceed for such Penalty, by the Nuisance Authority; but such Penalty shall not be recoverable unless it be sued for during the Continuance of the Offence, or within Six Months after it shall have ceased.

Daily penalty during the continuance of the offence.

25. In addition to the said Penalty of Two Hundred Pounds, (and whether such Penalty shall have been recovered or not,) the Person or Company so offending shall forfeit the Sum of Twenty Pounds (to be recovered in the like manner) for each Day during which such Washing or other Substance shall be brought or shall flow as aforesaid, or during which the Act by which such Water shall be fouled shall continue, after the Expiration of Twenty-four Hours from the Time when Notice of the Offence shall have been served on such Person or Company by the [Nuisance] Authority, or the Person into whose Water such Washing or other Substance shall be brought or flow, or whose Water shall be fouled thereby, and such Penalty shall be paid to the Parties from whom such Notice shall proceed; and all Moneys recovered by a [Nuisance] Authority under this or the preceding Section shall, after Payment of any Damage caused by the Act for which the Penalty is imposed, be applied towards defraying the Expenses of executing this Act.

Sec. 26, which relates to the inspection of unwholesome food exposed for sale, has been repealed by the 26 & 27 Vict., c. 117, and other provisions substituted. (See Page 154.)

27. If any Candle House, Melting House, Melting Place, or Soaphouse, or any Slaughter-house, or any Building or Place for boiling Offal or blood, or for boiling, burning, or crush-ing Bones, or any Manufactory, Building, or Place used for any Trade, Business, Process, or Manu-facture causing Effluvia, be at any time certified to the [Nuisance] Authority by any Medical Of-ficer, or any Two legally qualified Medical Practi-tioners,* to be a Nuisance or injurious to the Health of the Inhabitants of the Neighbourhood, the [Nuisance] Authority shall direct Complaint to be made before any Justice, who may summon before any Two Justices in Petty Sessions assem-bled at their usual Place of Meeting the Person by or in whose Behalf the Work so complained of is carried on, and such Justices shall inquire into such Complaint, and if it shall appear to such Justices that the Trade or Business carried on by the Person complained against is a Nui-sance,† or causes any Effluvia injurious to the Health of the Inhabitants of the Neighbourhood, and that such Person shall not have used the best

As to nui-sances aris-ing in cases of noxious trades, busi-nesses, pro-cesses, or manufac-tures.

* By Sec. 18 of the Sanitary Act, 1866, Page 13, a requisition in writing under the hands of any ten inhabitants of a place shall, for the purposes of this section, be deemed to be equi-valent to the certificate of the Medical Officer or Medical Prac-titioner herein-mentioned, and this section shall be enforced accordingly.

† The Nuisance, or the causing injurious Effluvia, must be proved, although slight evidence will be sufficient by the complainant that the defendant has not used the best practica-ble means for abating the Nuisance, or preventing or counter-acting the Effluvia.—*Stokes* v. *Grissel*, 23 L. J. C. P. 116.

SECTION 27. practicable* Means for abating such Nuisance or preventing or counteracting such Effluvia, the Person so offending (being the Owner or Occupier of the Premises, or being a Foreman or other Person employed by such Owner or Occupier,) shall, upon a summary Conviction for such Offence, forfeit and pay a Sum of not more than Five Pounds nor less than Forty Shillings, and upon a Second Conviction for such Offence the Sum of Ten Pounds, and for each subsequent Conviction a Sum double the Amount of the Penalty imposed for the last preceding Conviction, but the highest Amount of such Penalty shall not in any Case exceed the Sum of Two Hundred Pounds: Provided always, that the Justices may suspend their final Determination in any such Case, upon Condition that the Person so complained against shall undertake to adopt, within a reasonable Time, such Means as the said Justices shall judge to be practicable and order to be carried into effect for abating such Nuisance, or mitigating or preventing the injurious Effects of such Effluvia, or shall give Notice of Appeal in the Manner provided by this Act, and shall enter into Recognizances to try such Appeal, and shall appeal accordingly: Provided always, that the Provisions hereinbefore contained shall not extend or be applicable to any Place without the Limits of any City, Town, or populous District.

* See *Scholefield* v. *Schunck*, Page 16.

For the purposes of this section, the following notice may be useful, but must be altered, of course, as circumstances require.

To _____	NOTICE. SECTION 28.
of No. _____	*Under* 29 & 30 *Vict.*, *Cap.* 90,
and to the Owner or Occupier.	and the several Acts incorporated therewith.

The   being the Nuisance
Authority of this Borough, having ascertained that a nuisance
is caused to the inhabitants of this Borough, residing in and about
the neighbourhood of your works, at No.   Street,
by your acts, default, or sufferance in allowing quantities of
gases, vapours, and effluvia, to be given off into the open atmosphere from the several materials used in the process of
your manufacture so as to be a nuisance or injurious to the
health of the inhabitants residing in and about the neighbourhood of your works; and by your not using or not having
used the best practicable means for abating such nuisance
and for preventing or counteracting such gases, vapours, and
effluvia, and removing their injurious effects.

Now, take notice, that you are hereby required to prevent,
counteract, and abate the same, and for that purpose to do all
such things as may be necessary within   days from this
date; otherwise proceedings will be taken against you by the
said Nuisance Authority, without further notice, under the
provisions of 29 & 30 Vict., cap. 90, and the several Acts incorporated therewith, for the abatement or removal of such
nuisance, and for the prevention or counteraction of such gases,
vapours, and effluvia, and to enforce the provisions of said Acts
against you, and for the recovery of the penalties thereby imposed, in the event of your refusal or neglect to comply with
the terms of this notice.

This   day of   18

Signed——————,

Officer of said Nuisance Authority.

28. Provided also, That if, upon his Appearance before such Justices, the Party complained against object* to have the Matter determined by such Justices, and enter into Recognizances,

* But this objection must be taken immediately upon the
appearance in Court of the party complained against, and a
Justice will refuse to entertain the objection after he has heard
the complaint and adjudicated thereon.

SECTION 29. with sufficient Sureties to be approved by the Justices, to abide the Event of any Proceedings at Law or in Equity that may be had against him on account of the Subject Matter of Complaint, the Local Authority shall thereupon abandon all Proceedings before the Justices, and shall forthwith take Proceedings at Law or in Equity in Her Majesty's Superior Courts for preventing or abating the Nuisance complained of.

On certificate of Medical Officer to [Nuisance] Authority that House is overcrowded, proceedings may be taken to abate the same.

29. Whenever the Medical Officer of Health, if there be One, or, if none, whenever Two qualified Medical Practitioners, shall certify to the [Nuisance] Authority that any House is so overcrowded as to be dangerous or prejudicial to the Health of the Inhabitants, and the Inhabitants shall consist of more than One Family, the [Nuisance] Authority shall cause Proceedings to be taken before the Justices to abate such overcrowding, and the Justices shall thereupon make such Order as they may think fit, and the Person permitting such overcrowding shall forfeit a Sum not exceeding Forty Shillings.

The overcrowding of dwellings is declared to be a nuisance under Sec. 19 of the Sanitary Act, 1866, Page 13, without any reference to their being inhabited by one or more families, as mentioned in this section.

[Nuisance] Authority to order costs of prosecutions to be paid out of the rates.

30. The [Nuisance] Authority may, within the Area of their Jurisdiction, direct any Proceedings to be taken at Law or in Equity in Cases coming within the Purview of this Act, and may order Proceedings to be taken for the Recovery of any Penalties, and for the Punishment of any Persons offending against the Provisions of this Act, or in relation to appeals under this Act,

and may order the Expenses of all such proceedings to be paid out of the Rates or Funds admi-
nistered by them under this Act.

PART III.

As to Procedure under this Act.

And with regard to Procedure under this Act,
be it enacted, That

31. Notices, Summonses, and Orders under Service of
this Act may be served by delivering the same notices, summonses,
to or at the Residence* of the Persons to whom and orders.
they are respectively addressed, and where addressed to the Owner or Occupier of Premises
they may also be served by delivering the same
or a true Copy thereof to some Person upon the
Premises, or if there be no Person upon the Premises who can be so served, by fixing the same
upon some conspicuous Part of the Premises, or

---

* "Residence." As to the meaning of this word see the
decision in *Mason* v. *Bibby*, 33, L. J. N. S. M. C. 107, and
3 New Rep. 482, where service of notice on a clerk in defendant's place of business is held to be good service at "place of
abode" or residence. Service of notice on a person *de facto*
receiving the rent is a service on the owner.—33, L. J. N. S.
M. C. 11. The computation of the time of service through
the post of the notices, summonses, and orders mentioned in
this section must commence from the time when by the ordinary course of the Post Office, the letter containing the notice,
&c.,would be received by the person to whom it is addressed.—
Reg. v. *Slauston*, 21, L. J. M. C. N. S. 145. The five miles
distance from the office of the Inspector is to be measured in
a direct line "as the crow flies:"—*Lake* v. *Butler*, 24, L. J.
N. S. Q. B. 273.

SECTION 32. if the Person shall reside at a distance of more than Five Miles from the Office of the Inspector then by a registered Letter through the Post.

Proof of re-
solutions of
[Nuisance]
Authority.

32. Copies of any Orders or Resolutions of the [Nuisance] Authority or their Committee, purporting to be signed by the Chairman of such body or Committee, shall, unless the contrary be shown, be received as Evidence thereof, without Proof of their meeting, or of the official Character or Signature of the Person signing the same.

As to pro-
ceedings
taken
against
several per-
sons for the
same offence.

33. Where Proceedings under this Act are to be taken against several Persons in respect of One Nuisance caused by the joint Act or Default of such Persons, it shall be lawful for the [Nuisance] Authority to include such Persons in One Complaint, and for the Justices to include such Persons in One summons, and any Order made in such a Case may be made upon all or any Number of the Persons included in the Summons, and the costs may be distributed as to the Justices may appear fair and reasonable.

See Note at Sec. 12, Page 97.

One or
more joint
owners or
occupiers
may be
proceeded
against
alone.

34. In case of any Demand or Complaint under this Act to which Two or more Persons, being Owners or Occupiers of Premises, or partly the one or partly the other, may be answerable jointly or in common or severally, it shall be sufficient to proceed against any One or more of them without proceeding against the others or other of them; but nothing herein contained shall prevent the Parties so proceeded against

from recovering Contribution in any case in
which they would now be entitled to Contribution by Law.

See Note on Sec. 12, Page 97.
A nuisance cannot be justified by the existence of other nuisances of a similar character if it can be shown that the inconvenience is increased by the nuisance complained of.—*Crossley*
v. *Lightowler*, 36 L. J. Ch. 584.

35. Whenever in any Proceeding under this
Act, whether written or otherwise, it shall become necessary to mention or refer to the Owner
or Occupier of any Premises, it shall be sufficient to designate him as the " Owner" or " Occupier" of such Premises, without Name or further Description.

Designation
of "Owner"
or "Occu-
pier."

36. Whoever refuses to obey an Order of Justices under this Act for Admission on Premises
of the [Nuisance] Authority or their Officers, or
wilfully obstructs any Person acting under the
Authority or employed in the Execution of this
Act, shall be liable for every such Offence to a
Penalty not exceeding Five Pounds.

Penalty for
obstructing
execution of
this Act.

37. If the Occupier of any Premises prevent
the Owner thereof from obeying or carrying into effect the Provisions of this Act, any
Justice to whom Application is made in this Behalf shall by Order in Writing require such Occupier to desist from such Prevention or to
permit the Execution of the Works required to
be executed, provided that such Works appear
to such Justice to be necessary for the Purpose
of obeying or carrying into effect the Provisions
of this Act; and if within Twenty-four Hours

Penalty on
occupier ob-
structing
owner.

SECTION 38. after the Service of such Order the Occupier against whom it is made do not comply therewith he shall be liable to a Penalty not exceeding Five Pounds for every Day afterwards during the Continuance of such Non-compliance.

Penalties and expenses recoverable under 11 and 12 Vict., c. 43.

38. Penalties imposed by this Act for Offences committed and Sums of Money ordered to be paid under this Act may be recovered by Persons thereto competent in *England* according to the Provisions of the Act of the Eleventh and Twelfth Years of the present Reign, Chapter Forty-three; and all Penalties recovered by the [Nuisance] Authority under this Act shall be paid to them, to be by them applied in aid of their Expenses under this Act.*

* In Ireland, penalties are to be proceeded for in the manner directed by the Petty Sessions (Ireland) Act, 1851. See Sanitary Act, 1866, Sec. 60, Page 55.

Proceedings not to be quashed for want of form.

39. No Order, nor any other Proceeding,* Matter, or Thing done or transacted in or relating to the Execution of this Act, shall be vacated, quashed, or set aside for Want of Form, nor shall any Order, nor any other Proceeding, Matter, or Thing done or transacted in relation to the Execution of this Act, be removed or removable by *Certiorari*,† or by any other Writ or Pro-

* Although a party by appearing to an insufficient summons cures the defect therein, (*Reg.* v. *Magee*, 1, Leg. Rep., 220, Q. B.,) care must be taken to state the offence accurately with which the party is charged.

† But the Court quashed a conviction on *certiorari* in a case where a Justice had acted without jurisdiction in convicting under an illegal bye-law made by a Local Board of Health.—(*Reg.* v. *Wood*, 24, L. J. N. S. M. C. 130. Though the writ of *certiorari* be taken away by statute, the Court of Queen's

cess whatsoever, into any of the Superior Courts; and Proceedings under this Act against several persons included in One Complaint shall not abate by reason of the Death of any among the Persons so included, but all such Proceedings may be carried on as if the deceased Person had not been originally so included.

Bench may grant it under certain circumstances, as in *Reg.* v. *Dickenson*, 7 El. & Bl. 831. And this section is not applicable in a case where the Justices have acted without jurisdiction and contrary to the Act.—*Reg.* v. *Gosse,* 30, L. J. N. S. M. C. 41.

40. Appeals under this Act shall be to the Appeals Court of· Quarter Sessions held next after the Act to be to making of the Order appealed against; but the Sessions. Appellant· shall not be heard in support of the Appeal unless within Fourteen Days after the making of the Order appealed against he give to the [Nuisance] Authority Notice in Writing stating his Intention to bring such Appeal, together with a statement in Writing of the Grounds of Appeal, and shall within Two Days* of giving such Notice enter into a Recognizance before some Justice of the Peace, with sufficient Securities, conditioned to try such Appeal at the said Court, and to abide the Order of and pay such Costs as shall be awarded by the Justices at such Court or any adjournment thereof; and the said Court, upon hearing and finally determining the Matter of the Appeal, may, according to its Discretion, award such Costs to the

* Sunday is counted in the two days, and, therefore, where notice of appeal was given on Friday, but the recognizance was not entered into till the following Monday, it was held that the Sessions could not hear the appeal.—Ex parte *Simpkin,* 29, L. J. M. C. 23, Q. B., 6, Jur. N. S., 144.

SECTION 41. Party appealing or appealed against as they shall think proper, and its Determination in or concerning the Premises shall be conclusive and binding on all Persons to all Intents or Purposes whatsoever: Provided always, that if there be not Time to give such Notice and enter into such Recognizance as aforesaid, then such Appeal may be made to, and such Notice, Statement, and Recognizance be given and entered into for, the next Sessions at which the Appeal can be heard; provided also, that on the hearing of the Appeal no Grounds of Appeal shall be gone into or entertained other than those set forth in such Statement as aforesaid; provided also, that in any Case of Appeal the Court of Quarter Sessions may, if they think fit, state the Facts specially for the Determination of Her Majesty's Court of Queen's Bench, in which Case it shall be lawful to remove the Proceedings, by Writ of *Certiorari* or otherwise, into the said Court of Queen's Bench.

Forms to be used as in Schedule.

41. The Forms contained in the Schedule to this Act annexed, or any Forms to the like Effect, varied as Circumstances may require, may be used for Instruments under this Act, and shall be sufficient for the Purpose intended.

As to protection of [Nuisance] Authority and its officers.

42. The [Nuisance] Authority, and any Officer or Person acting under the Authority and in Execution or intended Execution of this Act, shall be entitled to such Protection and Privilege in Actions and Suits, and such Exemption from personal Liability, as are granted to Local Boards of Health and their Officers by the Law in force for the Time being.

No writ or process shall be sued out against or served upon the Local Authority, or any person or officer under the Authority and in execution, or intended execution of this Act until the expiration of one month next after notice in writing shall have been delivered to him, or them, or left at their or his office or place of abode, clearly and explicitly stating the cause of action, (in accordance with 5 & 6 Vict., c. 97, sec. 4,) and the name and place of abode of the intended plaintiff and of his attorney in the cause, &c.—*Reid* v. *Coker*, 13, C. B., 870. A letter from plaintiff's attorney, claiming compensation for his client, and intimating that he will commence proceedings if no arrangement is come to, would not be a sufficient notice of action. — *Mason* v. *Birkenhead*, 29, L. J. N. S. Exch., 407. As regards a notice of action in respect of a claim for compensation for injuries affecting premises by the construction of works according to the powers of an Act. — See *Delany* v. *The Metropolitan Board of Works*, 37, L. J. C. P., 59.

43. Nothing in this Act shall be construed to affect the Provisions of any Local Act as to Matters included in this Act, nor to impair, abridge, or take away any Power, Jurisdiction, or Authority which may at any Time be vested in any Commissioners of Sewers or of Drainage, or to take away or interfere with any Course of Proceedings which might be resorted to or adopted by such Commissioners if this Act had not passed, nor to impair any Power of abating Nuisances at Common Law, nor any Jurisdiction in respect of Nuisances that may be possessed by any Authority under the Act intituled *An Act to abate the Nuisances arising from the Smoke of Furnaces in the Metropolis, and from Steam Vessels above* London Bridge, or the Common Lodging Houses Acts, the Act for the Regulation of Municipal Corporations, the Public Health Act, or any Improvement Act respectively, or any Acts incorporated with such Acts, and Authorities may respectively proceed for the Abatement of Nuisances or in respect of any other Matter

[Act not to impair Jurisdiction of Sewers Commissioners, or Common Law Remedies for Nuisance, nor Jurisdiction of [Nuisance] Authority as to the Nuisances referred to in this Act.]

SECTION 44. or Thing herein-before provided or referred to either under the Acts mentioned in this Section or any other Act conferring Jurisdiction in respect of the Nuisances referred to in this Act, or any Byelaws framed under any such Act, as they may think fit; and the Local Authorities constituted under and for the Purposes of the Common Lodging Houses Act, 1851 and 1853, shall for the Purposes of those Acts have all the Powers of [Nuisance] Authorities under this Act.

Power of Local Authority as to New Sewers.

The 22nd Sec. of the Nuisance Removal Act for England enacts that where a watercourse used or partly used for the conveyance of sewage is a nuisance within the meaning of the Act, and cannot in the opinion of the Local Authority be rendered innocuous without the laying down of a sewer along the same or part thereof, or instead thereof, the Local Authority shall lay down such sewer, &c., the same section gives the Local Authority the same powers of entering lands as are given to the surveyor of highways by the 67th Section of the Highway Act. Those powers are to make and lay such trunks, tunnels, &c., as he shall deem necessary in and through lands or grounds adjoining or lying near to any highway upon paying the owner for the damages sustained by him, held (reversing the judgment of the Court of Exchequer) that the Local Authority in laying down a new sewer under this section are not bound to follow the course of the old watercourse, but may in the exercise of an honest discretion carry the new sewer across enclosed land adjoining the old watercourse.—The Earl of Derby *v.* the Bury Commissioners, 38 L. J. Ex.

Act not to affect navigation of rivers or canals. 44. Nothing herein contained shall enable any [Nuisance] Authority, Surveyor of Highways, or other Person, either with or without any Order of Justices, to injuriously affect the Navigation of any River or Canal, or to divert or diminish any Supply of Water of right belonging to any such River or Canal; and the Provisions of this Act shall not extend or be construed to SECTION 45. extend to Mines of different Descriptions, so as to interfere with or obstruct the efficient working of the same, or to the smelting of Ores and Minerals, or to the manufacturing of the Produce of such Ores and Minerals.

45. No Power given by this Act shall be exercised in such Manner as to injuriously affect the Supply, Quality, or Fall of Water contained in any Reservoir or Stream, or any Feeders of such Reservoir or Stream, belonging to or supplying any Waterwork established by Act of Parliament, or in Cases where any Company or Individual are entitled for their own Benefit to the Use of such Reservoir or Stream, or to the Supply of Water contained in such Feeders, without the Consent* in Writing of the Company or Corporation in whom such Waterworks may be vested, or of the Parties so entitled to the Use of such Reservoirs, Streams, and Feeders, and also of the Owners thereof in Cases where the Owners and Parties so entitled are not the same Person.

Saving as to rights of mill owners, &c

* And see pages 71 to 74.

46. In citing this Act in other Acts of Parliament, and in legal Instruments and other Proceedings, it shall be sufficient to use the Words "The Nuisances Removal Act for *England,* 1855."

Short title.

SCHEDULE OF FORMS.

FORM (A.)

Order of Justices for Admission of Officer of [Nuisance] Authority to inspect private Premises.

WHEREAS [*describe the (Nuisance) Authority*] have by their Officer [*naming him*] made Application to me *A. B.*, One of Her Majesty's Justices of the Peace having Jurisdiction in and for [*describe the Place,*] and the said Officer has made Oath to me of his Belief that a Nuisance, within the Meaning of the Nuisances Removal Act for England, 1855, as amended and extended to Ireland by the Sanitary Act 1866, viz. [*describe Nuisance*], exists on private Premises at [*describe Situation of Premises so as to identify them*], within my Jurisdiction, and Demand of Admission to such Premises for the Inspection thereof has been duly made under the said Act, and refused.

Now, therefore, I the said *A. B.*, do hereby require you to admit the said [*name the (Nuisance) Authority,*] [*or* the Officer of the said (*Nuisance*) *Authority*], for the Purpose of inspecting the said Premises.

Dated this   Day of   18 .

                                          A. B.

FORM (B.)
Notice of Nuisance.

To the [Nuisance] Authority (*describing it*).

I [*or* We,] the Person aggrieved by the Nuisance hereinafter described [*or* the undersigned and described Inhabitant Householders, Sanitary Inspector [*or other Officer (describing him,*)] do hereby give you Notice, That there exists in or upon the

FORM C.

[Dwelling House, Yard, *etc.*, *as the Case may be*], situate at   [*giving such Description as may be sufficient to identify the Premises*] in the Parish of   in your District, under the Nuisances Removal Act, 1855, as amended and extended to Ireland by the Sanitary Act, 1866, the following Nuisance, videlicet [*describing the Nuisance, as the Case may be, for instance*, a Dwelling House or Building, a Nuisance or injurious to Health for want of a Privy *or* Drain *or* sufficient Means of Ventilation, *or* so dilapidated *or* so filthy as to be a Nuisance or injurious to Health, *or for further instance*, a Ditch or Drain so foul as to be a Nuisance or injurious to Health, *or* an Accumulation of
a Nuisance or injurious to Health, *&c., or* Swine so kept as to be a Nuisance or injurious to Health] ; and that such Nuisance is caused by [*naming the Person by whose Act or Default the Nuisance is caused, or* by some Person unknown].

Dated this   Day of   in the Year of our Lord One thousand eight hundred and

[*Signed by Complainant under Section* 10.]

FORM (C.)*

Notice to Owner or Occupier of Entry for Examination.

To the Owner [*or* Occupier, *as the case may be*,] of [*describe the Premises*] situate at [*insert a Description sufficient to identify the Premises*].

Take notice, That under the Nuisance Removal Act for England, 1855, as amended and extended to

* Where a nuisance is ascertained by the Nuisance Authority to exist it is not necessary, before taking proceedings against the owner, under Sec. 21 of Sanitary Act, 1866, and Sec. 12 of the Nuisance Removal Act, 1855, to serve him with a notice in the form given in the Schedule of the latter Act (Form C.)—*Amys* v. *Creed*, 38 L. J. N. S. M. C. 22.

FORM D.   Ireland by the Sanitary Act, 1866, the [(*Nuisance*) *Authority, naming it,*] in whose District under the said Act the above Premises are situate, have received a Notice from [*name Complainant*], stating that in or upon the said Premises [*insert the Cause of Nuisance as set forth in the Notice.*]

And further take notice, That after the Expiration of Twenty-four Hours from the Service of this Notice the [*Nuisance*] *Authority* will cause the said Premises to be entered and examined under the Provisions of the said Act, and if the Cause of Nuisance aforesaid be found still existing, or, though removed or discontinued, be likely to be repeated, a Summons will be issued requiring your Attendance to answer a Complaint which will be made to the Justices for enforcing the Removal of the same, and prohibiting a Repetition thereof, and for recovering the Costs and Penalties that may be incurred thereby.

Dated this   Day of   in the Year of our Lord One thousand eight hundred and

A. B.

The Officer appointed by the [*Nuisance*] *Authority* to take Proceedings under the Nuisance Removal Act for England, 1855, as amended and extended to Ireland by the Sanitary Act, 1866.

FORM (D.)
Summonses.

To the Owner or Occupier of [*describe Premises*] situate at [*insert such a Description as may be sufficient to identify the Premises*], or to *A. B.*, of

County of [or Borough of &c. *or* District of *or as the Case may be*] to wit.	You are required to appear before Two of Her Majesty's Justices of the Peace [*or* One of the Magistrates of the Police

Courts of the Metropolis, or the Stipendiary Magis-
trate] of the County [*or other Jurisdiction*] of
at the Petty Sessions [*or* Court] holden at
on the   Day of   next, at the Hour of
     in the   noon, to answer the Com-
plaint this Day made to me by   [*or* by
on behalf of] [*naming the (Nuisance) Authority, as
the Case may be*], that in or upon the Premises above-
mentioned [*or* in or upon certain Premises situate at
No.   in the   Street in the Parish of
     *or such other Description or Reference as may
be sufficient to identify the Premises*], in their District,
under the Nuisances Removal Act for England, 1855,
as amended and extended to Ireland by the Sanitary
Act, 1866, the following Nuisance exists [*describing
it, as the Case may be*], and that the said Nuisance is
caused by the Act or Default of the Occupier [*or*
Owner] of the said Premises, *or* by you *A. B.* [*or in
case the Nuisance be discontinued, but likely to be repeated, say*, there existed recently, to wit, on or about
the   Day of   on the Premises the following Nuisance [*describe the Nuisance*], and that the
said Nuisance was caused [*&c.*], and although the
same has since the said last-mentioned Day been removed or discontinued there is reasonable Ground
to consider that the same or the like Nuisance is
like to recur on the said Premises.

Given under the Hand of me, *J. P.*, Esquire, One
     of Her Majesty's Justices of the Peace acting
     in and for the [*Jurisdiction*] stated in the
     Margin, *or* One of the Magistrates of the
     Police Courts of the Metropolis, *or* Stipendiary
     Magistrate of   Day of
     in the Year of our Lord One thousand eight
     hundred and

FORM (E.)

Order of Justices for Removal of Nuisances by Owner, &c.

To the Owner, [*or* Occupier] of [*describe the Premises*] situate [*give such Description as may be sufficient to identify the Premises,*] *or* to *A. B.* of or to, [*giving Name of the (Nuisance) Authority,*] or to their Servants or Agents, and to all whom it may concern.

County of
[*or* Borough, &c., of
    or
District of
or as the Case may be.]

WHEREAS on the Day of   Complaint was made before   Esquire, One of Her Majesty's Justices of the Peace acting in and for the County [*or other Jurisdiction*] stated in the Margin, [*or* before the undersigned, One of the Magistrates of the Police Courts of the Metropolis, *or as the Case may be,*] by [*or* by on behalf of] *the (Nuisance) Authority* [*naming it, as the Case may be,*] that in or upon certain Premises situate at   in the District under the Nuisances Removal Act for England, 1855, as amended and extended to Ireland by the Sanitary Act, 1866, of the Complainants above named, the following Nuisance then existed, [*describing it;*] and that the said Nuisance was caused by the Act or Default of the Owner [*or* Occupier] of the said Premises [or was caused by *A. B.*] (*If the Nuisance have been removed, say,* the following Nuisance existed on or about, [*the Day the Nuisance was ascertained to exist,*] and that the said Nuisance was caused, &c., and although the same is now removed, the same or the like Nuisance is likely to recur on the same Premises.)

And whereas   the Owner [*or* Occupier] within the meaning of the said Nuisances

FORM E.

Removal Act, 1855, as amended and extended to Ireland by the Sanitary Act, 1866, [or the said *A. B.*,] hath this Day appeared before us Justices, being Two of Her Majesty's Justices in and for   , sitting in Petty Sessions at their usual Place of Meeting, [*or* before me, the said Magistrate of the Police Courts of the Metropolis, *or as the Case may be*,] to answer the Matter of the said Complaint, [*or in case the Party charged do not appear, say*,] And whereas it hath been this Day proved to our [*or* my] Satisfaction that a true Copy of a Summons requiring the Owner [*or* Occupier] of the said Premises [*or* the said *A. B.*] to appear this Day before us [*or* me]   hath been duly served according to the said Act:

Now upon Proof here had before us [*or* me] that the Nuisance so complained of doth exist on the said Premises, and that the same is caused by the Act or Default of the Owner [or Occupier] of the said Premises, [*or* by the said *A. B.*,] we, [*or* I,] in pursuance of the said Act, do order the said Owner, [*or* Occupier, *or A. B.*,] within [*specify the Time*] from the Service of this Order or a true Copy thereof according to the said Act [*here specify the Works to be done, as for instance*, to cleanse, whitewash, purify, and disinfect the said Dwelling House; *or, for further instance*, to construct a Privy *or* Drain, *&c.*; *or, for further instance*, to cleanse *or* to cover *or* to fill up the said Cesspool, *&c.*,] so that the same shall no longer be a Nuisance or injurious to Health as aforesaid.

[*And if it appear to the Justices that the Nuisance is likely to recur on the Premises, say*, [And we, [or I] being satisfied that, notwithstanding the said Cause or Causes of Nuisances may be removed under this Order, the same is or are likely to recur, do therefore prohibit the said Owner [*or* Occupier *or A. B.*] from [*here insert the Matter of the Prohibition, as, for*

K

FORM E. *instance*, from using the said House or Building for Human Habitation until the same, in our Judgment, is rendered fit for that Purpose.]

And if the above Order for Abatement be not complied with, [*or* if the above Order of Prohibition be infringed,] then we [*or* I] do authorise and require you the said, [(*Nuisance*) *Authority, naming it,*] from Time to Time to enter upon the said Premises, and to do all such Works, Matters, and Things as may be necessary for carrying this Order into full Execution according to the Act aforesaid.

In case the Nuisance were removed before Complaint, say, [Now upon Proof here had before us, that at or recently before the Time of making the said Complaint, to wit, on   as aforesaid, the Cause of Nuisance complained of did exist on the said Premises, but that the same hath since been removed, yet notwithstanding such removal, we, [*or* I,] being satisfied that it is likely that the same or the like Nuisance will recur on the said Premises, do hereby prohibit, [*Order of Prohibition*;] and if this Order of Prohibition be infringed, then we [*or* I] [*Order on (Nuisance) Authority to do Works.*]

Given under the Hands and Seals of us, Two of Her Majesty's Justices of the Peace in and for [*or* the Hand and Seal of me, One of the Magistrates of the Police Courts of the Metropolis, *or as the Case may be.*] this   Day of in the Year of our Lord One thousand eight hundred and

FORM (F.)

Order of Justices for Removal of Nuisance by [Nuisance] Authority.

To the Town Council, &c., *as the Case may be.*

County, &c., } WHEREAS [*recite Complaint of Nui-*
to wit. } *sance as in last Form.*]
And whereas it hath been now proved to our [*or my*] Satisfaction that such Nuisance exists, but that no Owner or Occupier of the Premises, or Person causing the Nuisance, is known or can be found, [*as the Case may be:*] Now we, [*or I,*] in pursuance of the said Act, do order the said [*(Nuisance) Authority, naming it,*] forthwith to, [*here specify the Works to be done.*]

Given, &c.

FORM (G.)

Order to permit Execution of Works by Owners.

County of [*or* Borough of *or* Metropolitan Police District, *or as the Case may be*], to wit. _____ &c.] of _____ } WHEREAS Complaint hath been made to me, *E.F.*, Esquire, One of Her Majesty's Justices of the Peace in and for the County [*or* Borough, [*or* one of the Magistrates of the Police Courts of the Metropolis, *or as the Case may be, or* One of Her Majesty's Justices of the Peace, *as the Case may be*, of the County of], by *A. B.*, Owner within the Meaning of the Nuisances Removal Act for England, 1855, as amended and extended to Ireland by the Sanitary Act, 1866, of certain Premises, to wit, a Dwelling House [*or* Building, *or as the Case may be*], situate at [*insert such a Description of the Premises as may*

FORM G.   *be sufficient to identify them*], in the Parish of
in the said County [*or* Borough, &c.] that *C. D.*, the
Occupier of the said Premises, doth prevent the
said *A. B.* from obeying and carrying into effect the
Provisions of the said Act, in this, to wit, that he the
said *C. D.* [*here describe the Act of Prevention generally,
according to the Circumstances; for instance, thus*, doth
refuse to quit the said House the same having by the
Order of Justices been declared unfit for Human
Habitation, *or* doth prevent the said *A. B.* from
cleansing or whitewashing *or* purifying the said
Dwelling House, *or* erecting a Privy or Drain *or*
breaking an Aperture for ventilation, *or* cleansing a
Drain, Ditch, Gutter, Watercourse, Privy, Urinal,
Cesspool, *or* Ashpit which is a Nuisance or injurious
to Health]: And whereas the said *C. D.* has been
summoned to answer the said Complaint, and has
not shown sufficient Cause against the same, and it
appears to me that [*describe the Act or Works to be
done*] is necessary for the Purpose of enabling the
said *A. B.* to obey and carry into effect the Provisions of the said Act, I do hereby order that the
said *C. D.* do permit the said *A. B.* [*describe the Act
or Works to be done*] in the Manner required by the
said Act.

    Given under my Hand and Seal this
        Day of   in the Year of our Lord
        One thousand eight hundred and
                                E. F.   (L.S.)

FORM (H.)

Summons for Nonpayment of Costs, Expenses, or Penalties. Sec. 20.

To   [*Describe the Person from whom the Costs, Expenses, and Penalties are due*].

County of *or* Borough of *or* District of to wit.	You are required to appear before Two of Her Majesty's Justices of the Peace [*or* One of the Magistrates of

the Police Courts of the Metropolis, *or* the Stipendiary Magistrates] of the County [*or other Jurisdiction*] of   at the Petty Sessions [or Court] holden at   on the Day of   next, at the Hour of   in the   noon, to answer the Complaint this Day made to me by   [*or* by   on behalf of] [*naming the (Nuisance) Authority*], that the Sum of Pounds, being Costs and Expenses incurred by you under and in relation to a certain Complaint touching [*describe the Nuisance*], and an Order of [*describe the Person making the Order*] duly made in pursuance of the Nuisances Removal Act for England, 1855, as amended and extended to Ireland by the Sanitary Act, 1866, [*if Penalties are due, add*, and also the Sum of   being the Amount of Penalties payable by you for Disobedience of the said Order], remains unpaid and due from you.

Given under the Hand of me, *J. P.*, Esquire, One of Her Majesty's Justices of the Peace acting in and for the [*Jurisdiction stated in the Margin*] [*or* One of the Magistrates of the Police Courts of the Metropolis, *or* Stipendiary Magistrate of   ] the   day of   in the Year of Our Lord One thousand eight hundred and

FORM (I.)

Order for Payment of Costs, Expenses, and Penalties,
Sec. 20.

To   [*name the Person on whom
the Order is made*].

County, &c.,⎱ WHEREAS Complaint has been made
  to wit. ⎰ before us [*or* me] for that [*recite
Cause of Complaint*] :

And whereas the said [*naming the Person against
whom the Complaint is made*] has this Day appeared
before us the said Justices [*or* before me the said
Magistrate of the Police Courts of the Metropolis,
or as the Case may be*], to answer this Matter of the
said Complaint : [*Or, in case the Party charged do not
appear, say*],

And whereas it has been this Day satisfactorily
proved to us [*or* me] that a true Copy of the Summons requiring the said [*naming Person charged*] to
appear before us [*or* me] this Day hath been duly
served according to the said Act : Now, having heard
the Matter of the said Complaint, we [*or* I] do adjudge the said [*naming the Person charged*] to pay
forthwith [*or* by instalments of   payable respectively on or before the   ] to the said
[*naming the Person or (Nuisance) Authority to whom
the Costs adjudged are payable*], the Sum of
for Costs in this Behalf, and to [*naming the Person or
Authority to whom the Expenses are payable*], the Sum
of   for Expenses in this Behalf, [*if Penalties
are due, add,* and the Sum of   for Penalties
incurred in relation to the Premises], together with
the Sum of   being the Charges attending the
Application for this Order and Proceedings thereon ;
and if the said several Sums, amounting in the whole
to   [*or* if any One of the said Instalments]
be not paid within Fourteen Days after the same is
due as aforesaid, we [*or* I] hereby order that the same

be levied by Distress and Sale of the Goods and
Chattels of the said   and in default of sufficient Distress in that Behalf adjudge the said
to be imprisoned in the Common Gaol [*or* House of
Correction, *as the Case may be*,] at   in the
said County [*or as the Case may be*] for the space of
such Time, not exceeding Three Calendar Months,
as the Justices may think fit, unless the said several
Sums [*or* Sum], and all Costs and charges of the
said Distress [and of the Commitment and carrying
of the said   to the said House of Correction
or Common Gaol, *or as the Case may be*], shall be
sooner paid.

Given under our [*or* my] Hands, this   Day
of   in the Year of our Lord One thousand
eight hundred and   at   in the
[County, *or as the Case may be*], aforesaid.

FORM (K.)

Warrant of Distress. Sec. 20.

To the Constable of   and to all other Peace
Officers in the said County [*or as the Case may be*].

WHEREAS on   last past Complaint was
made before the undersigned, Two of Her Majesty's
Justices of the Peace in and for the said County of
[*or as the Case may be*] [*or* a Magistrate of the Police
Courts of the Metropolis *or* Stipendiary Magistrate,
as the Case may be] for that [*&c., as in the Order*] ;
and thereupon having considered the Matter of the
said Complaint, we [*or* I] adjudged the said
[*set out from Form K the Adjudication of Payment,
and the Order for Distress and for Imprisonment in
default of Distress*] : And whereas the Time in and
by the said Order appointed for the Payment of the
said several Sums of   and   hath
elapsed, but the said   hath not paid the same

FORM K.

or any Part thereof within Fourteen Days after the Date fixed by the Order for such Payment, but therein hath made default : These are therefore to command you in Her Majesty's Name forthwith to make Distress of the Goods and Chattels of the said *A. B.*, and if within the Space of   Days after the making of such Distress the said last-mentioned Sums, together with the reasonable Charges of taking and keeping the said Distress, shall not be paid, that then you do sell the said Goods and Chattels so by you distrained, and do pay the Money arising from such Sale over to the Clerk of the Justices of the Peace for the Division of   in the said [County, *or as the Case may be*], that he may pay and apply the same as by Law directed, and may render the Overplus, if any, on Demand, to the said   ; and if no such Distress can be found, then that you certify the same unto me, to the end that such Proceedings may be had therein as to the Law doth appertain.

Given under our [*or* my] Hands and Seal, this   Day of   in the Year of our Lord One thousand eight hundred and at   in the [County] aforesaid.

A. B.
C. D.

(L.S.)

FORM (L.)

Return of Proceedings under Nuisances Removal Act, 1855, *as amended and extended to Ireland by the Sanitary Act,* 1866, *by the* [name the (Nuisance) Authority at Length].

From 25th March, 1855, *to 25th March,* 1856.

Date of Notice.	By whom given.	Nature of Nuisance.	Proceedings taken.	Remarks:—With any special Work done under the Acts without any Notice.
16 April.	The Inspector.	Foul Drainage from House.	Owner put down good Drain, on Summons without Justices' Order.	Several Houses being in a like position, the Highway Surveyor laid down a Sewer in the old Watercourse, and each House was charged a proportionate sum for the same, of which the highest sum was 10s.
18 April.	Two Neighbours.	Offensive Cesspool.	Abated by [Nuisance] Authority.	Renewed once; but Penalty recovered, and no subsequent Renewal attempted.

Dated this 26th Day of March, 1856. [*To be signed by the Chairman of the (Nuisance) Authority.*]

DISEASES PREVENTION.

——◆——

THE DISEASES PREVENTION ACT, 1855.

———

18 & 19 Victoria, Cap. 116.

An Act for the better Prevention of Diseases.*

14th *August*, 1855.

Whereas the Provisions of "The Nuisances Removal and Diseases Prevention Act, 1848," amended by "The Nuisances Removal and Diseases Prevention Amendment Act, 1849," in so far as the same relate to the Prevention or Mitigation of epidemic, endemic, or contagious Diseases, are defective, and it is expedient to substitute other Provisions more effectual in that Behalf: Be it therefore enacted by the Queen's most Excellent Majesty, by and with the Advice and Consent of the Lords Spiritual and Temporal, and Commons, in this present Parliament assembled, and by the Authority of the same, as follows :—

* This Act is amended by the Act of 1860. (Page 145.)

In the application of these Acts to Ireland, the changes prescribed by the 62nd Sec. of the Sanitary Act, 1866, are to be observed. (Page 58.)

See, also, note on Sec. 40 of the Sanitary Act, 1866, Page 34.

1. This Act may be cited for all Purposes as the " Diseases Prevention Act, 1855."

SECTION 1
Short title.

[Sections 2 and 3, which define the Local Authority for executing the Act, and provide for the expenses incurred, are repealed by Section 10 of the 23 and 24 Vict., c. 77, p. 148.]

4. The Local Authority and their Officers shall have Power of Entry for the Purposes of this Act, and for executing or superintending the Execution of the Regulations and Directions of the General Board issued under this Act.

Power of entry.

5. Whenever any Part of *England* appears to be threatened with or is affected by any formidable epidemic, endemic, or contagious Disease the Lords and others of Her Majesty's Most Honourable Privy Council, or any Three or more of them, (the Lord President of the Council of One of Her Majesty's Principal Secretaries of State being One,)* may, by Order or Orders to be by them from Time to Time made, direct that the Provisions herein contained for the Prevention of Diseases be put in force in *England,* or in such Parts thereof as in such Order or Orders respectively may be expressed, and may from Time to Time, as to all or any of the Parts to which any such Order or Orders extend, and in like Manner, revoke or renew any such Order; and, subject to Revocation and Renewal as aforesaid, every such Order shall be in force for Six Calendar Months, or for such shorter Period as in such Order shall be expressed; and every such Order of Her Majesty's Privy Council, or of any Members

Power to PrivyCouncil to issue orders that provision herein contained for prevention of diseases may be put in force.

* The Lord Lieutenant in Council shall have the power with respect to Ireland, which the Privy Council has under these provisions in England.
Sec. 62 of the Sanitary Act, 1866, Page 58.

SECTION 6. thereof, as aforesaid, shall be certified under the Hand of the Clerk in Ordinary of Her Majesty's Privy Council, and shall be published in the *London Gazette;** and such Publication shall be conclusive Evidence of such Order, to all Intents and Purposes.

* In Ireland the *Dublin Gazette.*

Power to General Board of Health to issue regulations to carry out such provisions.
6. From Time to Time after the issuing of any such Order as aforesaid, and whilst the same continues in force, the General Board of Health* may issue Directions and Regulations as the said Board think fit—

For the speedy Interment of the Dead:

For House to House Visitation:

For the dispensing of Medicines, guarding against the Spread of Disease, and affording to Persons afflicted by or threatened with such epidemic, endemic, or contagious Diseases such Medical Aid and such Accommodation as may be required:

Local extent and duration of Regulations of General Board.
And from Time to Time, in like Manner, may revoke, renew, and alter any such Directions and Regulations as to the said Board appears expedient, to extend to all Parts in which the Provisions of this Act for the Prevention of Disease shall for the Time being be put in force under such Orders as aforesaid, unless such Directions and Regulations be expressly confined to some

* The Commissioners for administering the laws for the relief of the poor in Ireland. called the Poor Law Commissioners, shall be the Authority in Ireland for issuing regulations to carry the provisions of this Act into effect, and their regulations shall be authenticated in like manner as orders of theirs under the Dispensary Act, 1851, Sec. 2. See Sec. 62 of the Sanitary Act, 1866, Page 58.

SECTION 7.

of such Parts, and then to such Parts as therein are specified; and (subject to the Power of Revocation and Alteration herein contained) such Directions and Regulations shall continue in force so long as the said Provisions of this Act shall under such Order be applicable to the same Parts.

Publication of such Regulations.

7. Every such Direction and Regulation as aforesaid, when issued, shall be published in the *London Gazette,* and the Gazette in which such Direction or Regulation was published shall be conclusive Evidence of the Direction or Regulation so Published, to all Intents and Purposes.*

* In Ireland the *Dublin Gazette.* See Sec. 67 of the Sanitary Act, 1866, Page 62.

The Local Authority to see to the execution of such Regulations, &c. :

8. The Local Authority shall superintend and see to the Execution of such Directions and Regulations, and shall appoint and pay such Medical or other Officers or Persons, and do and provide all such Acts, Matters, and Things, as may be necessary for mitigating such Disease, or for superintending or aiding in the Execution of such Directions and Regulations, or for executing the same, as the Case may require.

and may direct prosecutions for violating the same.

9. The Local Authority may from Time to Time direct any Prosecutions or legal Proceedings for or in respect of the wilful Violation or Neglect of any such Direction and Regulation.

Orders of Council, Directions, and Regulations to be laid before Parliament.

10. Every Order of Her Majesty's Privy Council, and every Direction and Regulation of the General Board of Health, under this Act, shall be laid before both Houses of Parliament, forth-

SECTION 11. with upon the issuing thereof, if Parliament be then sitting, and if not, then within Fourteen Days next after the Commencement of the then next Session of Parliament.

Orders in
Council may
extend to
parts and
arms of the
sea.

11. Orders in Council issued in pursuance of this Act for putting in force the Provisions for the Prevention of Disease in the said Nuisance Removal and Disease Prevention Acts contained, in *Great Britain,* may extend to Parts and Arms of the Sea lying within the Jurisdiction of the Admiralty; and the Board of Health for *England** may issue under this Act Directions and Regulations for cleansing, purifying, ventilating, and disinfecting, and providing Medical Aid and Accommodation, and preventing Disease in Ships and Vessels, as well upon Arms and Parts of the Sea aforesaid as upon Inland Waters.

Medical
Officer of
Unions and
others
entitled to
costs of
attending
sick on board
vessels, when
required by
orders of
General
Board of
Health.

12. Whenever, in compliance with any Regulation of the General Board of Health,* which they may be empowered to make under this Act, any Medical Officer appointed under and by virtue of the Laws for the Time being for the Relief of the Poor shall perform any Medical Service on board of any Vessel, such Medical Officer shall be entitled to charge extra for any such Service, at the General Rate of his Allowance for his Services for the Union or Place for which he is appointed, and such Charges shall be payable by the Captain of the vessel, on behalf of the Owners, together with any reasonable Expenses for the Treatment of the Sick; and if such Services shall be rendered by any Medical

* The Poor Law Commissioners in Ireland—Sanitary Act, 1866, Sec. 62, Page 58.

Practitioner who is not a Union or Parish Officer, he shall be entitled to Charges for any Service rendered on board, with extra Remuneration on account of Distance, at the same Rate as those which he is in the habit of receiving from private Patients of the Class of those attended and treated on Shipboard, to be paid as aforesaid; and in case of Dispute in respect of such Charges, such Dispute may, where the Charges do not exceed Twenty Pounds, be determined summarily, at the Place where the Dispute arises, as in case of Seamen's Wages not exceeding Fifty Pounds, according to the Provisions of the Law in that Behalf for the Time being in force; and any Justice before whom Complaint is made shall determine summarily as to the Amount which is reasonable according to the accustomed Rate of Charge within the Place for Attendance on Patients of the like Class or Condition as those in respect of whom the Charge is made.

13. The Directions and Regulations of the General Board of Health under this Enactment shall be under the Seal of the said Board, and the Hand of the President or Two or more Members thereof; and any Copy of such Regulations purporting to bear such Seal and Signature, whether the said Signature and Seal be respectively impressed and written, or printed only, shall be Evidence in all Proceedings in which such Regulations may come in question.* *Authentication of Directions and Regulations, of General Board of Health.*

* In Ireland the directions and regulations of the Poor Law Commissioners are to be authenticated in like manner, as orders issued under the Medical Charities Act (14 and 15 Vict., c. 68, s. 2.) See Sanitary Act, 1866, Sec. 62, Page 58.

SECTION 14

Penalty for obstructing execution of Act.

14. Whoever wilfully obstructs any Person acting under the Authority or employed in the Execution of this Act, and whosoever wilfully violates any Direction or Regulation issued by the General Board of Health* as aforesaid, shall be liable for every such Offence to a Penalty not exceeding Five Pounds, to be appropriated in or towards the defraying the Expenses of executing this Act.

Certain provisions of Nuisances Removal Act to apply to this Act.

15. The Provisions of any General Act in force for the Removal of Nuisances, with regard to the Service of Notices, the Proof of Orders or Resolution of the Local Authority, and the Recovery of Penalties, shall extend and apply to this Act.

* In Ireland the Poor Law Commissioners.

THE NUISANCES REMOVAL AND DISEASES PRE-VENTION (AMENDMENT) ACT, 1860.

23 & 24 VICTORIA, CAP. 77.

An Act to Amend the Acts for the Removal of Nuisances and the Prevention of Diseases.*

[*6th August,* 1860.]

WHEREAS the Provisions of "The Nuisances Removal Act for *England,* 1855," and "The Diseases Prevention Act, 1855," concerning the Local Authority for the Execution of the said Acts, are defective, and it is expedient that the said Acts should be amended as herein-after mentioned: Be it enacted by the Queen's most Excellent Majesty, by and with the Advice and Consent of the Lords Spiritual and Temporal, and Commons, in this present Parliament assembled, and by the Authority of the same, as follows :— *18 & 19 Vict., cc. 121 & 116.*

Nuisances Removal.

I. Section Three, Section Six, Section Seven, and Section Nine of the said "Nuisances Removal Act for *England,* 1855," shall be repealed : Provided always, that such Repeal as aforesaid *Sections 3, 6, 7, and 9 of 18 & 19 Vict., c. 121, repealed.*

---

* In the application of this Act to Ireland, the changes prescribed by Sec. 62 of the Sanitary Act, 1866, must be observed. Page 58.

SECTION 5. shall not extend to any Charges or Expenses already incurred, but the same may be defrayed and recovered, and all Proceedings commenced or taken under the said Act, and not yet completed, may be proceeded with, and all Contracts under the said Act shall continue and be as effectual, as if this Act had not been passed.

[Section 2 defines the Local Authority to execute the Nuisances Removal Act in England. For the corresponding authority in Ireland, see the Sanitary Act, 1866, Sec. 57, (Page 53,) and the first Sceedule to that Act, (Page 64.)]

[Section 3 is repealed by Section 17 of the Sanitary Act, 1866.]   Page 12.

[Section 4, which provides for the expenses incurred by the Local Authority, appears to be applicable only to England. Provision on this subject, for Ireland, is contained in the 57th Section of the Sanitary Act, 1866, (Page 53.)]

Board of Guardians may appoint Committees for particular parishes

5. Provided, That the Board of Guardians for a Union may appoint a Committee or Committees of their own Body, under Section Five of the said Nuisances Removal Acts, to act in and for One or more of the Parishes or Places for which the Board is the [Nuisance] Authority; and every Committee so appointed shall have the full Power of executing the said Act in all respects, within the specified Place or Places for which it is appointed, unless its Power be expressly limited by the Term of its Appointment; and the Board of Guardians shall cause the Charges and Expenses of every such Committee to be paid out of the Poor Rates of the Place or Places for which such Committee is appointed; and where a Committee is so appointed for any such Place or Places, the Charges and Expenses of the Board as [Nuisance] Authority

for or in respect of the Place or Places for which a Committee is not appointed, shall be paid or contributed by such last-mentioned Place or Places in like Manner as the Expenses* of a Committee: Provided that where any one such Committee is appointed for all the Places for which the Board is the [Nuisance] Authority, its Charges and Expenses shall be contributed and paid in like Manner as the Charges and Expenses of the Board would have been contributed and paid if such Committee had not been appointed.

* Those expenses in Ireland are by this section chargeable to the electoral divisions for which committees are appointed, and the Dispensary Committees of those places would appear to be the best adapted to carry out the regulations, &c.

[Section 6 is not applicable to Ireland.]

7. All Wells, Fountains, and Pumps provided Wells, &c., under Section Fifty of "The Public Health Act, belonging to any place 1848," or otherwise, for the Use of the Inhabi- vested in Local Authority, &c. tants of any Place, and not being the Property of or vested in any Person or Corporation other than Officers of such Place, shall be vested in the [Nuisance] Authority under this Act for such Place, who shall from Time to Time cause to be kept in good Repair and Condition and free from Pollution all Wells, Fountains, and Pumps vested in them under this Act, and may also keep in good Repair and Condition and free from Pollution other Wells, Fountains, and Pumps dedicated to or open to the Use of the Inhabitants of such Place.

8. If any Person do any Act whatsoever Penalty for fouling whereby any Fountain or Pump is wilfully or water.

SECTION 9. maliciously damaged, or the Water of any Well, Fountain, or Pump is polluted or fouled, he shall, upon summary Conviction of such Offence before Two Justices, forfeit a sum not exceeding Five Pounds for such Offence, and a further sum not exceeding Twenty Shillings for every Day during which such Offence is continued after written Notice from the [Nuisance] Authority in relation thereto : but nothing herein contained shall extend to any Offence provided against by Section Twenty-three of the said "Nuisances Removal Act."

Appointment of Inspectors of Nuisances.

9. Local Authorities under this Act may, for the Purposes of the Act, severally appoint or employ Inspectors of Nuisances, and make such Payments as they see fit for the Remuneration and Expenses of such Inspectors.

This appointment need not be an instrument under seal, but it ought to be entered on the minutes, so as to be capable of being proved at any time.—Smart *v.* Westham, 24 L. J. N. S. Exch., 211.

A form of appointment, similar to the following, might be filled up, and given, to the person appointed, as his authority to act :—

We, the Committee of the Nuisance Authority of the
, pursuant to our powers in that behalf, DO
HEREBY *appoint and employ*

as an Inspector of Nuisances for the

*Chairman of the Committee of the
said Nuisance Authority.*

This   day of

Diseases Prevention.

Secs. 2 & 3 of 18 & 19 Vict., c. 116, repealed.

10. Sections Two and Three of "The Diseases Prevention Act, 1855," and every other Enact-

ment constituting a Local Authority for the Execution of the same Act, or providing for the Expenses of the Execution thereof, except those contained in the Eighteenth and Nineteenth of *Victoria*, Chapter One Hundred and Twenty, the Metropolis Local Management Act, shall be repealed.

11. The Board of Guardians for every Union, or Parish not within an Union, in *England* shall be the Local Authority for executing the said Diseases Prevention Act in every Place within their respective Unions and Parishes,* and in every Parish and Place in *England* not within a Union, and for which there is no Board of Guardians, the Overseers of the Poor shall be the Local Authority to execute the same Act; and the Expenses incurred in the Execution of such Act by the Board of Guardians for a Union shall be defrayed out of the Common Fund thereof, and the Expenses of the Board of Guardians or Overseers of the Poor of any single Parish or Place shall be defrayed out of the Rates for the Relief of the Poor of such Parish or Place; provided that every such Board of Guardians shall, for the Execution of the said Act for the Prevention of Diseases, have the like Powers of appointing Committees, with the like Authority, and where any such Committee is appointed the Expenses thereof and of the Board shall be paid in the same Manner, as hereinbefore provided where such a Board is the Local Authority for the Execution of the said Nuisances Removal Act; provided also, that any Expenses already

Marginal note: Guardians and overseers of the poor to be the Local Authorities for executing Diseases Prevention Act.

* This provision is made applicable to Ireland by the Sanitary Act, 1866, Sec. 62, (Page 57.)

SECTION 12. incurred by any Local Authority in the Execution of the said Act shall be defrayed as if this Act had not been passed; provided, moreover, that in respect of any Place where, under this Act, the Local Authority for executing the Nuisances Removal Act is any other Body than the Board of Guardians or the Overseers of the Poor, the Privy Council,* if it see fit, may, in the Manner provided for the Exercise of its Powers under the Public Health Act, 1858, authorize such other Body to be, instead of the Board of Guardians or the Overseers of the Poor, the Local Authority for executing the said Diseases Prevention Act ; provided also, that as regards the Metropolis the Vestries and District Boards under the Act of the Session holden in the Eighteenth and Nineteenth Years of Her Majesty, Chapter One Hundred and Twenty, within their respective Parishes and Districts, shall continue to be the Local Authorities for the Execution of the said " Diseases Prevention Act, 1855," and their Charges and Expenses shall be defrayed as if this Act had not been passed.

* By this section, the Lord Lieutenant and Privy Council may authorise Corporations, Town Commissioners, &c., to carry out this Act in their respective districts, which, if done, the expenses would be payable out of their respective moneys instead of the poor rates. See Sec. 58 of Sanitary Act, 1866, Page 54.

Local Authorities may provide carriages for conveyance of infected persons.

12. It shall be lawful for the Local Authority for executing the said " Diseases Prevention Act," to provide and maintain a Carriage or Carriages suitable for the Conveyance of Persons suffering under any contagious or infectious Disease, and to convey such sick and diseased Persons as may be residing within such Locality

to any Hospital or other Place of Destination,
and the Expense thereof shall be deemed to be
an Expense incurred in executing the said Act.

13. Upon Complaint before a Justice of the Justices, on
the applica-
Peace by any Inhabitant of any Parish or Place tion of householders, may
of the Existence of any Nuisance on any private order the
Premises in the same Parish or Place, such Jus- removal of
nuisances.
tice shall issue a summons requiring the Person
by whose Act, Default, Permission, or Sufferance the Nuisance arises, or if such Person
cannot be found or ascertained, the Owner or
Occupier of the Premises on which the Nuisance arises, to appear before Two Justices in
Petty Sessions assembled at their usual Place of
Meeting, who shall proceed to inquire into the
said Complaint, and act in relation thereto as in
Cases where Complaint is made by a [Nuisance]
Authority under Section Twelve of the said Nuisances Removal Act, and as if the Person
making the Complaint were such [Nuisance]
Authority; Provided always, that it shall be
lawful for the said Justices, if they see fit, to
adjourn the Hearing or further Hearing of such
Summons for an Examination of the Premises
where the Nuisance is alleged to exist, and to require the Admission or authorize the Entry into
such Premises of any Constable or other Person
or Persons, and thereupon the Person or Persons
authorized by the Order of the Justices may
enter and act as the Local Authority might under
a like Order made by any Justice under Section
Eleven of the said Act: Provided also, that the
Costs in the Case of every such Application
shall be in the Discretion of the Justices, and
Payment thereof may be ordered and enforced

SECTION 14.   as in other cases of summary Adjudication by
Justices : Any Order made by Justices under
this Enactment shall be attended with the like
Penalties and Consequences for Disobedience
thereof and subject to the like Appeal as any
Order made under Section Twelve of the said
Nuisances Removal Act, and the Justices making such Order may thereby authorize any Constable or other Person or Persons to do all Acts
for removing or abating the Nuisance condemned
or prohibited, and for executing such Order, in
like Manner as a Local Authority obtaining the
like Order might do under the said Act, and to
charge the Costs to the Person on whom the
Order is made, as is provided in the Case where
a like Order is obtained and executed by such
Local Authority.

> Whenever this Act is called into requisition, Sec. 13 gives to
> any person the same power and facilities in relation to prose-
> cuting for the removal or abatement of nuisances which, on
> ordinary occasions, can only be exercised by the Nuisance Au-
> thority.

Guardians
may procure
sanitary
reports and
pay for the
same.

14. The Guardians of any Union, or Parish
not within an Union, may at any Time employ
One of their Medical Officers to make Inquiry
and report upon the sanitary State of their Union
or Parish, or any Part thereof, and pay a reasonable Compensation for the same out of their
Common Fund.

Interpreta-
tion of terms.

15. The several Words used in this Act shall
be construed in the same Manner as is declared
with reference to the same Words in the above-
cited Act, termed "The Nuisances Removal Act
for *England,* 1855," and all the Provisions therein, and in "The Diseases Prevention Act, 1855,

contained, shall respectively be applicable to this Act, except so far as they shall be hereby repealed, or be inconsistent with anything herein provided.

16.*No Justice of the Peace shall, unless objected to at the Hearing of any Complaint or Charge, be deemed incapable of acting in Cases other than Appeals arising under the said Nuisances Removal Act by reason of his being a Member of any Body hereby declared to be the Local Authority to execute the said Act, or by reason of his being a Contributor, or liable to contribute, to any Rate or Fund out of which it is hereby provided that all Charges and Expenses incurred in executing the said Act, and not recovered as therein provided, shall be defrayed.

Justices not incapable of acting by being members of bodies to execute Nuisances Removal Act.

* This section (16) has been amended by 29 & 30 Vict., c. 41, Sec. 2, and now is as follows :—"No Justice of the Peace shall be deemed incapable of acting in cases under the Nuisances Removal Act, or the Act of the 23 & 24 Vict., c. 79 or 177, by reason of his being a member of any body thereby declared to be the Authority to execute the said Act, or by reason of his being a contributor or liable to contribute to any rate or fnnd out of which it. is thereby provided that all charges and expenses incurred in executing the said Act, and not recovered as therein provided shall be defrayed."

The following is the Justices of the Peace Act, 1867 (30 & 31 Vict., c. 115):—"A Justice of the Peace shall not be incapable of acting as a Justice at any Petty, or Special, or General, or Quarter Sessions, on the trial of an offence arising under an Act to be put in execution by a Municipal Corporation, or a Local Board of Health, or Improvement Commissioners, or Trustees, by reason only of his being as one of the several ratepayers, or as one of any other class of persons liable in common with the others to contribute to, or to be benefited by, any fund to the account of which the penalty payable in respect of such offence is directed to be carried, or of which it will form part, or to contribute to any rate or expenses in diminution of which such penalty will go."

NUISANCES REMOVAL ACT (1855) AMENDMENT,* 1863.

26 & 27 Victoria, Cap. 117.

An Act to amend the Nuisances Removal Act for *England*, 1855, with respect to the Seizure of diseased and unwholesome Meat.

[*28th July*, 1863.]

Whereas the Provisions of "The Nuisances Removal Act for *England*, 1855," with regard to the Inspection and Seizure of diseased and unwholesome Meat, are defective; and it is therefore expedient that the same should be repealed, and that other and more effectual Provisions in that Behalf should be substituted therefor: Be it therefore enacted by the Queen's most Excellent Majesty, by and with the Advice and Consent of the Lords Spiritual and Temporal, and Com-

---

* The 32 & 33 Vict., cap. 108, extends this Act to Ireland. (See Page 11.) It is not specifically referred to in the Sanitary Act, 1866. The 4th section, however, incorporates it with the Nuisances Removal Act of 1855; and it was, therefore, a question whether this Act applied to Ireland. In a case where a prosecution under Sec. 2 was instituted by the Nuisance Authority of the city of Dublin, it was held by the Recorder on appeal that this Act did not apply to Ireland, and the conviction was accordingly reversed. The case of *Webb* v. *Daly* was the first prosecution under Sec. 2 subsequent to the extension of the Act to Ireland. Page 156.

mons, in this present Parliament assembled, and _{SECTION 1.} by the Authority of the same, as follows:

1. From and after the passing of this Act, the _{Sec. 26 of recited Act repealed.} Twenty-sixth Section of the said Act is repealed.

2. The Medical Officer of Health or Inspector of Nuisances may at all reasonable Times inspect and examine any Animal, Carcase, Meat, Poultry, Game, Flesh, Fish, Fruit, Vegetables, Corn, Bread, or Flour, exposed for Sale, or deposited in any Place for the Purpose of Sale, or of Preparation for Sale, and intended for the Food of Man, the Proof* that the same was not exposed or deposited for such Purpose or Purposes, or was not intended for the Food of Man, resting with the Party charged; and in case any such Animal, Carcase, Meat, Poultry, Game, Flesh, Fish, Fruit, Vegetables, Corn, Bread, or Flour appear to him to be diseased, or unsound, or unwholesome, or unfit for the Food of Man, it shall be lawful for such Medical Officer of Health or Inspector of Nuisances to seize, take, and carry away the same, or direct the same to be seized, taken, and carried away by any Officer, Servant, or Assistant, in order to have the same dealt with by a Justice; and if it shall appear to the Justice that any such Animal, or any of the said Articles, is diseased, or unsound or un-

_{Power to Medical Officer of Health or Inspector of Nuisances to inspect any animal, &c.}

' * The *onus probandi* is clearly shifted by this provision. It was held in a case, (*Elias* v. *Nightingall*, 27, L. J. M. C. 151,) upon the construction of Sec. 26 of the 18 & 19 Vict., c. 121, which is repealed by this Act that, in order to justify either the officer or the Justice, the carcase, &c., should be shown to have been either exposed for sale, or to have been intended to be used for the food of man.

wholesome, or unfit for the Food of Man, he
he shall order the same to be destroyed, or so
disposed of as to prevent such Animal or Articles
from being exposed for Sale or used for such
Food; and the Person to whom such Animal,
Carcase, Meat, Poultry, Game, Flesh, Fish,
Fruit, Vegetables, Corn, Bread, or Flour belongs
or did belong at the Time of Sale or of Exposure
for Sale, or in whose Possession or on whose
Premises the same is found, shall, upon Conviction, be liable to a Penalty not exceeding
Twenty Pounds for every Animal, Carcase, or
Fish, or Piece of Meat, Flesh, or Fish, or any
Poultry or Game, or for the Parcel of Fruit, Ve-
getables, Corn, Bread, or Flour, so found, or at
the Discretion of the Justice, without the Inflic-
tion of a Fine, to Imprisonment in the Common
Gaol or House of Correction for a Term of not
more than Three Calendar Months.

The case of *Webb* v. *Daly* was the first prosecution under
this Act as extended to Ireland by 32 & 33 Vict., c. 108.
(Page 11.) The defendant, who was a foreman butcher,
residing in Dublin, was summoned by the officer of the Authority
for being the owner of, or possessed of a quantity of diseased,
unsound, or unwholesome meat, which was deposited in a
certain cart or place for the purpose of sale or of preparation
for sale, and intended for the food of man. A case was
stated to the Queen's Bench by the Magistrate, at the request
of the defendant, who submitted that a cart was not a " place"
within the meaning of the Act. The Queen's Bench, however, upheld the conviction, upon the ground that a cart upon
which meat is placed for the preparation for sale is such a
place as is within the meaning of Sec. 2; and although said
meat was not in the immediate possession of said owner, and
although it was not exposed for sale, it was held that the owner-
ship being proved, the owner was liable. The evidence of
the owner was held to be inadmissible. — *Webb* v. *Daly*,
3, I. L. T., 180.

A Defendant was a butcher, residing out of town, but
carrying on business in a shop in town. Diseased meat,
loaded in carts, was seized whilst being carried into the

yard; within this yard was a slaughter-house. Held—1st.,
That the yard was a place within the meaning of Sec. 2; 2nd.,
That assuming the word "place" was used in the same sense
in Sec. 2 as in Sec. 3; the word "place" in Sec. 3 is not to
be limited to places *ejusdem generis* with slaughter-house, shop,
building, or market. —*Young* v. *Gattridge*, 38, L. J. N. S.
M. C., 67.

3. In case any Person shall in any Manner Penalty for
prevent such Medical Officer of Health or In- obstructing Medical
spector of Nuisances from entering any Slaugh- Officer of Health, &c.
ter-house, Shop, Building, Market, or other Place
where such Animal, Carcase, Meat, Poultry, or
Fish is kept for the Purpose of Sale or of Preparation for Sale, or shall in any Manner obstruct or impede him, or his Servant or Assistant, when duly engaged in carrying the Provisions of this Act into execution, such Person
shall be liable to a Penalty not exceeding Five
Pounds.

4. This Act and "The Nuisance Removal This and
Act for *England*, 1855," shall be read and con- recited Act to be as one
strued together as One Act. Act.

5. This Act may be cited for all Purposes as Short title.
"The Nuisances Removal Act for *England*
(Amendment) Act, 1863."

EXTRACT FROM THE PUBLIC HEALTH ACT, 1848.

Private Improvement Rates.

90. And be it enacted, That whenever the Local Board of Health* have incurred or become liable to any Expenses which by this Act are or by the said Local Board shall be declared to be Private Improvement Expenses, the said Local Board may, if they shall think fit, make and levy upon the Occupier of the Premises in respect of which the Expenses shall have been incurred, except in the Cases herein-after provided, in addition to all other Rates, a Rate or Rates to be called Private Improvement Rates, of such Amount as will be sufficient to discharge such Expenses, together with interest thereon at a Rate not exceeding Five Pounds in the Hundred, in such Period not exceeding Thirty Years as the said Local Board shall in each Case determine: Provided always, that whenever any Premises in respect of which any Private Improvement Rate is made become unoccupied before the Expiration of the Period for which the Rate was made, or before the same is fully paid off, such Rate shall become a Charge upon and be paid by the Owner of the Premises so long as the same continue to be unoccupied.

* In Ireland the Sewer Authority. See Sanitary Act, 1866, Sec. 11, Page 9.

No such rate can be made in respect of premises not assessable to the Poor Rate. Property, therefore, not in the occupa-

tion of some person chargeable with Poor Rates in respect
thereof cannot be rated by the Local Board.—*Hodgson* v. *Car-
lisle*, 8 E. & B. 116. Places exempt from rates under any
Local Act by mere reason of their locality, will not, therefore,
be exempt from district rates under these acts when such places
are included within the district of a Local Board.—*Chelmsford*
v. *Chelmsford*, 2 E. & B. 500 ; *R. V. Luscombe*, 27 L. J. M. C.,
N. S. 299.

91. And be it enacted, That if the Occupier Proportion
by whom any Private Improvement Rate is paid of Private Improve-
holds the Premises in respect of which the Rate ment Rate may be
is made at a Rent not less than the Rackrent, deducted from Rent
he shall be entitled to deduct Three Fourths of
the Amount paid by him on account of such
Rate from the Rent payable by him to his Landlord, and if he holds at a Rent less than the
Rackrent he shall be entitled to deduct from the
Rent so payable by him such Proportion of Three
Fourths of the Rate as his Rent bears to the
Rackrent ; and if the Landlord from whose Rent
any Deduction is made under the Provision last
aforesaid is himself liable to the Payment of Rent
for the Premises in respect of which the Deduction is made, and holds the same for a Term of
which less than Twenty Years is unexpired, but
not otherwise, he may deduct from the Rent so
payable by him such Proportion of the Sum deducted from the Rent payable to him as the Rent
payable by him bears to the Rent payable to him,
and so in succession with respect to every Landlord (holding for a Term of which less than
Twenty Years is unexpired) of the same Premises
both receiving and liable to pay Rent in respect
thereof: Provided always, that nothing herein
contained shall be construed to entitle any Person to deduct from the Rent payable by him more
than the whole sum deducted from the Rent payable to him.

SECTION 92.

Redemption of special District and Private Improvement Rates.

92. Provided always, and be it enacted, That at any Time before the Expiration of the Period for which any Special District Rate or Private Improvement Rate is made, the Owner or Occupier of the Premises assessed thereto may redeem the same, by paying to the Local Board of Health the Expenses in respect of which the Rate was made, or such Parts thereof as may not have been defrayed by Sums already levied in respect of the same.

ARBITRATION.

Mode of referring to arbitration.

123. And be it enacted, That in case of Dispute as to the Amount of any Compensation to be made under the Provisions of this Act (except where the Mode of determining the same is specially provided for), and in case of any Matter which by this Act is authorized or directed to be settled by Arbitration, then, unless both Parties concur in the Appointment of a single Arbitrator, each Party, on the Request of the other, shall appoint an Arbitrator, to whom the Matter shall be referred; and every such Appointment when made on the Behalf of the Local Board of Health shall (in the Case of a Noncorporate District) be under their Seal and the Hands of any Five or more of their Number, or under the Common Seal in case of a Corporate District, and on the Behalf of any other Party under his Hand, or if such Party be a Corporation Aggregate under the Common Seal thereof; and such Appointment shall be delivered to the Arbitrators, and shall be deemed a Submission to Arbitration by the Parties making the same; and after

the making of any such Appointment the same shall not be revoked without the Consent of both Parties, nor shall the Death of either party operate as a Revocation ; and if for the Space of Fourteen Days after any such Matter shall have arisen, and Notice in Writing by one Party who has himself duly appointed an Arbitrator to the other Party, stating the Matter to be referred, and accompanied by a Copy of such Appointment, the Party to whom Notice is given fail to appoint an Arbitrator, the Arbitrator appointed by the Party giving the Notice shall be deemed to be appointed by and shall act on behalf of both Parties ; and the Award of any Arbitrator or Arbitrators appointed in pursuance of this Act shall be binding, final, and conclusive upon all Persons, and to all Intents and Purposes whatsoever.

A Local Board of Health having under Sec. 45 of the 11 & 12 Vict., c. 63, made a sewer through the land of A, he claimed compensation for the damage done thereby, under Sec. 144 (Sec. 8 of the Sewage Utilization Act, 1865, Page 79, is identical with Sec. 144 of this Act,) and proceeded to appoint an arbitrator. The Local Board of Health declined to appoint an arbitrator, on the ground that A had not sustained any damage, because his property was benefited by the making of the sewer, and the arbitrator of A made his award *ex-parte* : Held that this was a case in which the amount of drainage was disputed, and not a case in which the liability to make any compensation was denied, and therefore the award was valid.—In re *Bradley*, 4 El. & Bl. 1014, 1 Jur. N. S. 778, 24 L. J. Q. B. 239.

A *mandamus* to a Local Board of Health reciting that the Prosecutor has sustained damage by reason of the acts of the Board in the exercise of the powers of this Act, that he had demanded compensation according to the provisions of this Act, and that the Board had denied all liability, commanded the Board to make compensation out of the general or special rate to be levied under this Act. Return that the Board had not denied all liability, and was willing to make such compensation as soon as it should be duly ascertained ; that such compensation had not yet been ascertained, nor had the pro-

M

SECTION 124. secutor taken any steps towards having it ascertained, nor given notice of the cause or amount of his claim for compensation, nor informed the Board whether it had exceeded £20, nor given notice of his intention to appoint an arbitrator. The return being traversed, the jury found that the Board had denied their liability, but that the prosecutor had made no claim for any specific sum : Held (affirming the judgment of the Queen's Bench, 29 L. J. Q. B. 21,) first, that under Sec. 144 (which section is in substance the 8th Section of Sewage Utilization Act, 1865,) the proper course was to ascertain the liability of the Board in the first instance, and therefore the *mandamus* was good. Secondly, that it was not necessary that the prosecutor should claim any specific amount of compensation.—*Reg,* v. *Burslem Board of Health,* 6 Jur., N. S. 696.

Williams J.—*Prima Facie,* inasmuch as *mandamus* is the proper remedy to compel the performance of a public duty, this is a proper case for a *mandamus.—Ib.*

Death, &c., of one of several arbitrators ;

124. And be it enacted, That if before the Determination of any Matter so referred any Arbitrator die, or refuse or become incapable to act, the Party by whom such Arbitrator was appointed may appoint in Writing another Person in his Stead ; and if he fail so to do for the Space of Seven Days after Notice in Writing from the other Party in that Behalf the remaining Arbitrator may proceed *ex parte;* and every Arbitrator so appointed shall have the same Powers and Authorities as were vested in the Arbitrator in whose stead the Appointment is made; and

of single arbitrator.

in case a single Arbitrator die, or become incapable to act, before the making of his Award, or fail to make his Award within Twenty-one Days after his Appointment, or within such extended Time, if any, as shall have been duly appointed by him for that Purpose, the Matters referred to him shall be again referred to Arbitration under the Provisions of this Act, as if no former reference had been made.

125. And be it enacted, That in case there be
more than one Arbitrator, the Arbitrators shall, *Appointment*
before they enter upon the Reference, appoint by *of umpire by the parties;*
Writing under their Hands an Umpire, and if
the Person appointed to be Umpire die, or become incapable to act, the Arbitrators shall forthwith appoint another Person in his Stead; and
in case the Arbitrators neglect or refuse to appoint an Umpire for Seven Days after being requested so do by any Party to the Arbitration,
the Court of General or Quarter Sessions shall, *by Quarter Sessions.*
on the Application of any such Party, appoint
an Umpire; and the Award of the Umpire shall
be binding, final, and conclusive upon all Persons
and to all Intents and Purposes whatsoever; and
in case the Arbitrators fail to make their Award
within Twenty-one Days after the Day on which
the last of them was appointed, or within such
extended Time, if any, as shall have been duly
appointed by them for that Purpose, the Matters
referred shall be determined by the Umpire; and
the Provisions of this Act with respect to the
Time for making an Award, and with respect to
extending the same in the Case of a single
Arbitrator, shall apply to an Umpirage.

Under this section, arbitrators who have failed to make
their award within twenty-one days after the day upon which
the last of them was appointed, may nevertheless after the expiration of that period appoint an umpire.—Holdsworth *v.*
Barsham, 10 W. R., 646; 8 Jur. N. S., 672. Arbitrators
may appoint an umpire after the twenty-one days, limited by
Sec. 125 for making their award, have expired without their
having enlarged the time, provided such appointment be within
the time limited by Sec. 126 for making the umpirage.—*Holdsworth* v. *Wilson*, 32 L. J. Q. B., 289; 11 W. R. 733;
8 L. T. N. S., 434, Ex. Cham.

This section places an umpire, with respect to the time for
making his award, in the same position as a single arbitrator;

SECTION 126. and by Sec. 124, a single arbitrator is required to make his award within twenty-one days after his appointment, or within such extended time as shall have been appointed by him.— *Killett* v. *Board of Health of Tranmere*, 13 W. R. 207; 11 L. T. N. S., 457.

When an umpire, without extending the time for making his award, made his award after the twenty-one days from the time when he was appointed by the arbitrator had elapsed, held that the award was bad.—*Ib.*

An umpire did not extend the time, nor did he make his award within twenty-one days, but he appointed a day for the reference when both the parties attended; but the Board of Health, by their clerk, protested against the proceedings. The umpire, however, proceeded with the reference. Both the claimant and the Local Board went into their cases, examined witnesses, and addressed the umpire; held that the Local Board was not by its conduct before the umpire in going into the case, and examining witnesses, and addressing the umpire, estopped from afterwards disputing the umpire's jurisdiction. — *Ringland* v. *Lowndes*, 10 Jur. N. S., 850; 33 S. J. C. P., 337.

Time within which award must be made.

126. Provided always, and be it enacted, That the Time for making an Award under this Act shall not be extended beyond the Period of Three Months from the Date of the submission or from the Day on which the Umpire shall have been appointed (as the Case may be.)

Held on this section (126) that the provisions of the 17 & 18 Vict., c. 125, sec. 5, relating to the power of the Court to enlarge the time for making an award have no application to the case, and that after the time limited had elapsed the Court has no power to enlarge. — *Killett* v. *The Board of Health of Tranmere*, 13 W. R., 207; 11, L. T. N. S., 457.

Power to arbitrator to require production of documents.

127. And be it enacted, that any Arbitrator, Arbitrators, or Umpire, appointed by virtue of this Act, may require the Production of such Documents in the Possession or Power of either Party as they or he may think necessary for determining the Matters referred, and may examine the Parties or their Witnesses on Oath; and the

Costs of and consequent upon the Reference shall be in the Discretion of the Arbitrator or As to costs of Arbitrators, or of the Umpire (in case the Mat- reference. ters referred are determined by an Umpire under the Power herein-before contained in that Be-half); and any Submission to Arbitration under Submission the Provisions of this Act may be made a Rule may be made of any of the Superior Courts, on the Application court. of any Party thereto.

Arbitrators under this Act, before they entered on the re-ference, but after the twenty-one days within which they ought to make their award, appointed an umpire. By this section the costs are in the discretion of the umpire, and the submission may be made a rule of Court. The umpire awarded the amount of compensation to be made to the plaintiff, and that the costs of the reference should be paid by the Local Board of Health. Held that the appointment of the umpire was not too late, and that the plaintiff was entitled to maintain an action for the costs before they had been taxed.—*Holdsworth* v. *Wilson*, 4, B. & S., 1; 10, Jur. N. S., 171, Exch. Cham.

A dispute having arisen between a Local Board and an owner of property as to the amount of compensation to be paid for injury to premises belonging to the latter, and having been referred under Sec. 123, and the umpire awarded a specific sum by way of damages, and ordered that the costs consequent upon the reference should be borne by the Board, but without ascertaining their amount—it was held that no action would lie for the costs until the amount had been ascertained by taxation.—*Holdsworth* v. *Barsham*, 10, W. R., 646, 8, Jur. N. S., 672. But it was afterwards held that an award of costs, without ascertaining the amount, is good, and also that the taxation of costs is not a condition precedent to the other par-ty's right to bring an action to recover them. Ex Cham. re-versing the judgment of Queen's Bench in *Holdsworth* v. *Barsham*, 8, L. T. N. S., 434.

128. And be it enacted, That before any Arbi- Declaration trator or Umpire shall enter upon any such Re- by arbitrator ference as aforesaid he shall make and subscribe and umpire. the following Declaration before a Justice of the Peace; (that is to say,)

SECTION 128.   " I *A. B.* do solemnly and sincerely declare, That I will faithfully and honestly, and to the best of my Skill and Ability, hear and determine the Matters referred to me under the Public Health Act, 1848.

" A. B."

And such Declaration shall be annexed to the Award when made ; and if any Arbitrator or Umpire shall wilfully act contrary to such Declaration he shall be guilty of a Misdemeanour.

An Arbitrator's conduct should be unbiassed. —*Kemp* v. *Rose,* 32, L. T., 51.

THE WORKSHOP REGULATION ACT, 1867.

30 & 31 VICTORIA, CAP. 146.

An Act for regulating the Hours of Labour for Children, Young Persons, and Women employed in Workshops; and for other Purposes relating thereto. [*21st August,* 1867.]

WHEREAS by The Factory Acts Extension Act, 30 & 31 Vict, 1867, Provision is made, amongst other things, for c. 103. regulating the Hours during which Children, Young Persons, and Women are permitted to labour in any manufacturing Process conducted in an Establishment where Fifty or more Persons are employed:

And whereas it is expedient to extend Protection so far as respects the Regulation of the Hours of Labour to Children, Young Persons, and Women working in smaller Establishments, and further to make Provision respecting the Employment of a Fan or other mechanical Means for the Prevention of the Inhalation of Dust by Workmen in Processes of Grinding:

Be it therefore enacted by the Queen's most Excellent Majesty, by and with the Advice and Consent of the Lords Spiritual and Temporal, and Commons, in this present Parliament assembled, and by the Authority of the same, as follows:

1. This Act may be cited for all Purposes as Short Title. "The Workshop Regulation Act, 1867."

SECTION 2.   2. This Act shall apply to the whole of the United
Extent of   Kingdom.
Act.

Commence-   3. This Act shall come into operation on the
ment of Act.   First of *January* One thousand eight hundred and
                sixty-eight.

General   4. The following Words and Expressions shall in
Definitions.   this Act have the Meanings hereby assigned to them,
                unless there is something in the Context inconsis-
                tent with such Meanings; that is to say,

"Child" shall mean a Child under the Age of
    Thirteen Years:

"Young Person" shall mean a Person of the
    Age of Thirteen Years and under the Age of
    Eighteen Years:

"Woman" shall mean a Female of the Age of
    Eighteen Years or upwards:

"Parent" shall mean Parent, Guardian, or Per-
    son having the Custody of or Control over
    any such Child or Young Person:

"Employed" shall mean occupied in any Handi-
    craft, whether for Wages or not, under a
    Master or under a Parent as herein defined:

"Handicraft" shall mean any Manual Labour
    exercised by way of Trade or for Purposes
    of Gain in or incidental to the making any
    Article or Part of an Article, or in or inci-
    dental to the altering, repairing, ornamenting,
    finishing, or otherwise adapting for Sale any
    Article:

"Workshop" shall mean any Room or Place
    whatever, whether in the open Air or under
    Cover, in which any Handicraft is carried on
    by any Child, Young Person, or Woman, and
    to which and over which the Person by
    whom such Child, Young Person, or Woman
    is employed has the Right of Access and
    Control:

"The Court" shall include any Justice or Justices, Sheriff, or Sheriff Substitute, Magistrate or Magistrates, to whom Jurisdiction is given by this Act.

5. This Act shall not apply, *Application of Act.*

(1.) To any Factory or Part of a Factory, or other Place subject to the Jurisdiction of the Inspectors of Factories, in pursuance of any Act of Parliament already passed or which shall be passed during this present Session of Parliament :

(2.) To any Bakehouse as defined by "The Bakehouse Regulation Act, 1863."*

* See Page 215.

6. Subject to the Exceptions mentioned in the First Schedule† annexed hereto, the following Regulations shall be observed with respect to the Employment of Children, Young Persons, and Women in Workshops : *Regulations as to time of Labour.*

(1.) No Child under the Age of Eight Years shall be employed in any Handicraft :

(2.) No Child shall be employed on any One Day in any Handicraft for a Period of more than Six and a Half Hours, and such Employment shall take place between the Hours of Six in the Morning and Eight at Night :

(3.) No Young Person or Woman shall be employed in any Handicraft during any Period of Twenty-four Hours for more than Twelve Hours, with intervening Periods for taking Meals and Rest amounting in the whole to not less than One Hour and a Half, and such Employment shall take place only between the Hours of Five in the Morning and Nine at Night :

† See Page 179.

(4.) No Child, Young Person, or Woman shall be
employed in any Handicraft on *Sunday*, or
after Two o'Clock on *Saturday* Afternoon,
except in cases where not more than Five
Persons are employed in the same Establishment, and where such Employment
consists in making Articles to be sold by
Retail on the Premises, or in repairing Articles of a like Nature to those sold by
Retail on the Premises :

(5.) No Child under the Age of Eleven Years
shall be employed in grinding in the Metal
Trades or in Fustian Cutting.

Penalty for
Employment
of Children,
Young Per-
sons, and
Women con-
trary to the
Provisions of
this Act.

7. If any Child, Young Person, or Woman is employed in contravention of this Act the following
consequences shall ensue :

First, the Occupier of the Workshop in which
such Child, Young Person, or Woman is employed shall be liable to a Penalty of not
more than Three Pounds :

Second, the Parent of or the Person deriving
any direct Benefit from the Labour of or having the Control over the Child, Young Person, or Woman shall be liable to a Penalty
of not more than Twenty Shillings, unless it
appears to the Court before whom the Complaint is heard that the Offence has been
committed without the Consent, Connivance,
or wilful Default of the Parent or Person so
benefited, or having such Control.

Provision
with respect
to Use of
Fan in
grinding.

8. In every Workshop where grinding, glazing, or
polishing on a Wheel, or any other Process is carried on by which Dust is generated and inhaled by
the Workmen to an injurious Extent, if it appears
to the Local Authority or to any Inspector of Fac-

tories that such Inhalation could be to a great Extent prevented by the Use of a Fan or other mechanical Means, it shall be lawful for the Local Authority or for the Inspector of Factories, by Notice served on the Occupier of the Workshop in the Manner in which Notices given by such Local Authority or by the Inspector of Factories are usually served, to require a Fan or such mechanical Means as may from Time to Time be approved by One of Her Majesty's Principal Secretaries of State, under the Provisions of the Factory Acts, to be provided by the Occupier of the Workshop within a reasonable Time.

If the Occupier of any Workshop fails to provide a Fan or other mechanical Means in compliance with a Notice served on him in manner aforesaid he shall be deemed to be guilty of an Offence against this Act, and to be subject in respect of such Offence to a Penalty not exceeding Ten Pounds nor less than Three Pounds.

The Court having Jurisdiction to inflict any Penalty under this Act may, in addition to or instead of inflicting such Penalty in respect of an Offence under this Section, make an Order directing that within a certain Time to be named in such Order he do provide such Fan or other mechanical Means : The Court may upon Application enlarge any Time appointed for the Adoption of the Means directed by the Order, but any Non-compliance with the Order of the Court shall, after the Expiration of the Time as originally limited or enlarged by subsequent Order, be deemed to be a continuing Offence, and to be punishable by a Penalty not exceeding One Pound for every Day that such Non-compliance continues.

Power to Officers appointed by

9. If, on the Complaint of any Officer of Health, Inspector of Nuisances, or other Officer appointed

SECTION 10.
Local Authority, &c. to enter Workshops.

by a Local Authority, or of any Superintendent of Police, it appears to any Justice of the Peace that there is reasonable Cause for believing that any of the Provisions of this Act or of the Sanitary Act, 1866, are contravened in any Workshop, it shall be lawful for such Justice, by Order under his Hand, to empower the Complainant to enter into such Workshop at any Time within Forty-eight Hours from the Date of such Order, and to examine such Workshop; and any Person so empowered may examine, touching any Matter within the Provisions of this Act or of the Sanitary Act, 1866, so far as relates to such Workshop, any Person whom he finds in such Workshop.

Penalty on Persons refusing Admission.

Any Person refusing Admission to any Person so empowered, or obstructing him in the Discharge of his Duty, shall for each Offence incur a Penalty not exceeding Twenty Pounds.

Power to Inspector or Sub-Inspector of Factories to enter Workshops and inspect Condition thereof.

10. Any Inspector or Sub-Inspector of Factories may, when any Person is at work at any Handicraft, enter any Workshop and inspect the Condition thereof, and examine, touching any Matter within the Provisions of this Act or of the Sanitary Act, 1866, so far as relates to such Workshop, the Persons therein, provided that he report to One of Her Majesty's Principal Secretaries of State the Fact of such Entry. and the Condition of the Workshop, in his next half-yearly Report.

Penalty on obstructing Inspector, &c.

Any Person obstructing any Inspector or Sub-Inspector in making such Entry as aforesaid, or in his Inspection of a Workshop, shall for each Offence be liable to a Penalty not exceeding Twenty Pounds.

Liability of hirer of machine instead of occupier.

11. Where in any Workshop the Owner or Hirer of any Machine or Implement moved by Steam, Water, or other mechanical Power, in or about or in connection with which Machine or Implement Chil-

dren, Young Persons, or Women are employed, is SECTION 12. some Person other than the Occupier of the Workshop, and such Children, Young Persons, or Women are in the Employment and Pay of the Owner or Hirer of such Machine or Implement, in any such Case such Owner or Hirer shall so far as respects any Offence against this Act which may be committed in relation to such Children, Young Persons, or Women, be deemed to be the Occupier of the Workshop.

12. All Penalties under this Act may be recovered Recovery summarily, as to *England* before Two or more Jus- and application of tices in manner directed by an Act passed in the penalties. Session holden in the Eleventh and Twelfth Years of the Reign of Her Majesty Queen *Victoria*, Chapter Forty-three, intituled *An Act to facilitate the Performance of the Duties of Justices of the Peace out of* 11 & 12 Vict., *Sessions within* England *and* Wales *with respect to* c. 43. *summary Convictions and Orders*, or any Act amending the same ; as to *Scotland* in manner directed by " The Summary Procedure Act, 1864 ; as to *Ireland* in manner directed by the Act passed in the Session holden in the Fourteenth and Fifteenth Years of the reign of Her Majesty Queen *Victoria*, Chapter Ninety-three, intituled *An Act to consolidate and amend the Acts regulating the Proceedings of Petty* 14 & 15 Vict., *Sessions and the Duties of Justices of the Peace out of* c. 93. *Quarter Sessions in* Ireland, or any Act amending the same.

The Court imposing any Penalty under this Act may direct the whole or any Part thereof to be applied in or towards the Payment of such Costs of the Proceedings as the Court thinks just (including Compensation for Loss of Time to the Person upon whose Information such Penalty was recovered,) and, subject as aforesaid, all Penalties shall be ap-

SECTION 13. plied in the manner directed by the Acts referred to in this Section.

Description of Local Authority. 13. For the Purposes of this Act, in the several Places mentioned in the First Column* of the Second Schedule hereto annexed the Local Authority shall be the Bodies of Persons or Persons in that Behalf specified in the Second Column of the same Schedule, and such Schedule, with the Explanation annexed thereto, shall be deemed to be Part of this Act.

* See page 185.

Regulations for attendance at school of children employed in workshops. 14. The following Regulations shall be made (subject to the Provisions hereinafter mentioned) respecting the Education of Children employed in Workshops.

(1.) Every Child who is employed in a Workshop shall attend School for at least Ten Hours in every Week during the whole of which he is so employed :

(2.) In computing for the Purpose of this Section the Time during which a Child has attended School there shall not be included any Time during which such Child has attended either

(*a.*) In Excess of Three Hours at any One Time, or in Excess of Five Hours on any One Day ; or

(*b.*) On *Sundays;* or

(*c.*) Before Eight o'Clock in the Morning, or after Six o'Clock in the Evening :

Provided, that the Non-attendance of any Child at school shall be excused—

(1.) For any Time during which he is certified by the Principal Teacher of the School to have been prevented from Attendance by Sickness or other unavoidable Cause :

(2.) For any Time during which the School is closed for the customary Holidays, or for some other temporary Cause :

(3.) For any Time during which there is no School which the Child can attend within One Mile (measured according to the nearest Road) from the Workshop or the Residence of such Child.

15. The Parent of every Child employed in a Workshop shall cause that Child to attend School in manner required by this Act. *Parents to cause children to attend school.*

Every Parent who wilfully fails to act in conformity with this Section shall be liable to a Penalty of not more than Twenty Shillings for each offence.

16. Every Occupier of a Workshop who has employed a Child for any Time amounting in the whole to not less than Fourteen Days shall on *Monday* in every Week during the Employment of such Child obtain from the principal Teacher of some School a Certificate that the Child so employed has, in manner required by this Act, attended School during the preceding Week, if Attendance at School was so required during that Week. *Occupiers of workshops shall obtain certificates of attendance of children at school.*

The Certificate may be in the Form* contained in the Third Schedule hereto, or in such other Form as one of Her Majesty's Principal Secretaries of State may from Time to Time prescribe.*

The Employer shall keep the said Certificate for One Month, and shall produce the same to any Inspector or Sub-Inspector of Factories whenever required by him during that Period.

Every Person who acts in contravention of this Section shall be liable to a Penalty of not more Three Pounds.

* See page 186.

SECTION 17.

On appli-
cation of
teacher,
occupier to
pay sum for
schooling of
child, and
deduct it
from wages.

17. The principal Teacher of a School which is attended by any Child employed in a Workshop may apply in Writing to the Occupier of such Workshop to pay such sum as hereinafter mentioned on account of any Child in respect of whom he may have duly granted a Certificate* in pursuance of this Act, and after the Date of such Application the Occupier, so long as he employs the Child, shall pay to the principal Teacher of the said School for every Week that the Child attends that School the weekly Sum specified in the Application, not exceeding Twopence *per* Week, and not exceeding One-twelfth Part of the Wages of the Child. The Occupier may deduct the Sum so paid from the Wages so payable for the Services of such Child.

Any Occupier who, after such Application, refuses to pay on Demand any Sum that may become due as aforesaid, shall be liable to a Penalty not exceeding Ten Shillings.

Inspector
may disqua-
lify for grant-
ing certifi-
cates any
teacher who
is unfit.

If an Inspector of Factories is satisfied, by Inspection of a School or otherwise, that the principal Teacher of a School who grants Certificates of School Attendance required under this Act ought to be disqualified for granting such Certificates for any of the following Reasons : namely,

(1.) Because he is unfit to instruct Children by reason either of his Ignorance or Neglect, or of his not having the necessary Books and Materials ;

(2.) Because of his immoral Conduct ;

(3.) Because of his continued Neglect to fill up proper Certificates of School Attendance—

in any such Case he may serve on the Teacher a written Notice, stating the Reason for such Disqualification. At the Expiration of Two Weeks from the Date of such Notice the Teacher shall, subject to

---

* For the form of this certificate see page 186.

the Appeal hereinafter mentioned, be disqualified for granting Certificates.

The Inspector shall, so far as he can, serve on every Occupier of a Workshop who obtains Certificates from such Teacher a Notice to the like Effect as the Notice served on the Teacher, and also specifying a School which the Child employed in the Workshop of such Occupier can attend within One Mile (measured according to the nearest Road) from the Workshop or the Residence of the Child.

Any Teacher who is disqualified as aforesaid, and any Occupier of a Workshop who obtains Certificates from him, may, within Three Weeks after the Service of the Notice on the Teacher, appeal therefrom to One of Her Majesty's Principal Secretaries of State, who may confirm or reverse such Disqualification.

After a Teacher is disqualified for granting Certificates no Certificate given by him shall be deemed to be a Certificate in compliance with this Act, unless in the Case of there being no other School in which the Child employed in a Workshop can attend within One Mile (measured according to the nearest Road) from the Workshop or Residence of such Child, or unless with the written consent of an Inspector of Factories.

The Inspectors of Factories shall in their Reports to One of Her Majesty's Principal Secretaries of State report the Name of every Teacher disqualified under this section during the preceding Six Months, the Name of the School at which he taught, and the Reason for the Disqualification; and in the Case of such Teacher's continued Neglect to fill up proper Certificates, shall report the Fact of such Neglect to the Committee of Council on Education, if such Teacher be employed in any School in receipt of annual Grants made by the Committee of Council on Education.

SECTION 18.

Penalty for forging, &c., certificate.

Every Person who forges or counterfeits any Certificate required by this Act, or gives or signs any such Certificate falsely, or wilfully makes use of any forged, counterfeited, or false Certificates, or aids in or connives at any of the foregoing Offences, shall be guilty of a Misdemeanour, and be liable to be imprisoned for any Period not exceeding Three Months, with or without Hard Labour.

Local Authority to enforce Act.

18. It shall be the Duty of the Local Authority to enforce within their Jurisdictions the Provisions of this Act, so far as relates to any Powers or Authorities conferred on the Local Authority by this Act, and all Expenses incurred by them in enforcing the same may be defrayed out of any Funds in their hands, or any Rates leviable by them and applicable to any Purpose relating to the Improvement, paving, cleansing, or Management of the Places within their jurisdiction, or, in Cases where the Local Authority is in the Receipt of any Poor Rate, out of any such Rate.

Provision as to pleading that workshop is a factory.

19. Where any Proceedings are taken against any Person in respect of any Offence under this Act committed in or relating to a Workshop, it shall not be competent for the Defendant to prove that such Workshop is a Factory within the Meaning of any Act for regulating Factories unless he has previously given Notice of its being a Factory to the Inspector of Factories in manner required by any Act of Parliament in that Behalf.

Inspector or Sub-Inspector to be furnished with certificate of his appointment.

20. Every Inspector or Sub-Inspector of Factories shall be furnished with such Certificate of his Appointment as the Secretary of State may direct; and on applying for Admission to any Workshop, such Inspector or Sub-Inspector shall, if required, produce to the Occupier the said Certificate; every

Person who forges or counterfeits any such Certifi- SECTION 20.
cate, or makes use of any forged, counterfeited, or
false Certificate, or falsely pretends to be an Inspector
or Sub-Inspector of Factories, shall be guilty of a
Misdemeanor, and be liable to be imprisoned for
any Period not exceeding Three Months, with or
without Hard Labour.

FIRST SCHEDULE referred to in the foregoing
Act.

TEMPORARY EXCEPTIONS.

1. During the first Six Calendar Months next
ensuing the Day on which this Act is limited to
come into operation, herein-after referred to as the
Commencement of this Act, Children of not less
than Eleven Years of Age may be employed for the
same Time, and subject to the same Conditions, for
and subject to which Young Persons may be employed
under this Act :

2. During the first Thirty Calendar Months next
ensuing the Commencement of this Act, Children of
not less than Twelve Years of Age may be employed
for the same Time, and subject to the same Conditions, for and subject to which Young Persons may
be employed under this Act :

3. During the first Twelve Calendar Months next
ensuing the Commencement of this Act, Children,
Young Persons, and Women may be employed on
Saturdays until Half-past Four o'Clock in the Afternoon .

SECTION 4.

4. During the first Thirty Calendar Months next ensuing the Commencement of this Act, Children, Young Persons, and Women may be employed in the Manufacture of Preserves from Fruit in the same Manner as they were employed therein before the passing of this Act :

5. During the first Thirty Calendar Months next ensuing the Commencement of this Act, Male Young Persons of not less than Sixteen Years of Age may be employed in any Workshop where the Manufacture of Machinery is carried on in the same Manner as if they were Male Persons exceeding the Age of Eighteen Years.

PERMANENT EXCEPTIONS.

6. Whereas the Customs or Exigencies of certain Trades require that Male Young Persons of the Age of Sixteen Years and Upwards should be occasionally employed beyond the Hours allowed by this Act ; it shall be lawful for One of Her Majesty's Principal Secretaries of State, on due Proof to his Satisfaction that such Customs or Exigencies exist, and that such occasional Employment is not injurious to the Health of such Male Young Persons, from Time to Time, by Order to be advertised in the *London Gazette,** or otherwise published in such Manner as he may think fit, to give Permission that in the Case of any particular Workshop or Class of Workshops Male Young Persons of Sixteen Years of Age and upwards may be employed for a Period not exceeding Fifteen Hours on any One Day :

Provided that—

1st. They are not so employed except between the Hours of Six in the Morning and Nine in the Evening.

* In Ireland the *Dublin Gazette.*

2nd. In addition to the Time allowed under this Act for Meals, they shall be allowed Half an Hour for a Meal after the Hour of Five in the Evening.

3rd. They are not so employed for more than Twelve Days in any Period of Four Weeks, nor on the whole for more than Seventy-two Days in any Period of Twelve Months.

7. In any Workshop in which the mechanical Power is Water, and in any Workshop or Class of Workshops with respect to which One of Her Majesty's Principal Secretaries of State certifies by Order under his Hand that it has been proved to his Satisfaction, that by reason of the Nature of the Business it is necessary to carry on the same throughout the Night, it shall be lawful to employ Male Young Persons during the Night, subject to the same Intervals of Rest which they are allowed during the Day, and subject to this Provision, that no Male Young Person employed during the Night shall be employed during either the preceding or succeeding Day, and that no Male Young Person shall be employed more than Six Nights in any Fortnight.

For the Purposes of the last-mentioned Provision, Night shall mean any Time between Six o'Clock in the Afternoon of One Day and Six o'Clock of the Morning of the following Day.

8. So much of this Act as forbids the Employment of Young Persons and Women on any Saturday after Two o'Clock in the Afternoon shall not apply to Male Young Persons employed in Day and Night Turns, changing every alternate Week, nor in any Week to any Woman or Young Person whose Hours of actual Work have not in any Day in such Week exceeded Eight.

9. The said Secretary of State, on Proof to his Satisfaction that the Customs or Exigencies of Trade, or any other Special Circumstances, require the Alteration to be made, may, by Order to be advertised in the *London Gazette,** or otherwise published in such Manner as the Secretary of State may think fit, give Permission, with respect to any particular Workshop or Class of Workshops for all or any of the following Things ; namely—

(1.) That Children, Young Persons, or Women may be employed between Two and Eight o'Clock in the Afternoon on Saturday, provided that in any such Workshop or Workshops Arrangements are made to the Satisfaction of the said Secretary of State for giving on some Work-day in every Week to every Child, Young Person, or Woman employed, a Half Holiday of equal Length, either at the Beginning or at the End of their Day's Work ; or,

(2.) That in any Workshop in which it is proved to his Satisfaction that Work does not commence before the Hours of Seven or Eight in the Morning, Children, Young Persons, and Women may be employed on Saturday, or on any other Day on which the weekly Half Holiday is given, from the Hours of Seven in the Morning to Three in the Afternoon, or from Eight in the Morning to Four in the Afternoon, Subject to the usual Hours for Meals.

(3.) That Male Young Persons of not less than Sixteen Years of Age may be employed in the same Manner as if they were Male Persons exceeding the Age of Eighteen.

10. Where the Occupier of any Workshop is a

* In Ireland the *Dublin Gazette.*

Person of the Jewish Religion, and it is his Custom
to keep such Workshop closed on Saturday until
Sunset, it shall be lawful for him to employ Young
Persons or Women on that Day from after Sunset
until Nine o'Clock at Night.

SECOND SCHEDULE referred to in the preceding Act.

Column (1.)	Column 2.)
Places within Jurisdiction of Local Authority.	Description of Local Authority.

ENGLAND AND WALES.

The City of London and the Liberties thereof.	Commissioners of Sewers of the City of London.
Parishes within the Metropolis mentioned in Schedule (A.) to The Metropolis Management Act, 1855.	The Vestries incorporated by The Metropolis Management Act, 1855.
Districts within the Metropolis formed by the Union of the Parishes mentioned in Schedule (B.) to the Metropolis Management Act, 1855.	The Board of Works for the District incorporated by The Metropolis Management Act, 1855.
Boroughs, excepting Oxford.	The Mayor, Aldermen, and Burgesses, acting by the Council.
The Borough of Oxford and any Place not included in the above Description, and within the Jurisdiction of a Local Board constituted in pursuance of the Public Health Act, 1848, and the Local Government Act, 1858, or One of such Acts.	The Local Board.
Any Place not included in the above Descriptions, and under Jurisdiction of Commissioners, Trustees, or other Persons entrusted by any Local Act with Powers of improving, cleansing, or paving any Town.	The Commissioners, Trustees, or other Persons entrusted by the Local Act, with Powers of improving, cleansing, or paving the Town.
Any Parish not within the Jurisdiction of any Local Authority hereinbefore mentioned, and in which a separate Rate is or can be levied for the Maintenance of the Poor.	The Vestry, Select Vestry, or other Body of Persons, acting by virtue of any Act of Parliament, Prescription, Custom, or otherwise, as or instead of a Vestry or Select Vestry.

SCOTLAND.

Column (1).	Column (2.)
Places within Jurisdiction of Local Authority.	Description of Local Authority.
Burghs.	The Magistrates and Town Council.
Places where Police Commissioners or Trustees exercise the Functions of Police Commissioners acting under "The General Police and Improvement (Scotland) Act," or Trustees or Commissioners acting under General or Local Act.	The Police or other Commissioners or Trustees.
Any Place not included in the above Descriptions.	The Parochial Board having Jurisdiction in that Place.

IRELAND.

The City of. Dublin.	The Right Honourable the Lord Mayor, Aldermen, and Burgesses, acting by the Town Council.
Towns Corporate with Exception of Dublin.	The Mayor, Aldermen, and Burgesses, acting by the Town Council.
Towns having Town Commissioners under the Town Improvement (Ireland) Act, 1854 (17 & 18 Vict., c. 113,) or under any Local Acts.	The Town Commissioners.
Township having Commissioners under Local Acts.	The Township Commissioners
Towns under Commissioners appointed by virtue of an Act made in the Ninth Year of George the Fourth, intituled "An Act to make Provision for lighting, cleansing, and watching of Cities and Towns Corporate and Market Towns in Ireland in certain Cases."	The Commissioners.
Towns having Municipal Commissioners uuder 3 & 4 Vict., c. 108.	The Municipal Commissioners.
Any Place not included in the foregoing Descriptions.	The Guardians of the Poor of the Union in which such Place is situate.

EXPLANATION.

In this Schedule the following Words shall have the Meanings hereinafter assigned to them ; that is to say,

(1.) "Borough" in England shall mean any Place for the Time being subject to the Act passed in the Session holden in the Fifth and Sixth Years of the Reign of King William the Fourth, Chapter Seventy-six, intitutled "An Act to provide for the "Regulation of Municipal Corporations in England and Wales."

(2.) "Burgh" in Scotland shall mean any Place returning or contributing to return Members to Parliament.

THIRD SCHEDULE.

FORM OF CERTIFICATE OF SCHOOL ATTENDANCE.

School.

I do hereby certify that [*Christian Name and Surname of the Child*] has attended the above School for not less than Ten Hours during the Week ending on Saturday the　　　　of　　　　, 18 .

(Signed)　　*A. B.*
Principal Teacher of the above School.

Date　　　of　　　18 .
Address of School.

THE ADULTERATION OF ARTICLES OF FOOD OR DRINK ACT, 1860.

An Act for preventing the Adulteration* of Articles of Food or Drink.

[*6th August*, 1860.]

23 & 24 VICTORIA, CAP. 84.

WHEREAS the Practice of adulterating Articles of Food and Drink for Sale, in fraud of Her Majesty's Subjects, and to the great Hurt of their Health, requires to be repressed by more effectual Laws than those which are now in force for that Purpose : Be it therefore enacted by the Queen's most Excellent Majesty, by and with the Advice and Consent of the Lords Spiritual and Temporal, and Commons, in this present Parliament assembled, and by the Authority of the same, as follows :

1. Every Person who shall sell any Article of Food or Drink with which, to the Knowledge of such Person, any Ingredient or Material injurious to the Health of Persons eating or drinking such Article has been mixed, and every Person who shall sell as pure or unadulterated any Article of Food or Drink which is adulterated or not pure, shall for every such Offence, on a summary Conviction of

Penalty on Persons selling Articles of Food or Drink knowing the same to be injurious to Health.

---

* The word " Adulteration" means the putting anything into an article which is foreign to its nature or which lowers its value.

SECTION 2.   the same before Two Justices of the Peace at Petty Sessions in *England,* and in *Scotland* before Two Justices of the Peace in Justice of the Peace Court, or before the Sheriff Substitute of the County, or before Justices at Petty Sessions or a Divisional Justice in *Ireland,* forfeit and pay a Penalty not exceeding Five Pounds together with such Costs attending

As to subsequent Offences.   such Conviction as to the said Justices shall seem reasonable ; and if any Person so convicted shall afterwards commit the like Offence it shall be lawful for such Justices to cause such Offender's Name, Place of Abode, and Offence to be published, at the Expense of such Offender, in such Newspaper or in such other Manner as to such Justices shall seem desirable.

Power to appoint Analysts.   2. In the City of *London* and the Liberties thereof the Commissioners of Sewers of the City of *London* and the Liberties thereof, and in all other Parts of the Metropolis the Vestries and District Boards acting in execution of the Act for the better Local Management of the Metropolis, in *England* and *Ireland* the Court of Quarter Sessions of every County, and the Town Council of every Borough having a separate Court of Quarter Sessions, and in *Scotland* the Commissioners of Supply at their Ordinary Meetings for Counties, and Town Councils within their several Jurisdictions, may, from Time to Time for their respective City, Districts, Counties, or Boroughs, appoint and remove One or more Persons possessing competent medical, chemical, and microscopical Knowledge as Analysts of all Articles of Food and Drink purchased within the said City, Metropolitan Districts, Counties, or Borough, and may pay to such Analysts such Salary or Allowances as they may think fit ; but such Appointments and Removals shall at all Times be subject in *Great Britain* to the Approval of One of Her Majesty's

Principal Secretaries of State, and in *Ireland* to that SECTION 3. of the Lord Lieutenant.

The inhabitants of every town or borough, having a separate Court of Quarter Sessions, and whose Town Council has appointed public analysts, are provided with a ready means of procuring evidence to sustain a prosecution under Sec. 1. Inhabitants of counties have the same facilities where the Court of Quarter Sessions have in like manner appointed such officer or officers.

3. On the Hearing by the Justices of any Com- Protection plaint under this Act in any District, County, or against Articles of Borough wherein any Analyst shall have been ap- Food and pointed, the Purchaser shall prove to the Satisfaction Drink being of such Justices that the Seller of the Article of with by Food or Drink alleged to be adulterated, or his Ser- Purchaser. vants, had such Notice of the Intention of the Purchaser to have such Article analysed, and also such Opportunity of accompanying the Purchaser to an Analyst appointed by this Act, as the Justices shall think reasonable, in order to secure such Article from being tampered with by the Purchaser.

For the purposes of this section the Town Council of the Borough of Dublin has issued a notice in this form, to be served by the purchaser upon the vendor :—

. BOROUGH OF DUBLIN.

To , of , or to his servant.

I hereby give you notice that I intend to have the sold by you to me, examined by the City Analyst, and that I am now willing that you shall accompany me to him in order that you may secure the said article from being tampered with by any person whatever, in pursuance of 23 & 24 Vict., c. 84.

Signed———.

4. Any Purchaser of any Article of Food or Drink Power to in any District, County, City, or Borough where Purchasers of Articles of there is any Analyst appointed under this Act shall Food and

SECTION 5.

Drink to
have them
analysed.

be entitled, on Payment to the Analyst of a Sum
not less than Two Shillings and Sixpence nor more
than Ten Shillings and Sixpence, to have any such
Article analysed by any Analyst who may be appointed for such District, County, City, or. Borough,
and to receive from such Analyst a Certificate of the
Result of his Analysis, specifying whether in his
Opinion such Article is adulterated, and also
whether it is so adulterated as to be injurious to the
Health of Persons eating or drinking the same ; and

Certificate
of Analyst
made Evi-
dence.

such Certificate duly signed by such Analyst shall,
in the Absence of any Evidence to the contrary, be
sufficient Evidence before the Justices or in any
Court of Justice of the Matters therein certified, and
the Sum so directed to be paid for such Certificate
shall be deemed Part of the Costs.

Power to
Justices to
have Articles
of Food
and Drink
analysed.

5. The Justices before whom any Complant may
be made under this Act may, in their Discretion,
cause any Article of Food or Drink to be examined
and analysed by such skilled Person as they may
appoint for that Purpose, who may be required to
give Evidence of the same at the Hearing of the
Case ; and the Expense thereof, and of such Examination and Analysis, if not paid by the Complainant
or Party complained against, shall be deemed Part
of the Expenses of executing this Act, but nevertheless such Expense may be ordered by such Justices
to be paid by the Party so complaining or complained
against, as they shall think proper.

Appeal to
Quarter
Sessions.

6. Any Person who has been convicted of any
Offence punishable by this Act by any Justices may
appeal* to the next General or Quarter Sessions of
the Peace which shall be held for the City, County,
Town, or Place wherein such Judgment or Convic-

* As to Appeals in Ireland, see Sec. 11.

tion shall have been made, or in the Case of the SECTION 7
Conviction having been before a Sheriff Substitute in
Scotland, then the Appeal shall be to the Sheriff of
the County, provided that such Person enter into a
Recognizance within Two Days next after such Conviction, with two sufficient Sureties, conditioned to
try such Appeal, and to be forthcoming to abide the
Judgment and Determination of the Court at such
General or Quarter Sessions, or Sheriff, and to pay
such Costs as shall be by such Court awarded ; and
the Justices before whom such Conviction shall be
had are hereby empowered and required to take
such Recognizance ; and the Court at such General
or Quarter Sessions, or Sheriff, are hereby authorized and required to hear and finally determine the
Matter of every such Appeal, and may award such
Costs to the Party appealing or appealed against as
they shall think proper.

7. If any such Conviction or Judgment or Order Where Con-
of Forfeiture shall happen to be made within Six viction
within Six
Days before any General or Quarter Sessions of the Days of
Quarter
Peace shall be held for the City, County, Town, or Sessions,
Place wherein such Conviction shall have been Time allowed for
made, the Person who shall think himself aggrieved Appeal.
by any such Conviction may, on entering into a Recognizance in manner and for the Purposes before
directed, be at liberty to appeal either to the then next
or next following General or Quarter Sessions of the
Peace which shall be held for any such City, County,
Town, or Place wherein any such Conviction shall
have been made, on giving Six Days Notice to the
Complainant of his Intention to appeal.

8. Any Person who shall have been convicted by Persons convicted of
any Justices or Sheriff Substitute of any Offence selling
punishable by this Act, in respect of the selling of adulterated
patented
any Article of Food or Drink which shall have been Article may

SECTION 9.

have a Case
stated for
Opinion of
Superior
Court.
manufactured according to any Process patented before the passing of this Act, either by the Patentee or Owner of the Patent, or by any Person carrying on his Business or otherwise claiming under him during the Continuance of such Patent, may, instead of appealing to the General or Quarter Sessions of the Peace or Sheriff of the County, apply in Writing within Five Days after such Conviction to the Justices or Sheriff Substitute, to state and sign a Case for the Opinion of One of the Superior Courts of Law thereon, in like Manner as under the Statute of the Twentieth and Twenty-first Years of Her Majesty, Chapter Forty-three, he might have applied to the Justices to state and sign a Case, and thereupon all such Proceedings shall take place upon and in relation to such Application, and all such Provisions shall be applicable thereto as would have taken place upon and in relation thereto, and been applicable thereto, under the Provisions of the said last-mentioned Act; and in *Scotland,* for the Purposes of such Appeal, the Justices or Sheriff Substitute may state and sign a Case for the Opinion of the Court of Session, in like Manner as the Justices in *England* and *Ireland* may, for the Opinion of the Superior Courts of Law under the said Act, and the Court of Session shall have in relation thereto the like Powers as the Superior Courts have under the said Act, and all the other Provisions of the said Act shall be applicable to such Appeals.

9. In *England* the Provisions in the Nuisances Removal Act for *England,* 1855, as to Procedure, and the Provisions of the Act of the Eleventh and Twelfth Years of the Reign of Her present Majesty, intituled *An Act to facilitate the Performance of the Duties of Justices of the Peace and of Session within* England *and Wales with respect to summary Convictions and Orders,* and in *Scotland* the ordinary

Rules regulating the Procedure of Justices of the
Peace, so far as the same are respectively applicable,
shall extend and apply to Cases arising under this
Act in *England* or *Scotland;* and all Monies
arising from Penalties under this Act in any County, Application of Monies.
City, District, or Borough where there are Analysts
appointed under this Act shall, when paid or recovered, be paid in *England* and *Ireland* to the
Vestry, District Board, Commissioners, County
Treasurer, or Town Council for such County, City,
District, or Borough respectively, to be applied for
the general Purposes of such Vestry, District Board,
Commissioners, County, City, or Borough respectively, and to the Collector of Rogue Money for
each County in *Scotland.*

10. All Proceedings under this Act in *Ireland* as Proceedings in Ireland as to Com-plaints, &c. to be subject to Provisions of 14 & 15 Vict., c. 93, and 21 & 22. Vict., c. 100.
to compelling the Appearance of any such Person or
of any Witness, and as to the Hearing and Determination of such Complaints, and as to the making
and executing of such Orders, and as to the Applications of Fines, Amerciaments, and forfeited Recognizances imposed or levied under this Act at
Petty Sessions, shall be subject in all respects to the
Provisions of " The Petty Sessions (*Ireland*) Act,
1851," as the same is amended by " The Petty
Sessions Clerk (*Ireland*) Act, 1858," (when the Case
shall be heard in any Petty Sessions District,) and
to the Provisions of the Acts relating to the Divisional Police Offices (when the Case shall be heard in
the Police District of *Dublin* Metropolis,) so far as
the said Provisions shall be consistent with any
special Provisions of this Act ; and when any Fine or
Penalty is imposed at any of the Divisional Police
Offices of *Dublin* Metropolis, or by the Justices in
any Corporate Town, under the Provisions of this
Act, such Fines and Penalties shall be paid over to
the same Purposes and appropriated and applied in

SECTION 11. the same Manner as is now by Law authorized in respect of Fines and Penalties imposed at such Divisional Police Offices, or by the Justices in any such Corporate Town respectively.

Appeal to Quarter Sessions.

11. In *Ireland* any Person who has been convicted of any Offence punishable by this Act may appeal to the next Court of Quarter Sessions to be held in the same Division of the County where the Order shall be made by any Justice or Justices in any Petty Sessions District, or to the Recorder at his next Sessions where the Order shall be made by the Divisional Justices in the Police District of *Dublin* Metropolis, or to the Recorder of any Corporate or Borough Town when the Order shall be made by any Justice or Justices in such Corporate or Borough Town (unless when any such Sessions shall commence within Seven Days from the Date of any such Order, in which Case, if the Appellant sees fit, the Appeal may be made to the next succeeding Sessions to be held for such Division or Town) ; and it shall be lawful for such Court of Quarter Sessions or Recorder, as the Case may be, to decide such Appeal, if made in such Form and Manner, and with such Notices, as are required by the Petty Sessions Acts respectively herein-before mentioned as to Appeals against Orders made by Justices at Petty Sessions ; and all the Provisions of the said Petty Sessions Acts respectively as to making Appeals and as to executing the Orders made on Appeal, or the original Orders where the Appeals shall not be duly prosecuted, shall also apply to any Appeal or like Order to be made under the Provisions of this Act.

As to Expenses of executing Act.

12. The Expense of executing this Act shall be borne, in the City of *London* and the Liberties thereof, out of the Consolidated Rates raised by the Com.

missioners of Sewers of the City of *London* and the Liberties thereof, and in the rest of the Metropolis out of any Rates or Funds applicable to the Purposes of the Act for the better Local Management of the Metropolis, and in Counties out of the County Rate, and in Boroughs out of the Borough Fund, or out of the Rogue Money in Counties in *Scotland.*

13. Nothing in this Act contained shall be held to Indictment affect the Power of proceeding by Indictment, or to or other take away any other Remedy against any Offender Remedy under this Act. affected.

14. In the Construction of this Act the Words Interpre- " Articles of Food or Drink" shall (if not inconsis- tation of tent with the Context or Subject Matter) include Terms not only all alimentary Substances, whether Solids or Liquids, but also all Eatables or Drinkables whatsoever not being Medical Drugs or Articles usually taken or sold as Medicines,* but this Act shall not be construed so as to affect the ordinary Reduction of the Strength of Foreign, *British*, or Colonial Spirits by Persons licensed and paying Duties under the Excise.

* By the Pharmacy Act, 1868 (31 & 32 Vict., cap. 121, sec. 24,) these provisions are extended to all articles sold as medicines in England, and every adulteration of any such article shall be deemed an admixture injurious to health. Sec. 27 of the Pharmacy Act, however, expressly provides that it shall not apply to Ireland.

COMMON LODGING HOUSES ACT, 1851.

14 & 15 Victoria, Cap. 28.

An Act for the well-ordering of Common Lodging Houses.

[*24th July,* 1851.]

SECTION 1 WHEREAS it would tend greatly to the Comfort and Welfare of many of Her Majesty's poorer Subjects if Provision were made for the well-ordering of Common Lodging Houses: Be it therefore enacted by the Queen's most Excellent Majesty, by and with the Advice and Consent of the Lords Spiritual and Temporal, and Commons, in this present Parliament assembled, and by the Authority of the same, as follows ; to wit,

Short title.   1. In citing this Act for any Purpose, it shall be sufficient to use the Expression "The Common Lodging Houses Act, 1851."

Interpretation of terms in this Act.   2. The following Words and Expressions in this Act have, for the Purposes and Execution of this Act, the following Meanings ; to wit,

> The Word "Place" includes County, Riding, Hundred, and other Division or part of a County, City, Borough, Parish, District, and other Place whatsoever :
> The Word "Borough," and the Expressions

" Mayor, Aldermen, and Burgesses," and " Borough Fund," have respectively the same Meaning as in the Act for the Regulation of Municipal Corporations :

The Expression " Improvement Act" means an Act for regulating and managing the Police of, and for draining, cleansing, paving, lighting, watching, and improving a Place, and an Act for any of those Purposes :

The Expression " Common Lodging House" includes, in any Case in which only a Part of a House is used as a Common Lodging House, the part so used of such House.*

3. This Act shall be executed as follows ; to wit,

   1. Within and for all or any Part of the Metropolitan Police District, by "The Commissioners of Police of the Metropolis," or such One of them as is from Time to Time appointed in that Behalf by One of Her Majesty's Principal Secretaries of State :†

   2. Within and for all and any Part of any Place not being within the Metropolitan Police District, but being now or hereafter the District of a Local Board of Health, by the Local Board of Health for the District :

   3. Within and for all and any Part of any other Place not being within the Metropolitan Police District, and not being the District of a Local Board of Health, but being now or hereafter an incorporated Borough regulated under the Act for the Regulation of Municipal Corpo-

---

* In any proceeding under this Act, if the inmates of any house or part of a house allege that they are members of the same family, the burden of proving such allegation shall be on the persons making it. (See 41st section of the Sanitary Act, 1866, Page 34.)

† In Ireland the Lord Lieutenant.

rations, or any Act for the Amendment thereof, or any Charter granted in pursuance of any such Act, by the Mayor, Aldermen, and Burgesses of the Borough acting by the Council of the Borough :

4. Within and for all and any Part of any other Place not being within the Metropolitan Police District, and not being the District of a Local Board of Health, and not being such an incorporated Borough, but being now or hereafter the Place within the Limits of an Improvement Act, by the Commissioners, Trustees, or other Body, by whatever Name known, for executing the Improvement Act :

5. Within and for all and any Part of any other Place not being One of the Places hereinbefore specified, by the Justices of the Peace acting in Petty Sessions for the Place.

As to expenses of executing this Act.

4. The Expenses of and incident to the executing of this Act shall be borne and paid as follows; to wit,

1. With respect to the Metropolitan Police District, as part of the general Expenses of executing the Acts for the Time being in force relating to the Metropolitan Police Force :

2. With respect to the District of a Local Board of Health, as Part of the Expenses of executing the Acts for the Time being in force relating to the Local Board of Health, and as charged upon and payable out of the Monies carried, under the Public Health Act, 1848, to the District Fund Account of the Local Board of Health :

3. With respect to an incorporated Borough, as Part of the Expenses of carrying into execution within the Borough the Provisions of the Act for the Regulation of Municipal Corpora-

tions, and as charged upon and payable out of
the Borough Fund of the Borough :

4. With respect to a Place within the Limits
of an Improvement Act, as Part of the general
Expenses of executing that Act, and as charged
upon and payable out of the Monies from Time
to Time applicable for those Expenses :

5. With respect to a Place in which this Act
is executed by Justices in Petty Sessions, as
Part of the general Expenses of the Constable-
wick of the Place, and as charged upon and
payable out of the Monies from Time to Time
applicable for those Expenses :
And the Monies from Time to Time required for
the Payment of the Expenses of and incident to the
Execution of this Act shall be assessed, levied,
raised, recovered, and paid accordingly.

5. The Expression in this Act "the local Autho- Meaning of
rity" means, with respect to the Purposes and Execu- the term
"the local
tion of this Act with respect to any Place, the Body Authority."
or Person by this Act authorized to execute with
respect to the Place the several Provisions of this
Act.

6. Within Three Months after the passing of this Notice of
this Act to be
Act the local Authority shall, and from Time to given to the
Time thereafter the local Authority may, give to the keepers of
common
Keeper of every Common Lodging House already lodging-
or hereafter within the Jurisdiction under this Act of houses.
the local Authority Notice in Writing of this Act,
and shall give such Notice by leaving the same for
such Keeper at the House, and shall by such Notice
require the Keeper to register the House as by this
Act provided, and such Notice* may be in the Form
in the Schedule to this Act annexed, or to the like
Effect.

* See Page 203.

SECTION 7.
Registers
of common
lodging-
houses to
be kept.

7. The local Authority shall keep a Register in which shall be entered the Names and Residences of the Keepers of all Common Lodging Houses within the Jurisdiction of the local Authority, and the Situation of every such House and the Number of Lodgers authorized according to this Act to be received therein.

Lodgers
not to be re-
ceived in
common
lodging-
houses until
registered
under this
Act.

8. After One Month after the giving of such Notice to register as by this Act provided, the Keeper of any Common Lodging House or any other Person shall not receive any Lodger in such House until the same has been inspected and approved for that Purpose by some Officer appointed in that Behalf by the local Authority, and has been registered as by this Act provided.

Power to
local Autho-
rity to make
Regulations
respecting
common
lodging-
houses.

9. The local Authority may from Time·to Time make Regulations respecting Common Lodging Houses within its Jurisdiction for all or any of the Purposes respecting the same for which the Local Board of Health are by the Public Health Act, 1848, authorized to make Byelaws, and for the well-ordering of such Houses, and for the Separation of the Sexes therein : Provided always, that the Regulations made under this Act by the local Authority shall not be in force until they have been confirmed by One of Her Majesty's Principal Secretaries of State.*

Power to
local Autho-
rity to im-
pose penal-
ties for
offences
committed
against
regulations.

10. The local Authority shall have the same Power of imposing Penalties on Offenders against the said Regulations, subject to the same Restrictions, as the Local Board with respect to Offenders against such Byelaws, and such Penalties shall be recoverable in the same Way as is provided in the said Act with respect to the Penalties imposed on Offenders against such Byelaws ; and a Copy of the said

* In Ireland the Lord Lieutenant.

Regulations, purporting to be signed by the Secretary of State, and also to be signed by the local Authority, (or to be sealed with the Seal of the same, in case it have a Seal,) shall be receivable in Evidence of such Regulations, and of the duly making and confirming thereof.

11. The Keeper of a Common Lodging House shall, when a Person in such House is ill of Fever or any infectious or contagious Disease, give immediate Notice thereof to the local Authority, or some Officer of the local Authority, and also to the Poor Law Medical Officer and the Poor Law Relieving Officer of the Union or Parish in which the Common Lodging House stands. *Keepers of common lodging-houses to give notice of fever, &c., therein.*

12. The Keeper of a Common Lodging House, and every other Person having or acting in the Care or Management thereof, shall, at all Times when required by any Officer of the local Authority, give him free Access to such House or any Part thereof. *As to inspection of common lodging-houses.*

13. The Keeper of a Common Lodging House shall thoroughly cleanse all the Rooms, Passages, Stairs, Floors, Windows, Doors, Walls, Ceilings, Privies, Cesspools, and Drains thereof, to the Satisfaction of and so often as shall be required by or in accordance with any Regulation or Byelaw of the local Authority, and shall well and sufficiently, and to the like Satisfaction, limewash the Walls and Ceilings thereof in the First Week of each of the Months of *April* and *October* in every Year. *As to cleansing of common lodging-houses.*

14. If the Keeper of a Common Lodging House, or any other Person having or acting in the Care or Management thereof, offend against any of the Provisions of this Act, or any of the Byelaws or Regulations made in pursuance of this Act, or if any *Penalty for offences against this Act.*

SECTION 15. Person in any Common Lodging House be confined to his Bed for Forty-eight Hours by Fever or any infectious or contagious Disease, without the Keeper of such House giving Notice thereof as required by this Act, every Person so offending shall for every such Offence be liable to a Penalty not exceeding Five Pounds, and to a further Penalty not exceeding Forty Shillings, for every Day during which the Offence continues : Provided always, that this Act shall not exempt any Person from any Penalty or other Liability to which he may be subject irrespective of this Act.

Recovery of Penalties.

15. The Clauses and Provisions of the Railways Clauses Consolidation Act, 1845, "with respect to the Recovery of Damages not specially provided for, and of Penalties, and to the Determination of any other Matter referred to Justices," are for the Purposes and Execution of this Act incorporated with this Act.

General Powers of local Authority, &c.

16. The local Authority, and all Justices, Constables, and others, shall respectively have full Jurisdiction, Powers, Authorities, and Indemnities for executing the several Provisions of this Act; and the Restrictions of the Public Health Act, 1848, as to the Hours within which Common Lodging Houses may be entered by Persons authorized by a Local Board of Health, shall not apply to this Act.

Act not to extend to the City of London ;

17. That this Act shall not extend to the City of *London* or the Liberties thereof.

nor to Scotland.

18. That nothing in this Act shall extend to *Scotland.*

SCHEDULE.

FORM OF NOTICE.

TAKE notice, That on the [   ] Day of
[   ] an Act called " The Common Lodging Houses Act, 1851," was passed, and that before
the [   ] Day of [   ] you, being
the Keeper of a Common Lodging House within
[*here state the Place over which the Jurisdiction of the
local Authority giving the Notice extends*], must have
your Common Lodging House registered, and that the
Register is to be kept at [*here state where the Register is to be kept*], and that if you do not have your
Common Lodging House so registered you will be
liable to a Penalty not exceeding Five Pounds for
every Lodger whom you receive in your Common
Lodging House while it is not so registered; and that
on your applying to [*here give the Name and Address
of the Person to keep the Register*] he will register your
Common Lodging House free of all Charge to you.
Dated [*&c.*   .]

THE COMMON LODGING HOUSES ACT, 1853,

16 & 17 VICTORIA, CAP. 41.

An Act for making further Provisions with respect to
Common Lodging Houses.

[*4th August,* 1853.]

SECTION 1. WHEREAS it is expedient to extend the Provisions of
"The Common Lodging Houses, Act, 1851:" Be it
therefore enacted by the Queen's most Excellent
Majesty, by and with the Advice and Consent of the
Lords Spiritual and Temporal, and Commons, in
this present Parliament assembled, and by the Authority of the same, as follows :

Short Title. 1. This Act may be cited for any Purpose as
" The Common Lodging House Act, 1853."

Recited Act 2. The Common Lodging Houses Act, 1851, and
and this Act this Act shall be construed and executed as if they
to be as One. were One Act.

All Common 3. After Three Months after the passing of this
Lodging
Houses to be Act a Person shall not keep a Common Lodging
registered House or receive a Lodger therein until the House
before being
used, and to have been inspected and approved for that Purpose
be kept only by some Officer appointed in that Behalf by the local
by registered
Keepers. Authority, and have been registered as by the recital
Act provided ; and a Person shall not keep a Com-

mon Lodging House unless his Name as the Keeper thereof be entered in the Register kept under the recited Act : Provided always, that when the Person so registered dies, his Widow or any Member of his Family may keep the House as a Common Lodging House for not more than Four Weeks after his Death without being registered as the Keeper thereof.

4. The local Authority may refuse to register as the Keeper of a Common Lodging House a Person who does not produce to the local Authority a Certificate of Character in such Form as the local Authority shall direct, signed by Three Inhabitant Householders of the Parish respectively rated to the Relief of the Poor of the Parish within which the Lodging House is situated for Property of the yearly rateable Value of Six Pounds or upwards.

Local Authority may refuse to register Houses if Keepers do not produce Certificate of Character.

5. A Copy of an Entry made in a Register kept under the recited Act, certified by the Person having the Charge of the Register to be a true Copy, shall be received in all Courts and before all Justices and on all occasions whatsoever as Evidence, and be sufficient Proof of all Things therein registered, without Production of the Register or of any Document, Act, or Thing on which the Entry is founded ; and every Person applying at a reasonable Time shall be furnished gratis by the Person having such Charge with a Certified Copy of any such Entry.

Evidence of Register.

6. Where it appears to the local Authority that a Common Lodging House is without a proper Supply of Water for the use of the Lodgers, and that such a Supply can be furnished thereto at a reasonable Rate, the local Authority may by Notice in Writing require the Owner or Keeper of the Common Lodging House, within a Time specified therein, to obtain such Supply, and to do all Works necessary for that Purpose ; and if the Notice be not complied with

Power to Local Authority to require an additional supply of Water to Common Lodging Houses.

SECTION 7. accordingly, the local Authority may remove the Common Lodging House from the Register until it be complied with.

As to Removal of sick Persons from Common Lodging Houses to Hospitals, &c.

7.   When a Person in a Common Lodging House is ill of Fever or any infectious or contagious Disease the local Authority may cause such Person to be removed to an Hospital or Infirmary, with the Consent of the Authorities thereof, and on the Certificate of the Medical Officer of the Parish, Place, or District that the Disease is infectious or contagious, and that the Patient may be safely removed, and may, so far as the local Authority think requisite for preventing the Spread of Disease, cause any Clothes or Bedding used by such Person to be disinfected or destroyed, and may, if the local Authority think fit, award to the owners of the Clothes and Bedding so disinfected or destroyed reasonable Compensation for the Injury or Destruction thereof, and such Compensation shall be paid to such Owners by the proper Officer of the Parish or Union in which the Common Lodging House is situate, out of the Rates applicable to the Relief of the Poor of such Parish, the Amount of such Compensation being first certified in Writing upon a List of such Articles.

Power to order Reports from Keepers of Common Lodging Houses kept for Beggars and Vagrants.

8. The Keeper of a Common Lodging House in which Beggars or Vagrants are received to lodge, or other Person having the Care or Management thereof, shall from Time to Time, if required by any Order of the local Authority served on such Keeper or Person, report to the local Authority, or to such Person or Person as the said local Authority shall direct, every Person who resorted to such House during the preceding Day or Night, and for that Purpose Schedules shall be furnished by the local Authority to the Person so ordered to report, which Schedules they shall fill up with the Information required, and transmit to the local Authority.

9. The Town Council, Trustees, Commissioners, Guardians, and other Officers and Boards specified in the First Section of the " Nuisances Removal and Diseases Prevention Act, 1848," shall, on the Receipt of a Certificate of any Police Constable or of any Officer appointed for the Inspection of Common Lodging Houses by the Local Authority, stating the Existence in or about any Common Lodging House of any of the Causes of Complaint specified in that Section, take all such Proceedings as by that Section are required to be taken by the Town Council, Trustees, Commissioners, Guardians, and other Officers and Boards specified therein on a Notice signed by Two Inhabitant Householders, and in like Manner as nearly as may be as if such Notice had been given ; and the Local Authority shall have the like Powers, and shall take all such Proceedings, on Receipt of any such Certificate of the Existence of any such Cause of Complaint, as the Town Council, Trustees, Commissioners, Guardians, and other Officers or Boards have and are empowered and required to take under the Provisions of that Act.

SECTION 9.

Power to Town Councils, &c., to remove Causes of Complaint certified under Nuisances Removal, &c. Act.

10. Provided always, notwithstanding any Provision contained in this Act, That within the City of *Oxford*, or the Parts within the Jurisdiction of the Commissioners for amending certain Mileways leading to *Oxford*, and making Improvements in the University and City of *Oxford*, the Suburbs thereof, and the adjoining Parish of *Saint Clement*, (which Commissioners are herein-after called the *Oxford* Commissioners,) the several Powers and Duties assigned by this Act to any Local Authority shall, in so far as they are consistent with the Laws under which the said *Oxford* Commissioners act, be exercised by the said *Oxford* Commissioners ; and within the Borough of *Cambridge*, or the Parts within the Jurisdiction of the Commissioners acting under an

The Oxford Commissioners and the Cambridge Commissioners to act as the local Authority under this Act.

SECTION 11. Act of the Thirty-fourth Year of the Reign of King *George* the Third, for amending and enlarging the Powers of a former Act of the same Reign, for the better paving, cleansing, and lighting the Town of *Cambridge*, for removing and preventing Obstructions and Annoyances, and for widening the Streets, Lanes, and other Passages within that Town, (which Commissioners are herein-after called the *Cambridge* Commissioners,) the several Powers and Duties aforesaid shall, in so far as they are consistent with the Laws under which the said *Cambridge* Commissioners act, be exercised by the *Cambridge* Commissioners.

As to Offences against this Act.

11. The Fourteenth Section of the recited Act extends to Offences against any of the Provisions of this Act, so as to render the Offenders liable to the Penalties therein expressed, and any Person convicted of any Offence against the recited Act and this Act, or either of them, may, in default of Payment of the Penalty imposed, be imprisoned for any Term not exceeding Three Months in the Manner provided by Law in that Behalf.

Conviction for Third Offence to disqualify Persons from keeping Common Lodging House.

12. Where a Keeper of a Common Lodging House, or a Person having or acting in the Care or Management of a Common Lodging House, is convicted of a Third Offence against the recited Act and this Act, or either of them, the Justices before whom the Conviction for such Third Offence takes place may, if they think fit, adjudge that he shall not at any Time within Five Years after the Conviction, or within such shorter Period after the Conviction as the Justices think fit, keep or have or act in the Care or Management of a Common Lodging House without the previous Licence in Writing of the Local Authority, which Licence the Local Authority may withhold or may grant on such Terms and Conditions as they think fit.

13. In a Case in which there are not Petty Sessions for a Place fifthly mentioned in Section Acts may be Three of the recited Act, that Act and this Act may executed by Justices at be executed within and for all and any Part of such Petty Sessions. Place by the Justices of the Peace acting in Petty Sessions in the Petty Sessional Division within which such Place is comprised.

14. Where in any Place the recited Act and this As to expenses of Act are executed by Justices in Petty Sessions, the executing Expenses of and incident to the executing of the re- Act by Justices, cited Act and this Act with respect to such Petty Sessional Division shall be borne by and paid out of the Rates for the Relief of the Poor of the several Parishes or other Places comprised therein in which any Common Lodging House is situate, (except so far as there are other Monies applicable to the Purpose,) and the Amount of such Expenses shall be ascertained and apportioned by such Justices, and shall be paid accordingly as they order.

THE COMMON LODGING HOUSES (IRELAND) ACT, 1860.

---◆---

23 VICTORIA, CAP. 26.

An Act to remove Doubts as to the Application of
" The Common Lodging Houses Acts" to *Ireland,*
and to amend the Provisions of the same so far as
they relate to *Ireland.*

[*25th May,* 1860.]

SECTION 1

14 & 15Vict.,
c. 28.
16 & 17 Vict.,
c. 41.

WHEREAS Doubts have arisen as to whether " The
Common Lodging Houses Act, 1851," and " The
Common Lodging Houses Act, 1853," extend to
Ireland, and Difficulties have occurred in the Execution of the said Acts therein ; and it is expedient
that such Doubts and Difficulties should be removed,
and for that Purpose that the said Acts should be
explained and amended with reference to the Execution thereof in *Ireland:* Be it therefore enacted by
the Queen's most Excellent Majesty, by and with the
Advice and Consent of the Lords Spiritual and
Temporal, and Commons, in this present Parliament
assembled, and by the Authority of the same as follows ; (that is to say,)

Short Title.

1. In citing this Act for any Purpose it shall be
sufficient to use the Expression "The Common
Lodging Houses Act, *Ireland,* 1860.

Recited Acts
and this Act
to be con-

2. This Act and " The Common Lodging Houses
Act, 1851," and " The Common Lodging Houses

Act, 1853," shall, for the Purpose of the Execution
thereof in *Ireland*, be construed as if they were One strued as
Act, and the said Acts as hereby amended shall be One, and to
deemed to extend to *Ireland*. extend to
Ireland.

3. For the Purpose of the Execution of the said Explanation
recited Acts and of this Act in Ireland, certain Terms in
Words and Expressions used in the said Acts are recited Acts
hereby declared and explained to have been in- Act.
tended to bear the following Meanings ; (that is to
say,)

The Word " Place" includes Electoral Division :

The Words " Poor Law Medical Officer," and
" Medical Officer of the Parish, Place, or District," mean the Medical Officer of the Dispensary District within which any Common Lodging
House is situate :

" The Act for the Regulation of Municipal Corporations" means the Act passed in the Third
and Fourth Years of the Reign of Her Majesty,
intituled *An Act for the Regulation of Municipal
Corporations in* Ireland :

The Term "Common Lodging House" shall mean
a House in which Persons are harboured or
lodged for Hire for a single Night, or for less
than a Week at a Time, or any Part of which is
let for any Term less than a Week :

The Term " Local Authority" shall have the following Meanings : In Boroughs, incorporated
under the above-mentioned Act for the Regulation of Municipal Corporations, or any Charter
granted or to be granted in pursuance of it, it
shall mean the Town Council of such Borough;
in Towns having Town Commissioners elected
or appointed under any Act of Parliament it
shall mean such Town Commissioners ; in all
other Places it shall mean the Poor Law Guardians of the Union.

SECTION 4.

Local Authority to make Byelaws respecting Common Lodging Houses, but such Byelaws to be confirmed by the Lord Lieutenant.

4. The Ninth and Tenth Sections of "The Common Lodging Houses Act, 1851," are hereby repealed as to *Ireland,* and the following Provisions substituted therefor as to *Ireland* : The Local Authority may make Byelaws respecting Common Lodging Houses, for the well-ordering of such Houses, and for the Separation of the Sexes therein, and for fixing the Number and Sex of the Lodgers who may be received into each such House, and for promoting Cleanliness and Ventilation therein, and with respect to the Inspection thereof; provided that such Byelaws shall not be repugnant to Law, and shall not be in force until they shall have been confirmed by the Lord Lieutenant or other the Chief Governor or Governors of *Ireland* for the Time being ; and that

Old Byelaws to continue until new ones are confirmed.

any Byelaws heretofore made under the Provisions of the said recited Acts shall continue in full Force and Effect until new Byelaws shall have been made and confirmed in lieu thereof, under the Provisions of this Act.

Copy of Byelaws to be received in Evidence.

5. A Copy of the Byelaws made by the Local Authority under the Provisions of this Act, purporting to be signed by the Chief or Under Secretary for *Ireland* on behalf of the Lord Lieutenant, and also signed by the Local Authority (or sealed with the Seal of the same, in case it have a Seal), shall be received as Evidence of such Byelaws, and of their having been duly made and confirmed.

Penalties imposed by 14 & 15 Vict., c. 28, to apply to Byelaws made under this Act.

6. The Penalties imposed by "The Common Lodging, Houses Act, 1851," for Offences against Byelaws made under the Provisions of the said recited Act, shall apply to the Byelaws made under the Provisions of this Act, and such Penalties shall be recoverable before Justices of the Peace at Petty Sessions ; and all the Provisions of the Petty Sessions Act, *Ireland,* shall apply to the Proceedings for Recovery of such Penalty.

7. The Expenses of the Execution of the said Acts and of this Act are to be defrayed in Boroughs Expense to out of the Borough Fund, in Towns having Town be levied off the whole of . Commissioners out of the Rates levied by such Com- an Electoral missioners, and in other Places out of the Rates for Division. the Relief of the destitute Poor.

8. Nothing herein contained shall affect any Pro- Not to affect vision of the Towns Improvement, *Ireland*, Act, or Provisions of 17 & 18 Vict., any Byelaw duly made under its Provisions. c. 103.

9. All Acts and Proceedings for the Execution and Former Pro- ceedings Enforcement of the Provisions of the said Common validated. Lodging Houses Acts shall be as valid as if said Acts had originally included *Ireland*, but no Adjudi- cation already pronounced shall be affected hereby.

10. This Act shall extend to *Ireland* only. Extent of Act.

THE BAKEHOUSE REGULATION ACT, 1863.

26 & 27 Victoria, Cap. 40.

An Act for the Regulation of Bakehouses.*

[13th *July*, 1863.]

SECTION 1. WHEREAS it is expedient to limit the Hours of Labour of Young Persons employed in Bakehouses, and to make Regulations with respect to Cleanliness and Ventilation in Bakehouses: Be it enacted by the Queen's most Excellent Majesty, by and with the Advice and Consent of the Lords Spiritual and Temporal, and Commons, in this present Parliament assembled, and by the Authority of the same, as follows:

Short title. 1. This Act may be cited as "The Bakehouse Regulation Act, 1863."

Interpretation of terms. 2. For the Purposes of this Act the Words hereinafter mentioned shall be construed as follows; that is to say,

"*Local Authority*" shall, as respects any Place, mean the Persons or Bodies of Persons defined to be the Local Authority in that Place by the

* Bakehouses are not affected by the provisions of the Workshop Regulation Act, 1867, 30 & 31 Vict., Cap. 146, Page 169.

One hundred and thirty-fourth Section of the SECTION 2. Act passed in the Session holden in the Eighteenth and Nineteenth Years of the Reign of Her present Majesty, Chapter One hundred and twenty, or by the Nuisances Removal Acts herein-after mentioned; that is to say, as to *England*, by the Act passed in the Session holden in the Eighteenth and Nineteenth Years of the Reign of Her present Majesty, Chapter One hundred and twenty-one, as amended by the Act passed in the Session holden in the Twenty-third and Twenty-fourth Years of the Reign of Her present Majesty, Chapter Seventy-seven; as to *Scotland*, by the Act passed in the Session holden in the Nineteenth and Twentieth Years of the Reign of Her present Majesty, Chapter One hundred and three; and as to *Ireland*, by the Acts passed, the one in the Session holden in the Eleventh and Twelfth Years of the Reign of Her present Majesty, Chapter One hundred and twenty-three, and the other in the Session holden in the Twelfth and Thirteenth Years of the Reign of Her present Majesty, Chapter One hundred and eleven :

" Bakehouse" shall mean any Place in which are baked Bread, Biscuits, or Confectionery, from the baking or selling of which a Profit is derived :

" Employed," as applied to any Person, shall include any Person working in a Bakehouse, whether he receives Wages or not :

" Occupier" shall include any Person in possession :

" The Court" shall include any Justice or Justices, Sheriff or Sheriff Substitute, Magistrate or Magistrates, to whom Jurisdiction is given by this Act.

SECTION 3.

Limitation
of hours of
labour of
persons
under 18
years of age.

3. No Person under the Age of Eighteen Years shall be employed in any Bakehouse between the Hours of Nine of the Clock at Night and Five of the Clock in the Morning.

If any Person is employed in contravention of this Section, the Occupier of the Bakehouse in which he is employed shall incur the following Penalties in respect of each Person so employed ; that is to say,

For the First Offence, a Sum not exceeding Two Pounds :

For a Second Offence, a Sum not exceeding Five Pounds :

For a Third and every subsequent Offence, a Sum not exceeding One Pound for each Day of the Continuance of the Employment in contravention of this Act, so that no greater Penalty be imposed than Ten Pounds.

4. The inside Walls and Ceiling or Top of every Bakehouse situate in any City, Town, or Place containing according to the last Census a Population of more than Five Thousand Persons, and the Passages and Staircase leading thereto, shall either be painted with Oil or be limewashed, or partly painted and partly limewashed : Where painted with Oil there shall be Three Coats of Paint, and the painting shall be renewed once at least in every Seven Years, and shall be washed with hot Water and Soap once at least in every Six Months : Where limewashed the limewashing shall be renewed once at least in every Six Months.

Every Bakehouse wherever situate shall be kept in a cleanly State, and shall be provided with proper Means for effectual Ventilation, and be free from Effluvia arising from any Drain, Privy, or other Nuisance.

If the Occupier of any Bakehouse fails to keep the same in conformity with this Section, he shall be deemed to be guilty of an Offence against this Act, and to be subject in respect of such Offence to a Penalty not exceeding Five Pounds.

The Court having Jurisdiction under this Act may, in addition to or instead of inflicting any Penalty in respect of an Offence under this Section, make an Order directing that within a certain Time to be named in such Order certain Means are to be adopted by the Occupier for the Purpose of bringing his Bakehouse into conformity with this Section ; the Court may upon Application enlarge any Time appointed for the Adoption of the Means directed by the Order, but any Non-compliance with the Order of the Court shall, after the Expiration of the Time as originally limited or enlarged by subsequent Order, be deemed to be a continuing Offence, and to be punishable by a Penalty not exceeding One Pound for every Day that such Non-compliance continues.

5. No Place on the same Level with a Bakehouse As to sleeping- situate in any City, Town, or Place containing ac- places near cording to the last Census a Population of more bakehouses. than Five Thousand Persons, and forming Part of the same Building, shall be used as a Sleeping Place, unless it is constructed as follows ; that is to say,

Unless it is effectually separated from the Bake- house by a Partition extending from the Floor to the Ceiling :

Unless there be an external glazed Window of at least Nine Superficial Feet in Area, of which at the least Four and a Half Superficial Feet are made to open for Ventilation:

And any Person who lets, occupies, or continues to let, or knowingly suffers to be occupied, any Place contrary to this Act, shall be liable for the First Offence to a Penalty not exceeding Twenty Shillings,

The Bakehouse Regulation Act, 1863.

SECTION 6. and for every subsequent Offence to a Penalty not exceeding Five Pounds.

Power to local Authority to enforce provisions of this Act.

6. It shall be the Duty of the Local Authority to enforce within their District the Provisions of this Act, and in order to facilitate the Enforcement thereof any Officer of Health, Inspector of Nuisances, or other Officer appointed by the Local Authority, herein-before referred to as the Inspector, may enter into any Bake-house at all Times during the Hours of baking, and may inspect the same, and examine whether it is or not in conformity with the Provisions of this Act; and any Person refusing Admission to the Inspector, or obstructing him in his Examination, shall for each Offence incur a Penalty not exceeding Twenty Pounds; and it shall be lawful for any Inspector who is refused Admission to any Bakehouse, in pursuance of this Section, to apply to any Justice for a Warrant authorizing him, accompanied by a Police Constable, to enter into any such Bakehouse for the Purpose of examining the same, and to enter the same accordingly.

As to expenses of local Authority acting under this Act.

7. All Expenses incurred by any Local Authority in pursuance of the Provisions of this Act may be paid out of any Rate leviable by them, and applicable to the Payment of the Expenses incurred by the Local Authority under the said Nuisances Removal Acts, and the said Authority may levy such Rate accordingly.

Penalties.

Recovery of penalties.

8. All Penalties under this Act may be recovered summarily before Two or more Justices; as to *England,* in manner directed by an Act passed in the Session holden in the Eleventh and Twelfth Years of the Reign of Her Majesty Queen *Victoria,*

Chapter Forty-three, intituled *An Act to facilitate the* SECTION 9.
Performance of the Duties of Justices of the Peace out
of Sessions within England *and* Wales *with respect to*
summary Convictions and Orders, or any Act amending the same ; as to *Ireland*, in manner directed by
the Act passed in the Session holden in the Fourteenth and Fifteenth Years of the Reign of Her
Majesty Queen *Victoria*, Chapter Ninety-three, intituled *An Act to consolidate and amend the Acts regu-*
lating the Proceedings of Petty Sessions and the Duties
of Justices of the Peace out of Quarter Sessions in
Ireland, or any Act amending the same ; and as to
Scotland, upon summary Conviction, with Power for
the Justices having Cognizance of the Case to sen-
tence the Offender to Imprisonment for a Period not
exceeding Three Months until the Penalty and the
Expenses of Conviction are paid.

9. Any Act, Power, or Jurisdiction hereby autho- Jurisdiction of certain Magistrates.
rized to be done or exercised by Two Justices may
be done or exercised by the following Magistrates
within their respective Jurisdictions; that is to say,
as to *England*, by any Metropolitan Police Magistrate or other Stipendiary Magistrate sitting alone at
a Police Court or other appointed Place, or by the
Lord Mayor of the City of *London*, or any Alderman
of the said City sitting alone or with others at the
Mansion House or *Guildhall;* as to *Ireland*, by any
One or more Divisional Magistrates of Police in the
Police District of *Dublin*, and elsewhere by One or
more Justice or Justices of the Peace in Petty Sessions; and as to *Scotland*, by the Sheriff or Sheriff
Substitute, or by any Police Magistrate of a Burgh.

INDEX.

2.40   INDEX.

R

INDEX.

256

INDEX.

Page

ORDER, (continued):

Copies of orders of Nuisance Authority may be received in evidence, ... 116

Justices may make an order requiring occupier to allow the owner to execute the works directed by the Nuisance Authority, ... 117

No order to be set aside nor quashed for want of form or removable by certiorari, ... 118

Of Justices for admission of officer of Nuisance Authority to inspect private premises, ... 124

Form of order of Justices for the removal of nuisances by the owner or occupier, ... 128

Form of order of Justices for the removal of nuisance by the Nuisance Authority, ... 131

Form of order of Justices upon occupier to permit the execution of works by the owner, ... 131

Form of order of Justices for payment of costs, and expenses, and penalties, ... 134

Lord Lieutenant has power to issue orders putting in force the provisions of the Diseases Prevention Act, 1855, where any part of Ireland is threatened or affected by any epidemic, ... 139

Poor Law Commissioners shall be the Authority in Ireland for issuing orders to carry the provisions of the Diseases Prevention Act into effect, ... 140

Of Lord Lieutenant under the Nuisances Removal Act to be laid before Parliament, ... 141

Justices may order, upon the application of the Medical Officer of Health or the Inspector of Nuisance, any animal, meat, fish, vegetables, &c., to be destroyed if same appear unfit for the food of man, ... 156

ORDERS IN COUNCIL:

To be laid before Parliament, ... 141

For putting in force Diseases Prevention Act, may extend to parts and arms of the sea lying within the jurisdiction of the Admiralty, ... 142

OVERCROWDING:

Where two convictions relating to overcrowding of house or occupation of a cellar as a dwelling have taken place within three months, Justices may order the premises to be closed, ... 31

On certificate of Medical Officer or two Medical Practitioners that a house is so overcrowded as to be dangerous to the health of the inhabitants, Nuisance Authority may take proceedings before the Justices, ... 114

Page

SEWAGE UTILIZATION ACT, *(continued)*:
Powers given by, to be in addition to, and not in derogation of
any other powers, ... 82
Sewage may be collected for sale by the Sewer Authority, so as
it does not cause a nuisance, ... 69
Utilization Act, 1865, not to extend to any place in which the
Public Health Act, 1848, is in force, or in which the Local
Government Act is in force, ... 67
Powers of the Sewer Authority under the Act accumulative, ... 82

SEWER AUTHORITY:
Definition of I
Amended definition in regard to Ireland, ... 47
May require occupiers to obtain a supply of water under certain
circumstances, ... 48
May supply water for public baths or wash-houses, or for manu-
facturing purposes, ... 49
May construct and maintain public cisterns, &c., for gratuitous
supply of water, ... 49
May form committees of its own members and ratepayers, ... 2
Mad add to or diminish the number of members of the commit-
tee, alter its constitution or dissolve it, ... 3
Chairman of, ... 3
Quorum of committee, ... 3
Committee to be deemed the agents of, ... 4
To allow owner or occupier within its district to drain into its
sewers, ... 6
To allow owner or occupier beyond its district to drain into its
sewers, ... 7
May require owners of houses to make drains, ... 8
May make drains in default of, but at the expense of owner, 8
Powers of, in relation to the supply of water, ... 9
Expenses of, in relation to the supply of water, ... 10
May close communication between drains and sewers made in
contravention of the provisions of the Act, ... 6
May require owners of houses to make drains, ... 8
Or in default may may do the work required, and recover the
expenses from owner, ... 8
Powers in relation to the supply of water, ... 9
Property in wells, fountains, and pumps vested in Nuisance
Authority by 23 & 24 Vict., cap. 77, to vest in Sewer Autho-
rity where that Authority supplies water, ... 10
May provide hospitals or temporary places for the reception of
the sick, ... 32
Appearance of Nuisance Authority in legal proceedings, ... 40
Incorporated, ... 38, 57
On default of Sewer Authority, Lord Lieutenant may, after in-

Page

SEWER AUTHORITY *(continued)*:

make an order authorizing them to enter, examine, or lay open land or premises, ... 75

Shall pay all expenses incurred by them in carrying the Sewage Utilization Act into effect out of the fund or rate mentioned in the schedule to that Act, ... 75

May exercise the borrowing powers of the Local Government Act, 1858, ... 76

Shall have the power to take lands, as is conferred by the 75th section of the Local Government Act, 1858, ... 76

Regulations as to the purchase of land by the Sewer Authority, ... 77

May, upon the dissent of the owners or occupiers of such lands, petition the Lord Lieutenant to put in force the compulsory power of the Sewer Authority to take lands, ... 77

Private improvement expenses of Sewer Authority to be levied upon the occupier of the premises by a rate not exceeding £5 in the hundred, ... 158

Appointment of an Arbitrator by Sewer Authority must be under the seal and the hands of any five or more of their number, ... 160

Appointment of an Arbitrator shall be deemed a submission to arbitration by the parties making such appointment ... 160

Such appointment not to be revoked without consent of both parties, nor shall the death of either party operate as a revocation, ... 161

If for the space of fourteen days after notice in writing shall have been given by one party who has appointed an Arbitrator, the party to whom notice is given fail to appoint an Arbitrator, the Arbitrator appointed shall act on behalf of both parties, ... 161

Award of such Arbitrator shall be binding and conclusive, ... 161

Liability of Sewer Authority must first be ascertained to make compensation, ... 162

SEWERS :

Such sewers may be constructed by the Sewer Authority, as they may think necessary, for keeping their district properly drained, ... 68

If Sewer Authority close a sewer they must provide another as effectual, ... 69

Canal companies, &c., may, if sewers of the Sewer Authority interfere with their rights or navigation, substitute other sewers at their own expense, ... 74

Open sewers may be covered, improved, or closed up by Nuisance Authority, ... 106

Owner or occupier within the district may cause his drains to

T

276 CONTENTS.

Page

WOMAN:

No woman shall be employed in any handicraft for more than twelve hours a-day, including one hour and a-half for meals; such an employment to take place between five in the morning and nine at night, ... 169
Nor on Sundays, ... 170
Nor after two o'clock on Saturday afternoon, where not more than five persons are employed in the same establishment, and where articles made are sold by retail or repaired on the premises, ... 176
If any woman is employed in contravention of the Workshop Regulation Act of 1867, a penalty is inflicted upon the occupier of the workshop, ... 170

WORDS:

Meaning of Adulteration, ... 187
,, Borough Rate, ... 54, 87
,, Borough Fund, ... 54, 87
,, Consuming, as far as possible, smoke, 14, 16
,, Child, ... 168
,, Court, ... 168
,, Council, ... 54, 87
,, Employed, ... 168
,, Guardians, ... 87
,, Handicraft, ... 166
,, Improvement Act, ... 88
,, Improvement of Land, ... 82
,, Inhabitants, ... 9
,, Justices making an order, ... 56
,, Justices, two, ... 89
,, Lord Lieutenant in Council, ... 2
,, Mayor, Aldermen, Burgesses, ... 55, 87
,, Nuisances, ... 13
,, Nuisance Authority, ... 12
,, Nuisances Removal Act, ... 11
,, Owner, ... 88, 104
,, Parent, ... 168
,, Person, ... 89
,, Parish, ... 88
,, Premises, ... 88
,, Place, ... 87, 156, 157
,, Poor Rate of Union, ... 55
,, Person by whose act, default, permission, or sufferance a nuisance arises, ... 97
,, Quarter Sessions, ... 88
,, Suffer, ... 109
,, Sewage Utilization Act, 1865, ... 2

Porteous and Gibbs, Printers, 18 Wicklow Street, Dublin.

www.ingramcontent.com/pod-product-compliance
Lightning Source LLC
Chambersburg PA
CBHW020513270326
41926CB00008B/849